Two Worlds of Liberalism

Eldon J. Eisenach

Two Worlds of Liberalism
Religion and Politics in Hobbes, Locke, and Mill

The University of Chicago
Chicago and London

ELDON J. EISENACH is associate professor of
political science at the University of Arkansas at
Little Rock.

The University of Chicago Press, Chicago 60637
The University of Chicago Press, Ltd., London

© 1981 by The University of Chicago
All rights reserved. Published 1981
Printed in the United States of America

85 84 83 82 81   1 2 3 4 5

Library of Congress Cataloging in Publication Data

Eisenach, Eldon J
    Two worlds of liberalism.

    A revision of the author's thesis, University
of California at Berkeley.
    Includes bibliographical references and index.
    1. Liberalism—Great Britain—History.
    2. Hobbes, Thomas, 1588–1679—Political science.
    4. Locke, John, 1632–1704—Political science.
    5. Mill, John Stuart, 1806–1873—Political science.
    I. Title.
JC599.G7E37   1981   320.5'12'0941   80-27255
ISBN 0-226-19533-3

To the Memory of My Father

Contents

vii

Acknowledgments

Thomas Hobbes was right when he said that benefits oblige and that obligation is a kind of bondage which, if not requited, becomes "perpetuall thraldome." As I have received benefits from so many teachers, colleagues, and students over the years, so I have incurred obligations which no private expressions of gratitude could begin to repay. It is with some relief, then, to thank publicly those who have a share in this project and who have waited almost in perpetuity for its completion. Professor Sheldon Wolin, now at Princeton, provided encouragement and advice which were indispensable when I began the study of English liberalism as a doctoral candidate at Berkeley. Professor John Pocock of Johns Hopkins helped me, long before we met, through his writings on the historical dimensions of political theory and, after we met, by his advice on the early chapters of the manuscript. Professor Richard Ashcraft of UCLA, a friend since undergraduate days, has always generously shared his research findings and ideas with me. I am especially grateful to two of my colleagues from Cornell, Professors Werner Dannhauser and Isaac Kramnick, who helped me in ways beyond recounting. Although Werner did not teach me to write, he did teach me how to rewrite and to rethink many parts of the manuscript. Isaac taught me that one can often say something more forcefully by deletion than by addition. Professor Benjamin Barber of Rutgers read two versions of the manuscript; to him I owe much of the improvement in the second version. Two generations of graduate students at Cornell continually amazed me by their tolerance and enthusiasm when first presented with materials which became parts of the book. Over the years, their seminar papers and essays were engaged in a dialogue with my own writing, and it was this dialogue which made my task so rewarding. The William Andrews Clark Library at UCLA provided both summer fellowship funds and access to seventeenth-century pamphlet literature on the English Civil War. My wife, Valerie, was witness

ix

and participant at every stage of this project. At all hours and seasons she typed, edited, and retyped the manuscript and checked and rechecked the notes. More important, she knew more than my own diffidence would allow—that friends and colleagues are more generously giving of their help than reason can explain or justice can measure. Her own conduct is the most admirable testament of this knowledge.

Introduction

In the midst of the English Civil War, a pamphleteer urging obedience to Cromwell's side appealed both to interest and to duty. Conscientious Christians "are born to two worlds and are made of matter proportionable to both, and therefore cannot but naturally have some kinde of affection for both."[1] Throughout this pamphlet, two different assumptions are made about man's condition. According to the first, he is born in liberty and thus is free to choose the best means of securing his preservation; according to the second he is born in servitude and thus is bound to the commands of God, who intervenes at particular moments in history. The logic of interest is best seen in a "state of nature" in which no human artifacts distort the exercise of natural liberty. The logic of duty and supernatural rewards and punishments is best found in the Bible, a record of sacred history and divine prophecy.

Thomas Hobbes's *Leviathan,* published shortly after this pamphlet, is addressed to men born to both worlds. The first half of the book constructs a world of interest and calculation, as durable and universal as the unceasing play of man's appetites and aversions. The second half of *Leviathan* places men in a stream of history whose collective past is irrevocable and whose future is sustained only by faith. The two worlds seem profoundly at odds with one another. Like the pamphleteer, Hobbes seems to suspend man and political life between these worlds.

John Locke's writings display this same division. In the early Restoration period, when the magistrates' power over religion was again an issue, Locke wrote two tracts on the question. In the course of his argument, he examines the source of civil power. "Some suppose men to be born in servitude, others, to liberty," Locke says, but he refuses to take sides. His refusal is a considered one. To suppose that men are born free and equal requires that civil power be created by each man's surrender of his "native liberty" and by the transfer of the latter to a magistrate. The right to rule would then be anchored in the consent of the governed. The countersupposition asserts that the power of the magistrate is possessed "by divine institution and by the distinction of his character and nature." This ruler manifests the biblical Word in history; other men should obey him as children should obey their parents and Christians their God. Locke abjures a choice on fundamental grounds: "a right to govern will not easily be derived from the paternal right nor a right of life and death from the popular."[2] Political life requires the sanction of death. Popular consent cannot give this power to a magistrate because no man has a natural right over another man's life. Hobbes put this same distinction in terms of political power. In the first half of *Leviathan*, he says that words which promise are worthless without the sword. In the second half, he says that the sword is powerless unless it is believed by the subjects to be wielded to protect the Word in history and prophecy.

Whether we mark the origins of English liberalism with Hobbes or Locke, we have been trained to see its coherence within only one of the two worlds they address. There are many plausible reasons for this. We are taught that political philosophers write philosophy, not religion and not history. Liberal political philosophy, we are told, starts with the assumption that men are born free, no matter what historical chains might suggest the contrary. If a god is required at all in this philosophy, he is at most discoverable by reason and made manifest in the regularities of timeless nature, including human nature. To take seriously a god who says different things to different men at different times seems to compromise the intentions of liberal political philosophy from the very start.

Liberalism as a philosophy of natural liberty and individual interest does have a well-documented coherence. The logic of civil law and private contractual exchange complements a psychology portraying men as creatures who seek to maximize their interests. By providing a realm of moral freedom, a political order that guarantees the integrity of civil society makes it possible for individual men to be responsible for their actions. To be sure, critics and defenders alike have disagreed on the particular shape and center of liberalism's coherence, but all have found it within the confines of one world alone. Thus, socialist critics and capitalist defenders of liberalism have isolated the "hedonistic" elements of interest, the centrality of private property, and the protection of contractual relationships. Liberalism tested against the canons of humanism is seen as a moral theory—whether adequate or not—based on the capacity of man's reason to shape a common life. In short, the tradition of thought called liberalism—whatever one considers its starting point—is said to begin with individual interest and individual reason.

History, too, has been a means of teaching us to see liberalism completely within the confines of individual liberty. That history is found both in the writings of the major liberal theorists themselves and in later histories of ideas. Locke's *Two Treatises of Government* constitutes an obvious attempt to substitute a state of nature for biblical and "paternal" theories of origins. Locke, however, does more than assert the sovereignty of nature and reason against history—whether religious or political. The state of nature itself has a "natural history," which consists of the progressive articulation of economic and contractual relationships. The latter, through time, teach men the value of liberty. If the first rulers were in fact father-kings, the last will be legislators demanding a government of laws. Social and economic life has a developmental history requiring appropriate political forms.

The implicit teaching of Locke's natural history becomes of paradigmatic importance in the writings of Adam Smith and David Hume, and it is a commonplace of twentieth-century histories of ideas. Much of our own interpretation of the place of liberal political ideas in history is conveniently provided by the very writings we interpret. We can hardly err: the progress of ideas yields a commitment to natural rights, individual interest, and the efficacy of reason. This result is in part simply the appropriate response of sensitive minds to the conditions increasingly dominating their day. An audience receptive to these ideas is both creature and creator of the new material conditions. In such an understanding, all other features of liberal thought become somewhat peripheral. The call for supernatural belief, for reliance on habit or superstition, the appeals to illusion and mystery—all this can be explained either as occasional lapses into an earlier language or as rhetoric designed to make new doctrines more attractive to audiences historically a step behind the authors.

However, we have good reason to suspect such historical understandings of liberalism. The assumption that man is born in servitude is also a part of historical explanation. Locke, who does outline a materialist explanation of the rise of liberal politics, sees his own role in this development quite differently. In his theological writings, he maintains that the progress of reason in the world is dependent not upon material conditions but upon the state of religious belief. Philosophical truth is always hostage to religious truth. Locke concludes that his own religious duty is to further the progress of philosophy by examining the entire range of political and moral duties on the basis of reason—in short, to construct a demonstrable moral philosophy. Yet, Locke does not do this; he ended his life writing and defending a reasonable theology. For Locke at least, liberal politics is as much dependent upon the world of faith (men are born to duty) as it is upon the world of works and reason (men are born to liberty).

A century and a half later, John Stuart Mill provides additional cause for doubting that liberal ideas entail the primacy of individual interest and reason. On first inspection, this doubt seems misplaced: Mill appears to be the unambivalent votary of liberty; his ideas seem far removed from the lingering religious elements found in the writings of Hobbes and Locke. Mill's critique of the utilitarian philosophy of his father and Jeremy Bentham is both widely known and supportive of this secular view. Mill holds that the progress of human freedom requires the rational cultivation of the higher, nonmaterial pleasures: indeed, he sometimes suggests that a kind of enslavement results from an exercise of liberty dominated by the pursuit of lower ends. Almost as familiar to us is Mill's explanation of the relationship of intellectual, moral, and material progress. Material and moral progress requires intellectual freedom in an atmosphere of toleration. As if to quiet the doubts which Locke had raised, Mill can be said to have fulfilled the "true" spirit of Locke as philosopher of freedom—as expressed in Locke's *Letter on Toleration* and *Essay Concerning Human Understanding*. A skeptical reason in the service of men born to liberty is the most powerful weapon in the arsenal of freedom, and the use of that reason is the highest proof that freedom is possible.

Many criticisms are levelled at Mill's writings, especially those which seek to amend the older utilitarianism. And many doubts are expressed regarding the argument in *On Liberty*—whether its teachings are appropriate only for an intellectual elite, whether liberty on this absolute a scale would endanger other values, and whether the distinction between self- and other-regarding actions is adequately drawn. But Mill's most trenchant critic is Mill himself. An inspection of Mill's writings on religion and history compels us to confront the question of whether Mill's liberalism can be contained at all within a secular world bounded by interest *and* reason. In these writings, Mill not only casts doubt on the liberating power of self-interest in history but also on the liberating power of reason itself. His strictures are as much against the dissolving power of reason as they are against the corrosive effects of interest. For Mill, too, men are born to two worlds. Analytic reason and material interest belong to only one world and often mirror each other: combined, they are insufficient to sustain a politics or a culture of freedom.

Mill's affection for the other world of liberalism—the world of duty and belief—is most apparent in his theory of historical change. The objects of happiness which all men seek are, according to Mill, dependent upon ideas and opinions which change over time. Moral progress is marked by the quality of those objects and the consistency of men's commitment to them. The true agents of progress, then, are those who shape more worthy ends of life. In the past, these agents have been prophets, not philosophers, and the spread of their ideas has been accomplished by believing disciples, not by self-interested men. Moreover, he suggests that this holds true *even of liberalism*.

The overthrow of old ideas always comes from within, so moral progress demands men who are both committed and courageous. Paradoxically, this process of change preserves the leading ideas of the past as much as it destroys them. Mill sometimes writes as if this chain of world-organizing ideas must remain unbroken, lest men fall back into the barbarism of natural passion. Those who would act most freely in history—those who shape the world's ruling opinions—are precisely men who are born in servitude to ends outside the range of interest and reason:

> Their impulse [is] a divine enthusiasm—a self-forgetting devotion to an idea . . . a phenomenon belonging to the critical moments of existence, not to the ordinary play of human motives, and from which nothing can be inferred as to the efficacy of the ideas which it sprung from . . . in overcoming ordinary temptations and regulating the course of daily life.[3]

Mill's "religion of humanity" enshrines such past ideas and men in order to encourage the creation of new ideas in the future. The freest intellects are not those beginning with unaided reason but those firmly bound to a story of ideas through time.

These ideas of history and religion from Mill do not prove that he thereby entirely repudiates a liberalism bounded by individual interest and reason. They are meant to suggest that Mill, too, often repaired to the other world of English liberalism. The distance between Thomas Hobbes and John Stuart Mill is great. My hope is, however, that this preliminary survey has induced the reader to entertain the possibility that liberal political theory from its beginning to the present has been based on *two* distinct foundations. The difference between them is not the difference of interest and reason (they are bound by the same logic); both interest and reason vie with religious belief, collective loyalties, and self-sacrifice. Two specific features of this other world bear mention: first, it contains elements which liberalism has often been accused of lacking, such as a theory of political education. A second feature relates to the problem of death. Rousseau asked the question which dogged every formulation that began with the single assumption that man is born to liberty: "Does a man go to death from self-interest?"[4] Liberal models of civil society presume the primacy of the motive of self-preservation; yet the establishment of a liberal regime in the face of divine-right monarchy, traditions of patriotism, and systems of privilege requires the opposite: the risk and taking of life. Moreover, once established, the maintenance of civil society built on motives of interest brings to prominence the importance of death. Stated symbolically, were liberal political philosophy simply confined to the limits given to it by contemporary scholarship, its teachings would be as compelling to the thoughtful man as they might be to the soldier in Locke's *Second Treatise:* "The general [cannot] dispose of one farthing of that soldier's estate or seize one jot of his goods, whom yet he can command anything, and hang for the least disobedience."[5] Locke assumed that both soldiers and citizens gave more than a farthing for their lives. From Hobbes through Mill, the problem of establishing and defending a liberal society is closely related to questions of religious belief and theories of history.

A liberal theory of politics defined only by individual reason and interest points away from these questions and turns instead to features in society and government designed to protect civil society from the depredations of political power. Indeed, the political and power resources implicit in religion, patriotism, and other kinds of affective connections are often seen as threats to individual liberty. And instead of tapping those resources for public ends, liberal theory often seems to banish them forever into the utterly private realm of conscience and subjective belief. From Hobbes through Mill, however, these attempts not only failed but, I suggest, were rarely undertaken with the expectation of success. By far the more serious endeavor was to subsume the logic of interest and reason within the larger and more comprehensive framework of history and duty.

Issues of criminal punishment, political power, and supernatural religious belief are so persistently raised within liberal political philosophy that it is important to attempt their recovery as a coherent tradition. This study is an attempt to do so. The other source of coherence within liberalism, built on the twin pillars of interest and reason, takes many well-known forms: the psychological empiricism begun by Hobbes and Locke is essentially intact in Bentham and James Mill; a positivist theory of law can be traced from Hobbes through Jeremy Bentham and John Austin; consent as a basis of political obligation and obligation as the central issue of political philosophy are found in many of the major writings. I think it is equally possible, however, to discover persistent themes which run counter to these patterns, themes which begin with the assumption that man is born to duty as well as with rights. Hobbes ends the first half of *Leviathan* musing on the question of rewards and punishments after death; Locke begins the *Second Treatise* by raising the issue of a right to kill in the state of nature; Bentham spent a lifetime devising penitentiary schemes and legal codes to avoid the need for bodily punishment and death sentences; John Stuart Mill defends capital punishment by declaring flatly that some ways of life are worse than death no matter what the opinion of the miscreant.

Religion is a second obvious thread: the familiar liberal attack on priesthoods, rituals, and church establishments might deter us from recognizing that the basis of this critique was often itself religious, and from seeing how the theological perspectives of Reformed Protestantism were consciously incorporated into liberal thought—even in the case of Mill. Another theme which might constitute a coherent pattern in liberal thought involves "manners"—that combination of opinion and motives concerning judgments of good and evil. A moral theory grounded in interest and pain-pleasure calculation is familiar to all students of liberalism. Less obvious is the persistence of a question slightly subversive of that postulate: how does one convince men to act out of self-interest? How is it possible to shape men's opinions so that they want to do what the theory says they must do and the legal order compels them to do? Insofar as the stability of the government rests on these motives, the question broadens to one of political education: what conditions must be imposed or what teachings inculcated to insure proper moral opinion?

Yet another reason exists for attempting to reconstruct this other world of liberalism. Traditions of political ideas are not merely themes and issues repeated over time; intellectual traditions also involve structures of thought containing their own imperatives and vocabulary. For those participating in the religious and political turmoils of seventeenth-century England, the world was "turned upside down" and the basis of all social relationships was examined afresh. No matter under whose auspices political order was to be reconstituted, the ideas and opinions which pointed the way could no longer be voiced in the prevailing structure of ideas. Hobbes's response was the most daring and thus the most instructive: the first half of *Leviathan* reconstructs human nature, moral philosophy, and the political order ex nihilo, as if the static space of a state of nature swallowed all political time and memory. The philosopher himself is part of this space, for he, too, begins by feigning the destruction of ideas legitimated by history. The other half of *Leviathan* also destroys history as tradition, memory, and institutional continuity, but with an older and more epochal (and apocalyptic) history from the Bible. In the hands of Hobbes and many reform Protestants, the Bible as sacred history and prophecy becomes the great destroyer of secular history and institutions. On this reading, the signal political event for Christians is the setting aside of the law for the Gospel and the substitution of saving faith for the idolatrous world of works.

The two halves of *Leviathan* codify a systemic disjunction between these two means of destroying the relevance of the historic past, even as they establish two ways of reconstituting authority. The state of nature (a product of reason) and sacred history (the record and prophecy of God's intervention in time) seem so contradictory that contemporary students of Hobbes suggest that one can ignore the latter entirely and still comprehend Hobbes's entire political philosophy—as if the enterprise of modern philosophy itself can only begin with a state of nature or at least with a heavy veil of ignorance. But if *Leviathan* is one book and the author a philosopher throughout, the great disjunction ascribed by scholars today might in fact be a greater complementarity. To raise this possibility is to suggest that the defects of one assumption—man's freedom—might be the strengths of the other—man's duty. Were this the case at the very outset of a new way of thinking about politics, all who start where Hobbes did in the first half of *Leviathan* are preordained to run up against the same order of difficulties which the second half of *Leviathan* is designed to address.

Because *Leviathan* in its entirety is my point of departure in examining writings in the liberal canon from Locke through Mill, I will examine many texts not considered today as containing political theory. Through this examination, the evidence mounts that Locke and Mill also did not see the task of political philosophy as unambiguously beginning outside of history in a state of nature or from universally valid psychological postulates. As the author of the second half of *Leviathan*, Hobbes could not presume men were born to liberty: he neither wrote the Bible nor controlled the meanings in the events and prophecies recorded. Those who came after Hobbes and raised issues dominating the last half of *Leviathan* were under a double servitude. They were bound both to the periodizations of biblical history and, willy-nilly, to the structure of *Leviathan* itself.

Beginning with the achievement of *Leviathan* (many books have been written from its paragraphs), one necessarily places one's own scholarly enterprise within an ongoing history of thought, often making the role of philosopher merge with that of commentator. As both Locke and Mill were to assert, this condition is not necessarily a limit on the intellectual freedom of the philosopher. In fact, to start with the premise that the philosopher is entirely free—the governing assumption of the first half of *Leviathan* and of all analytic philosophy—might only end with the assertion that what he can teach us is infinitely less than what political life requires. Conversely, to be bound to a history of ideas—the governing assumption of the second half of *Leviathan* and of all commentaries—might liberate thought and politics from the negative and dissolving conclusions of analytic philosophy. Students of liberalism today might inhabit both of its worlds, if only provisionally, in order to understand liberalism's larger structure and logic.

Possibilities of this sort will be considered at the conclusion of this study. At this point, some utilities and some hazards of my approach should be indicated. First the hazards. For all of the writers discussed, I take their writings on religious belief and theology seriously, that is, not only as context but also as text, integral to their theories of politics. This author shares with most of his readers a lack of training in theology and a lack of specific knowledge of seventeenth- and eighteenth-century religious disputation. And like most students of political philosophy, I have been trained to judge the consistency of theories of political obligation but not the quality and use of biblical interpretation. Despite these handicaps, I think it is possible for me to demonstrate the systematic use of religious categories in liberal political philosophy, in ways which preclude the assumption that their use is simply a refuge of failed logic.

I should also warn the reader of the stress I place upon history or notions of time in understanding liberalism. I treat theories of history in these writings as integral to the structure and logic of liberal political philosophy. As will become evident later, the use of "historical" versus "universal" or 'logical" forms of argument is more appropriate to some topics than to others. For example, *super*natural religion is almost always discussed as a mode of history, natural religion as a mode of logic. So, too, with more obviously political things: political executives and magistrates are more usually perceived as existing in time, while legislatures and judges in civil disputes are seen as inhabiting a world devoid of historical location and movement. A parallel distinction is found between criminal and civil law and between the notions of political loyalty and legal obligation. The weight I give to subjects discussed in the historical mode is much greater than that given in most studies of Hobbes, Locke, and Mill. To some extent, this weighting proves what I want to prove—the centrality of historical argument—and is thus open to the charge of circularity. My initial response is that our understanding of their nonhistorical arguments is enhanced in the process as well, and that many gaps and logical absurdities alleged in these writings are transformed when placed alongside their theories of history and religion.

   A last hazard which requires warning is related to the previous two. Stressing religion and giving prominence to historical modes of argument in liberal political theory necessarily effects the location and meaning of politics in these writings. Politics in a world bounded by interest and reason is usually centered in the realm of what Locke termed "civil interests"—physical health and safety and objects of economic value. The meaning and purpose of politics, therefore, is closely allied to the interests, institutions, and psychological mechanisms which constitute civil society. Issues which touch directly on government—obedience to and enforcement of law, the relationship of public power to economic life, and the selection and control of officials—are then discussed in terms of the norms of civil society. In contrast, politics in a world marked by supernatural religious belief and distinct historical epochs assumes a different aspect. In some respects, politics seen this way becomes disconnected from the laws, moral rules, and economic necessities of civil society. As politics acquires a broader and more autonomous meaning, its location in men also changes. Psychological principles quite adequate to account for obedience to law, the keeping of agreements, and political choice are no longer sufficient, while the psychological principles used to explain popular religion, altruism, and expressive modes of action come into prominence. In this view, political man cannot be comprehended as a bundle of legal rights and duties or as a physical container for the endless play of desire and aversion. In a historical and religious perspective, the political capacity of man is his ability to act on his conscious commitment to a way of life. By stressing this other world of liberal political theory, I am not suggesting that politics is thereby placed beyond the reach of philosophical understanding. On the contrary, by showing how philosophers within the liberal tradition deal with these themes systematically and often profoundly, I would hope that our critical understanding of their philosophic enterprise may become more sympathetic as the reach of philosophy itself is seen as expanded.

Some of the uses of this study have already been suggested. I must add that it makes possible the examination from a new perspective of the role of de facto theories of political obligation in the liberal tradition. Obligation grounded in conquest or in the sheer power of the ruler is a familiar formulation of the maxim that might makes right. But religious belief and theories of action based on habit, tradition, and the matrix of historical institutions also constitute a kind of de facto argument: they are ways of describing the existence of public power which, in this case, happens to protect a liberal social, economic, and legal order. These complex explanations differ from formal de facto theories of obligation, however, and may even constitute a means of escaping the grip of de facto argument. Reliance on the formal necessity of de facto power is most typically found in the logic and psychology of men presumed to be born in liberty (a state of nature). In contrast, justifications of political power from the standpoint of habit, tradition, or prevailing belief presume man to be born in servitude (history and religion). But some forms of servitude bestow a greater degree of *political* freedom on men than the liberty of men in the state of nature. Elements of considered choice and self-consciousness mark the historical and religious formulations of de facto obligation; timeless necessity marks the more analytic and rational ones. On this reading, the freedom specifically relevant to political life and action is of a different order from the liberties embedded in the legal, moral, and economic mechanisms of civil society—even a civil society ruled by de facto power.

It remains to claim one utility which may not be desired by all students of political philosophy. An implicit assumption of my study is that the lines dividing criticism, interpretation, and construction of political philosophy are often blurred. The humblest glossarist of Hobbes or Locke today should be made aware of the dual nature of his enterprise by remembering that some of the boldest and most original political argument formulated by Hobbes and Locke was in their interpretation of the Bible. To be bound by allegiance to "texts" in philosophy is not necessarily a hindrance to freedom of the mind. The other side of this conclusion also holds: criticism consisting of the detection of logical error and absurdity in the major texts, followed by amendment and tighter reformulation is usually less significant an enterprise than first appears. If it is indeed the case that liberal political philosophy is a complex structure created by and addressed to men "born to two worlds," the errors and absurdities so proudly exposed might only indicate the inherent limits of discourse in one world and a shift to the logic of another. Hannah Arendt puts it best: "The truth of the matter is that elementary logical mistakes are quite rare in the history of philosophy; what appear to be errors in logic [are so only] to minds disencumbered of questions that have been uncritically dismissed as 'meaningless.' "[6] By seeking to recover a tradition of discourse within, but seemingly counter to, prevailing understandings of liberal political philosophy, we might better understand the patterns of interpretation and criticism which mark our own studies.

To accomplish the purposes of this study requires that I often introduce complex ways of seeing familiar and even simple teachings. I am compelled to surround books and chapters familiar to students of political thought with writings and vocabulary unfamiliar to them. By surrounding what is generally known with what is generally unknown in the writings of Hobbes, Locke, and Mill, I hope that I will not obscure the familiar in new shadows but that I will clarify and even transform it by different lights.

Part One

Thomas Hobbes

Reason . . . so farre from teaching us any thing of God's nature . . . cannot teach us our own nature, nor the nature of the smallest creature living.

Hobbes, *Leviathan*

For the law is all the . . . reason we have.

Hobbes, "The Questions Concerning
Liberty, Necessity, and Chance"

This study begins by addressing the structure and dynamics of the first half of *Leviathan* in three contexts: in past history, in a state of nature, and in a political society established in history according to standards discovered by natural reason. My initial purpose in isolating these contexts is to show that each is radically deficient. Man in history fights, exploits, turns illusion into law, restlessly throws away his life and the lives of others in sacrifice to idols of his own imagination. Man in the state of nature is uncorrupted by history but is unable to turn intentions into action: poverty, savagery, and conflict mark his short and miserable life. Man in Hobbes's rational commonwealth is absurd: he joins with others to preserve his own life by creating a sovereign who has the power to destroy him at will. Moreover, this artificially created sovereign on whom all else depends is pitifully weak: the loyalty of his subjects stops when the safety of their skin begins. Moreover, natural reason and natural religion teach the subjects that the ultimate reward for a life of virtue and sacrifice is the same as the punishment for a life of unmitigated vice: eternal death. Any private man or foreign prince promising a greater reward for obedience or a greater punishment for disobedience—and whose promises are believed—would quickly replace the Leviathan.

13

Hobbes's rationally constructed commonwealth is as empty of historical purpose as its institution is devoid of historic possibility; he ends the
first half of *Leviathan* hoping that his handbook of scientific politics "derived from the Principles of Natural Reason" will fall into the hands of
an incorruptible prince and so "convert this Truth of Speculation, into
the Utility of Practice."[1] But Hobbes does not end his politics with this
vain hope. A second half to *Leviathan* remains, containing an interpretation of Judeo-Christian history and its meaning for man's political and
moral life. The second half of *Leviathan* is not a new and entirely separate enterprise. Its subject matter, mode of argument, and psychological
assumptions are all introduced in the early chapters (10–12) of the book.
These three chapters, bounded on one side by psychology and epistemology (1–9) and on the other by the state of nature and its laws (13–16), are
a philosophically coherent explanation of the rise and fall of political regimes in history. This theory of history early in *Leviathan* needs explaining for two important reasons: first, Hobbes utterly ignores what he says
in these chapters for the remainder of Part I and all of Part II; and second, all of the major elements of these chapters are reintroduced in Part
III and Part IV, but there in the context of biblical laws and (corrupt)
ecclesiastical history (IV) and biblical faith and redemptive prophecy (III).

Contemporary scholarship has ignored the connection between
Hobbes's three-chapter general theory of politics in history and the entire
second and "religious" half of *Leviathan*. The result has been a variety of
alternative approaches, each containing prima facie weaknesses. The simplest and most widely used alternative is to write off the entire second
half of *Leviathan* as "nonphilosophy" and unworthy of serious attention.
The result is to write off as well (or radically misread) the philosophical
account of history and religion given in Part I.[2] Another alternative is to
conflate supernatural and natural religion under the general rubric of
"theism," thereby reducing the second half of *Leviathan* to an application
(Christianity) of a more general principle (natural religion, the god of nature).[3] This alternative not only confuses two notions of religion which
Hobbes consistently distinguishes but ignores the fact that Hobbes denies
all efficacy in the world to a religion based on what unaided reason can
tell us. As Hobbes makes plain, even as early as Chapters 11 and 12, no
civil or moral philosophy in the past has made its way in the world without the aid of supernatural gods, real or imagined; in all of man's past,
prophets and not philosophers have given intellectual birth to the opinions creating power among men.

A third and more plausible alternative is to see the second half of *Leviathan* as "policy"—Hobbes's artful manipulation of prevailing belief patterns designed to make the political and moral teachings acceptable to his
contemporaries.[4] Curiously, this alternative often destroys itself by adding

that Hobbes's theology is so obviously outrageous, so far removed from respectable Christian opinion, that no informed contemporary believer would be fooled. But even without such a self-destroying feature, this alternative view makes the implicit assumption that Hobbes's politics does not require any particular kind of supernatural belief and that societies with markedly different religious principles or none at all are equally capable of instituting and maintaining Hobbes's commonwealth. To assume the contrary, that the two halves of the *Leviathan* are integrally connected, is not to deny the "policy" of the second half but to insist that such policy is a necessary part of Hobbes's political philosophy. Put differently, the philosophy of the first half and the theology of the second are joined together in *Leviathan* by history: political life exists in time, created and sustained by all men who act within the constraints imposed by memory, present desires, and prophecy. Before one enters into the text itself, then, some preliminary remarks are needed to make clear the ways in which concepts of time and history help one to see *Leviathan* as one book.

Supernatural religion is itself history: a belief in a particular story of past, present, and future, and the acceptance by the believers of the religious, political, and moral duties which honor and vindicate that story.[5] Thus, the first justification for taking Parts III and IV of *Leviathan* seriously is found in Hobbes's psychological principles: every man seeks a meaning for his life by connecting his personal history and destiny to some larger story of the history and destiny of the world. To know this is to understand that the power of political regimes in history is generated by supernatural religious belief motivating men to die willingly in defense of their "interests," i.e., their ultimate destinies.

A second use of the dimension of history in understanding the *Leviathan* involves the issue of the many paradoxes and/or absurdities which commentators claim to have discovered in the first half of the book. By viewing the first half from the perspective of the "revealed history" of the second half, one can show many of these claims to be without foundation, while many of the central concepts of Hobbes's politics (authorization, obligation, covenant) take on an altered meaning.[6] A third way in which history is valuable as a connecting link is that it permits us to see more clearly the place of *Leviathan* in the context of the political crises of seventeenth-century England. The remarkable outpouring of writings on political obligation occasioned by the "Engagement" controversy combined theological, historical, and philosophical discourse. A view of *Leviathan* in its entirety not only permits us to benefit from a comparative perspective provided by historical scholarship but also provides additional clues for understanding the particular structuring of *Leviathan*.[7]

A final way of stressing history as a means of understanding the relevance of religion to the politics of the *Leviathan* is retrospective. With the aid of the second half of *Leviathan*, we can more clearly understand the place of Hobbes's politics in the later intellectual development of liberalism. Hobbes's theology and interpretation of church history is often echoed by Locke and, through Locke, in later liberal philosophy. Moreover, in constructing a rudimentary "philosophical" or "natural" history to parallel and complement his sacred and ecclesiastical one, Locke also provides a means of disengaging liberal politics from biblical theology altogether. In the hands of eighteenth-century Scottish philosophers and later utilitarians, this form of history seems to replace its religious counterpart altogether as a source of explanation and justification of liberal truths. Lest we think that *this* development signals an end of the relevance of *Leviathan*'s second half, however, we should remember that this form of history was soon criticized in almost the same terms used to discredit the first half of *Leviathan:* it posits a society which cannot generate political support. In this view, natural history is to sacred history what natural religion is to supernatural religion: it has no hold on the opinions and motives of men.

In the nineteenth century, John Stuart Mill and other liberal critics of utilitarianism do not so much doubt the psychological, moral, and legal truths posited by utilitarianism as they question the sufficiency of those truths for politics. As if to recreate the tension between the two halves of *Leviathan*, these writers increasingly come to see liberalism in historical terms—as a story and as a tradition of ideas. This development makes the second half of *Leviathan* as important for understanding liberalism in the mid-nineteenth century and after as the first half is for understanding the utilitarianism that preceded it. Not only do these nineteenth-century critics reintroduce religious belief into their historical understanding of the rise of liberal values, they incorporate variants of these same beliefs into ways of justifying contemporary liberal values. Moreover, those most instrumental in this process of revision lead the way in creating a liberal "history of ideas." This history is important in two ways: first, it provides an alternative to natural history and, second, it constitutes a nonrational source of obligation for the philosophical truths of liberalism. Like the second half of *Leviathan*, the history of ideas begins with authoritative texts which, through interpretation, can yield knowledge of our highest duties. The penultimate testament to the relevance and power of *Leviathan*, then, is its importance as one of the authoritative texts in the nineteenth-century history of ideas. The ultimate testament to its power over twentieth-century liberalism is that, despite all of the definitive refutations of its teachings by the "unaided reason" of analytic philosophy, we continue to study it in order to understand who we are—in Hobbes's words, to understand "our own nature."

1

Rules, Rulers, and Kingdoms

When men are intellectually stripped of ties binding them together, when they are viewed apart from laws, customs, extended family connection, political loyalty, and religious belief, a new mode of political speculation begins: liberalism. According to Hobbes in particular and liberalism in general, this world begins without gods, rulers, or churches, justice or injustice, virtue or vice. For the next two centuries after Hobbes, this world was to be filled and filled again with a variety of new authorities, standards, and patterns of discipline. But the beginnings of this new world are not entirely empty: it begins with natural man, the most potent symbol of the liberal imagination. This natural man is the primary unit for the construction of a new world, a world filled with explicitly rational rules of conduct that are institutionalized in sovereigns, civil laws, churches, and property. This new man and these new worlds, however, are in some ways haunted. Just beneath their hypothetically constructed surfaces lie demonic fears, godlike hopes, and the capacity for madness and transcendence.

Men without Rules

Hobbes begins all three of his major political writings with a discussion of "natural man."[1] In *Elements of Law,* he defines men's natural faculties in terms of "powers" of body and mind. Bodily powers are "power nutritive, power motive and power generative." The "powers of mind" consist of the "cognitive . . . and motive." In *De Cive*, these faculties are "reduced unto four kinds: bodily strength, experience, reason, passion." In *Leviathan,* Hobbes defines the faculties of natural man in terms of how the latter acquire "thoughts."[2] From this perspective, the faculty of sense is "the Originall" of all thoughts, for ideas, considered "singly . . . are every one a Representation or Apparence, of some quality, or other Accident of a body without us." The faculty of imagination is "decaying sense." Simple imagination is to "recall" an object "formerly perceived by Sense." Compounded imagination consists of combining isolated former sense impressions; Hobbes uses the example of a "Centaure" as a compound of the idea of man and horse. Imagination is the same as memory, except that the latter expresses more clearly the idea of decayed sense impression. Experience is simply "much memory, or memory of many things."[3] When Hobbes considers trains of thought or imagination, he introduces the faculty of passion or, more specifically, appetite and aversion. Guided thought is "passionate thought" in that ideas are "regulated by some desire, and designe." Guided trains of thought or "mental discourse" are a form of "seeking." Men "seek the causes, or means that produce" some remembered idea (literally, an "object" of sense impression).[4]

Thus far in Hobbes's learning theory, the mental discourse or "thinking capacity" of men does not differ from that of other animals. All animals receive sensory impressions and regulate their "images" of past sense impressions by seeking the means or causes of desired objects. Men differ from other animals, however, in regulating their thoughts by a distinctly human form of seeking. Men, "when imagining any thing whatsoever, seek all the possible effects, that can by it be produced; that is to say, we imagine what we can do with it, when wee have it." To be able to imagine what to do with something is to introduce a range much beyond the simple sensual desires "such as . . . hunger, thirst, lust, and anger."[5] Men can project new uses for desired objects into the future; men thus have the mental capacity to "desire" a future which is different from the past. The difficulty, however, is in attaining that future.

The relationships among "seeking," "thoughts," and "mental discourse" on the one hand, and the "future" on the other, constitute a difficulty for Hobbes's natural man. Only present time exists in nature. The past exists "in the Memory only, but things *to come* [have] no being at all; the Future [is] but a fiction of the mind, applying the sequels of actions Past, to the actions that are Present." To act in the present on the basis of experience is to act on a "praesumption of the Future, contracted from the Experience of time Past."[6] This is prudence. The more experience a man has, the more certain is his presumption as a guide for his mental discourse and his actions. Both prudential knowledge and prudent actions typify man and beast. Because of the limited range of the objects of the beast's simple passions, prudential "thinking" and prudential acting suffice for it. By contrast, man's passion-directed "mental discourse" can encompass distantly imagined futures. Lacking the gift of true prophecy, his thoughts and actions are hazardous guesswork.

In the discussion of man's natural faculties up to this point, Hobbes's epistemological framework assumes an intimate relationship between acting (external motion) and thinking. Passion, the "cause" of regulated thoughts, is itself a kind of action, defined as "endeavor," or "the small beginnings of Motion, within the body of man, before they appear in . . . visible actions." This "internal motion," in turn, depends on "a precedent thought of wither, which way, and what; it is evident [then], that the Imagination is the first internall beginning of all Voluntary [external] Motion."[7]

But man, according to Hobbes, has unique capacities beyond those of sense and memory. Natural man is also distinguished from other animals by his capacity for *industry*—in its original meaning of "contrivance." Hobbes's definition of reason rests on this capacity for industry:

> Reason is not as Sense, and Memory, born with us; nor gotten by Experience onely, as Prudence is; but attayned by Industry; first in apt imposing of Names; and secondly by getting a good and orderly Method in proceeding from the Elements, which are Names, to Assertions made by Connexion of one of them to another; and so to Syllogisms, which are the Connexions of one Assertion to another, till we come to a knowledge of all the Consequences of names appertaining to the subject in hand; and that is it, men call Science. And whereas Sense and Memory are but knowledge of Fact, which is a thing past, and irrevocable; Science is the knowledge of Consequences.[8]

Industry in the form of naming is not, however, related simply to man's capacity for "knowledge of consequences," or science. Naming is more generally related to speech, the overall use of which is "to transferre our Mental Discourse, into Verbal . . . the Trayne of our Thoughts, into a Trayne of Words." Speech consists of the use of names for "Markes, or Notes of remembrance," and for

> Signes . . . to signifie (by their connexion and order) one to another, what [men] conceive, or think of each matter; and also what they desire, feare, or have any other passion for.[9]

Both mental and verbal discourse hold great hope and great danger for men. The great hope lies in the possibility of true knowledge of consequences, or science; the great danger lies in opinion and absurdity:

> they that have *no* Science, are in better, and nobler condition with their naturall Prudence; than men, that by mis-reasoning, or by trusting them that reason wrong, fall upon false and absurd generall rules. For ignorance of causes, and of rules, does not set men so farre out of their way, as relying on false rules, and taking for causes of what they aspire to, those that are not so. . . .[10]

"Natural sense and imagination," which are the origin of both passion and experience (prudence), "are not subject to absurdity. Nature itself cannot erre: and as men abound in copiousness of language; so they become more wise, or more mad than ordinary."[11]

Hobbes's argument concerning the relationship between language and "madness" is a complex one, because it involves a relationship among passion, discourse, and action. We have already mentioned that "mental discourse" is "regulated by some desire, and designe." When this "mental discourse" consists of names, absurdity and "madnesse" become a distinct possibility.

The use of names in discourse yields only the true or false "knowledge" of the consequence "of one *name* of a thing, to another *name* of the same thing" and is, therefore, only conditional. When men deliberate, "the Appetites, and Aversions are raised by foresight of the good and evil consequences, and sequels of the action whereof we deliberate." Deliberation, then, is the internal "motion," alternately, of "Appetites, and Aversions, Hopes and Feares, concerning one and the same thing." Good and evil are names which men give to the objects of appetite and aversion. Similarly, pleasure is the "apparance, or sense of Good" and "displeasure," or pain, "the apparance, or sense of Evill."[12]

The problem in the process of deliberation, then, revolves around the "forsight of good and evill consequences." The good or evil effect of an action "dependeth on the foresight of a long chain of consequences, of which very seldome any man is able to see to the end." Despite this failing, appetite and aversion depend on this "foresight" of good and evil consequences. Felicity is the "continuall successe" in obtaining objects of appetite.[13] The future construed as consequences of actions, however, is "but a fiction of the mind." Prudence, based on experience, can never yield universally true consequences. Moreover, each man has only a limited set of experiences or memories. Men are not animals, to be sure, and can transcend prudence through industry, and acquire science, the knowledge of consequences. But, through industry, they can also manufacture absurdity and "opinion," both in "naming" and in connecting names. Both forms of industry constitute "acquired wit," which constitutes the decisive source of inequalities or differences among men.

Both science and opinion constitute collective as well as individual futures. Buttressed by the natural capacity for industry and speech, the natural faculties of men provide a foundation for Hobbes's discussion of inequality. Just as man is unique in having the privilege of reason, attainable by industry, so, through industry, does he uniquely possess "the Privilege of Absurdity."[14]

Natural Passion, Acquired Wit, and Historical Madness

Hobbes discusses madness in Chapter 8 of *Leviathan*, "of the Vertues commonly called Intellectual, and their contrary Defects." This discussion is closely related to Hobbes's concern with absurdity, belief, and opinion, begun briefly in Chapter 5 of *Leviathan* ("Of Reason and Science") and continued in Chapters 10 ("Power"), 11 ("Manners"), and 12 ("Religion"). It will be useful to outline Hobbes's various definitions of opinion, both in order to distinguish opinion from reason and to show how Hobbes relates power inequalities to opinion, and opinion to forms of madness.

Opinion is defined by Hobbes in the following contexts.

Supposition or presumption: Either in discourse or deliberation, we often admit a proposition, without it being evidently true, in order to join it to other propositions to see if the conclusion reached "will lead us into any absurdity." If the conclusion is not absurd, it still remains an opinion.[15]

Error or absurdity: To accept as true a proposition resulting from false reasoning from a mere supposition, is to hold an opinion.[16]

Faith and belief: To trust another man's statement is an "opinion of the veracity of the man" or "an opinion of the truth of the saying," or both.[17]

Conscience: In *Elements of Law,* conscience is defined as "opinion of evidence." In *Leviathan,* Hobbes begins with the idea of two or more men each being *conscious* that the other "know[s] of one and the same fact." Conscience was the term to signify this mutual knowledge. Thus it was thought wrong for a "man to speak against his Conscience; or to corrupt or force another so to do." Metaphorically, conscience signifies "knowledge of men's own secret facts, and secret thoughts." Thus, conscience is used by men to protect obstinately held opinion.[18]

From the perspective of the holder (as opposed to the maker) of opinion, Hobbes's most general definition occurs in Chapter 7 of *Leviathan,* in a summary of a statement concerning belief in the Christian creed:

> From whence we may inferre, that when wee believe any saying
> whatsoever it be, to be true, from arguments taken, not from the thing
> itselfe, or from principles of naturall Reason, but from Authority, and
> good opinion wee have, of him that hath sayd it; then is the speaker,
> or person we belief in, or trust in, and whose word we take, the object
> of our faith; and the Honour done in Believing, is done to him onely.

Thus, "whatsoever we believe, upon no other reason, then what is drawn from authority of men onely . . . is Faith in men onely."[19]

Authority, opinion, and belief: what causes men to believe, have faith in, other men? And how is it that these other men come to be focal points of belief? How do some men come to manufacture certain forms of speech that inspire trust?

The beginning of an answer to the last question is found primarily in Hobbes's discussion of intellectual "virtues and defects." Intellectual virtue consists of natural or acquired wit. The former, attained "by Use onely, and Experience; without Method, Culture, or Instruction," consists largely of [c]elerity of imagining [fancy] . . . and steddy direction to some approved end [discretion]." Differences in natural wit among men can be traced to differences in men's passions. However, Hobbes is hard put to see much difference among men regarding "natural wit" as a virtue. Great fancy alone is "a kind of madness," while discretion is really prudence, depending upon "much Experience, and Memory of the like things, and their consequences heretofore." Since experience depends on age, men of equal age do not differ much as to quantity of experience, but only in "different sorts of businesse." Thus, differences in prudence are largely dependent upon the steady direction toward a "designe in hand" and observation of the various means that "conduce to that designe." Hobbes's discussion of natural wit, then, is essentially the same as his earlier discussion of "traynes of thought." Only with regard to "Fancy" does he admit significant differences among men, but he has difficulty defending even this, since *natural* fancy or quick imagining is simply the "swift succession of one thought to another."[20] To deal only with the individual and his mind is to reach an impasse in explaining either power differentials among men or the rise of opinion, for opinion is expressed in speech and is symbolized and buttressed by power-wielding institutions. Only acquired wit can shade into acquired power over the actions and beliefs of other men, because opinion is a form of predicition or prophecy and men will shape their actions in accordance with their opinions. Those who shape opinions, then, have a control over other men's powers and faculties.

When Hobbes turns to "acquired wit"—that is, reason and/or opinion based not on "thoughts" but on names and speech—the differences among men are radically increased. Acquired wit is attained by industry. As a virtue, this wit is "none but Reason; which is grounded on the right use of Speech; and produceth the Sciences."[21] To explain the causes of difference in acquired wit, both as a virtue and as a "defect," Hobbes shifts to an explicitly social and contrived context.

> The causes of this difference of Witts, are in the Passions. . . . The Passions that most of all cause the differences of Wit, are Principally, the more or less Desire of Power, of Riches, of Knowledge, and of Honour. All of which may be reduced to the first, that is Desire of Power.[22]

In this context, "Fancy" becomes crucial to inequality of acquired wit:

> For the Thoughts, are to the Desires, as Scouts, and Spies, to range abroad, and find the way to the things Desired: All Stedinesse of the minds motion, and all quicknesse of the same, proceeding from thence. For as to have no Desire, is to be Dead: so to have weak Passions, is Dulnesse; and to have Passions indifferently for every thing, Giddinesse, and Distraction; and to have stronger, and more vehement

Passions for any thing, than is ordinarily seen in others, is that which men call Madnesse.[23]

In this social context, the mark of madness is known by external action and effect. "In summe," says Hobbes, "all Passions that produce strange and unusuall behavior, are called by the generall name of Madnesse. . . . [T]here is no doubt, but the passions themselves, when they tend to Evill, are degrees of the same." Thus, for example,

> in them, that are possessed of an opinion of being inspired, [acts of folly] be not visible alwayes in one man . . . yet when many of them conspire together, the Rage of the whole multitude is visible enough. For what argument of Madnesse can there be greater, than to clamour, strike, and throw stones at our best friends? . . . And if this be Madnesse in the multitude, it is the same in every particular man.

Indeed, Hobbes continues, the "very [fact of] arrogating such inspiration to themselves, is argument enough [of madness]."[24]

More ominous than "inspiration" is the attribution of madness Hobbes makes to "everyman":

> For, [I believe] the most sober men, when they walk alone without care and employment of the mind, would be unwilling the vanity and Extravagance of their thoughts at that time should be publiquely seen: which is a confession, that Passions unguided, are for the most part meere Madnesse.

After examining competing explanations for madness, Hobbes concludes this discussion of intellectual virtues by adding "amongst the sorts of Madnesse . . . that abuse of words" called "by the name of Absurdity," found particularly in the writings of scholastic theologians.[25]

What has "Passion for Power" to do with theology? Even in his discussion of natural wit, Hobbes speaks of "The secret thoughts of [men running] over all things, holy, prophane, clean, obscene, grave, and light, without shame or blame."[26] Are secret thoughts ultimately as mysterious as unguided passions and, therefore, "mad"? More generally, how can the distinction between science and opinion be viewed as an attack on historical ways of thinking about politics? These are perplexing questions. That Hobbes raises them at all while purportedly dealing with natural man is strange enough. That he raises them even before he discusses the position of man in a state of "meer Nature" is stranger yet. After a brief outline "Of the Severall Subjects of Knowledge," Hobbes attempts to bring all of these themes together in three chapters concerning power, manners, and religion.

When Hobbes turns to these topics, he shifts to historical analysis and tries to show that history is a record of individual prudence become "mad" within frameworks of collective belief and therefore of collective power. He

relationship of opinion and madness is closely connected to Hobbes's
ry of the relationship between opinion and political authority in past
ory. Involved in both relationships is acquired wit as a product of the
ion for power. This passion motivates men to construct chains of thought
discourse in order to plot the consequences of proposed action toward
e imagined or "fancied" object felt to be good. When this "plotting"
"reckoning" takes place among men, power becomes important. "The
er of a Man, (to take it Universally,) is his present means, to obtain
e future apparent Good. And is either Originall [natural] or Instru-
tal."[1]

Iobbes's distinction between natural and instrumental power is discussed
ost wholly in terms of acquired power. Natural power is simply the
inence of the Faculties of Body, or Mind." But in a social context, most
ver consists of "strengths united," of the "compounded Powers
. . men." Thus, instrumental power is acquired by natural power or by
ches, Reputation, and the secret working of God" (good luck) to be
d as "means and Instruments to acquire more" instrumental power. In
cial context power is, "like to Fame, increasing as it proceeds."[2]

Iobbes's discussion of power is a kind of vicious circle: natural power
minence of natural faculties; instrumental power is based partly on this
nence and partly on acquired trappings which increase the eminence of
an. But how does a man acquire riches and a reputation for good luck,
"popularity," and even for power itself?

he Value, or Worth of a man is . . . his Price: that is to say, so much
s would be given for the use of his Power: and therefore is not
bsolute; but a thing dependent on the need and judgment of another.[3]

identifies three chief threats to liberal man. The first is "priv
unregulated by desire for material objects in the material worl
consists of these same "private thoughts" made systematic
philosophy and religion. Finally, one finds public power, politi
and law "sanctioned" by opinions whose origins and reasons
cannot be known because they cannot be connected directly
dential calculation or to science. One might say that Hobbe
between rational trains of thought and "madness" and his para
between science and collective madness or opinion provide t
attack on historical politics. This attack begins with the argui
past political history and political discourse can be explaine
in a new way.

Hobbes's argument proceeds on three related levels. Firs
logical origins of nonrational ideas can be found in humar
Second, the social or collective explanation of historical polit
showing that these ideas become externalized in absurd spe
moral opinion, and, most importantly, invisible power (gods) i
in religious doctrines and institutionalized religion. Third, t
litical connection between the individual and historical polit
a linkage between invisible power and psychological mechan
to all men.

If the power of a man is the opinion of power by other men and if his value is also dependent upon opinion, how does it arise in the first place? In his discussion of power, Hobbes only tells us that to value a man is to honor him, but "Honour consisteth onely in the Opinion of Power."[4]

Thus, the mechanics of human connection and the generation of power among men depend on opinion. Within the limits of Hobbes's discussion of power in Chapter 10, this opinion is not "mad" or irrational; on the contrary, each man calculates how the powers of other men might hinder or help his own pursuit of felicity. The search for "connection" with other men is instrumental and prudential. Some men need the protection of other men, and a protector increases his own power if it "pays" him to protect another.

In Hobbes's discussion of manners, he continues his analysis of power. Manners are "those qualities of man-kind that concern their living together in Peace and Unity." The consideration of manners is also a discussion of men's desires and actions in a social context because it concerns morals or "goods." Earthly felicity "is a continuall progresse of the desire, from one object to another; the attaining of the former, being still but the way to the latter." Because objects of desire differ, so do voluntary actions of men, "aris[ing] partly from the diversity of the passions, in divers men; and partly from the difference of the knowledge, or *opinion* each one has of the causes, which produce the effect desired." Even a moderate man "cannot assure the power and means to live well, which he hath present, without the acquisition of more." In a social context, differences in manners produce "a perpetual and restless desire of Power after power, that ceaseth onely in Death."[5]

This discussion of manners is strikingly similar to Hobbes's earlier discussion of the regulation of men's thoughts, of the process by which "deliberation" leads to voluntary action, and of the acquisition of "wit" through industry. Once again, the future is portrayed as troubling for men who search for causes "which produce the effect desired." Hobbes's discussion of manners, then, occurs in a context both of society and power, but here he seeks to discover how bonds of political unity are created among men.

Prudential seeking among "private men" is not absurd insofar as the power differentials which result are "merited." The problem Hobbes raises when he turns to politics and religious belief, however, is that "estimates" (prudence) and "goods" change their character. Prudential calculation is normally an estimate of future causes and effects based on experience of past causal linkages. But the more men "think ahead" the less confidence do they have in their estimates. Within the framework of a limitless future, prudence produces anxiety. Anxiety gives rise to the dependence of most men on the "invisible," entirely personal, and "unmerited" authority of other men. Everyday prudential manners are necessarily colored by this authority which is expressed in laws, moral rules, and religious duties.

Thus, Hobbes shifts to a consideration of common power, or political power, and then to invisible power, or the realm of religious mystery, personality, and gods.

> Ignorance of causes, disposeth, or rather constraineth a man to rely on the advise, and the authority of others. For all men whom the truth concerns, if they rely not on their own, must rely on the opinion of some other, whom they think wiser than themselves, and see not why he should deceive them.[6]

At the most simple level, men want to know the outcome of events in the future "because the knowledge of them, maketh men better able to order the present to their best advantage." At this level anxiety is a necessary concomitant of human desire, given the limits of prudential knowledge. But when man "cannot assure himselfe of the true causes of things[,] he supposes causes of them" either by relying on his own "fancy" or that of others. Thus, "men have created in the world innumerable sorts of Gods. And this Feare of things invisible, is the naturall Seed of . . . Religion." Knowing of this fear, some men "nourish, dresse, and forme [this seed] into Lawes; and . . . adde to it of their own invention, any opinion of the causes of future events, by which they thought they should best be able to govern others, and make unto themselves the greatest use of their Powers."[7]

Hobbes is able to move from personal anxiety to collective gods because

> it is peculiar to the nature of Man, to be inquisitive into the Causes of the Events they see, some more some lesse; but in *all men,* so much, as to be curious in the search of the causes of their own good and evill fortune.[8]

Such a search ultimately ends in mystery because "it is impossible for a man, who continually endeavoreth to secure himselfe against the evill he fears, and procure the good he desireth, not to be in a perpetuall solicitude of the time to come." Unable to find an object of this "perpetuall feare," men first invent, then accuse or praise, "some Power, or Agent Invisible."[9]

To produce gods out of fear, however, is to hinder men "from the search of the causes of other things; and thereby gives occasion to feigning of as many Gods, as there be men that feigne them." And men, "not knowing that such apparitions are nothing else but creatures of the Fancy, think [them] to be reall, and externall Substances."[10] Having invented these gods, men can rely only on their own prudence when seeking to understand how these "invisible Agents" act to cause events. But this prudence necessarily ends in superstition and personal political authority.

Finally, since these gods are thought to "declare to men the things which shall hereafter come to passe, especially concerning their good and evill fortune," men are likely to conjecture on the basis of a few events, and take this conjecture for "Prognostiques of the like encounter ever after" or to "believe the . . . Prognostiques from other men." Thus prudential calculation shades into anxiety and thence into those structures of religion and politics which define historical men. The natural faculties of men lead them into "opinion of Ghosts, Ignorance of second causes, Devotion towards what men fear, and Taking of things Causall for Prognostiques." These constituent parts of the "Naturall seed of Religion . . . by reason of the different Fancies, Judgements, and Passions of severall men, hath grown up into ceremonies so different, that those which are used by one man, are for the most part ridiculous to another."[11]

On these "ridiculous" results, actual political orders are founded. Men who have "nourished and ordered" these seeds "according to their own invention," do so "with a purpose to make those men that [rely] on them, the more apt to Obedience, Laws, Peace, Charity, and civill Society." Hobbes calls such religion and political orders "Government of Religion" and "humane Politiques."[12]

A kind of madness haunts these political kingdoms, for men's desires and their "reckoning" of consequences are projected into time without limit. The gods invented are products of unguided passion, secret thoughts and fancies. Power among men in these kingdoms is really power based on belief in other men, to be sure, but it is backed ultimately by a belief in the "mad" product of men's fears. Desire for "power after power" may cease in death, but men who are living can place no time limit on their attempt to foresee future consequences. Within man lie unregulated thoughts and passions; without him lies an unknowable future. Prudence, experience, and external sense impression cannot cope with these mysteries. And yet, political orders are built on the mad products invented to cope with these mysteries. All men require surcease from potentially endless personal anxiety. What Hobbes terms "mystery," or that which cannot be known rationally, necessarily requires an answer, for the desire to know the unknowable future is a product of systematic self-interest.

Human Politics and the Gods of Fear

According to Hobbes, all commonwealths allegedly based on invisible power are founded on faith in men only. But the "seeds of religion" are natural and "can never be so abolished out of humane nature, but that new Religions may again be made to spring out of them, by the culture of such men, as . . . are in reputation."[13] Human or historical politics resembles a realm of "false prophecy," in that "formed Religion"

> is founded . . . upon the faith which a multitude hath in some one
> person, whom they believe not only to be a wise man, and to labor to

procure their happiness, but also to be a holy man, to whom God himselfe vouchsafeth to declare his will supernaturally.[14]

This faith in men is unstable because it is necessarily founded on opinion. Human politics and the consequent distribution of power among men is thus constantly threatened by the "failing of faith" in men. Human politics, as in all forms of power among men, is "a thing dependent upon the need[s] and judgement[s] of . . . others."[15] But political power differs from other power in that it binds men under the aegis of invisible power. By the same token, however, men are motivated to disobey political power when the reputation of men in power is undermined.

When the reputation of wisdom, sincerity, and love becomes suspect, belief in religion suffers likewise. As Hobbes states, "it followeth necessarily." For example, if men are asked to believe things obviously contradictory, the reputation for wisdom enjoyed by ministers declines. If "private ends" can be detected in the clergy in the acquisition of "Dominion, Riches, Dignity, or secure Pleasure, to themselves onely, or specially," it "taketh away the reputation of Love."[16]

Given these problems, human politics can be sustained only by the maintenance of intellectual and moral virtue on the part of the clergy. If ministers cannot maintain their virtue, human politics rests only on "the feare of the Civill Sword." Yet the stability of "invented religion" and historical politics suffers from a final failing which cannot be overcome by clerical virtue:

> Lastly, the testimony that men can render of divine Calling, can be no other, than the operation of Miracles; or true Prophecy, (which is also a Miracle). . . . And therefore, to those points of Religion, which have been received from them that did such Miracles; those that are added by such, as approve not their Calling by some Miracle, obtain no greater beliefe, that what the Custome . . . wrought into them. For as in naturall things, men of judgement require naturall signes, and arguments; so in supernaturall things, they require signes supernaturall, (which are Miracles,) before they consent inwardly, and from their hearts.[17]

Human politics is power backed by madness unless supernatural signs are in evidence in its support. Hobbes's judgment of "historical politics" is profoundly skeptical: "Seeing . . . Miracles now cease, we have no signe left."[18] In historical politics, rules of worship, moral rules, and civil rules are enforced by men who fear only the tortured imaginings of their own or other unregulated minds.

Hobbes begins the chapter on manners by inquiring into the desires which motivate men to obey "a common Power." He speaks of the "Desire of Ease, and sensuall delight," of the "Desire of Knowledge," and of the "Fear of Death and Wounds." These motivate a man to "abandon the protection

[that] might be hoped for from his own Industry, and Labor."[19] But this same man cannot escape "anxiety for the future time." "Every man," Hobbes argues, *"especially those that are over provident, . . .* has no repose, nor pause of his anxiety, but in sleep."[20]

Throughout his discussion of power, manners, and religion, Hobbes refers to men in social contexts; indeed, "manners" is a consideration of "those qualities of man-kind that concern their living together in Peace and Unity." These social contexts, however, are also historical contexts. In Chapter 10, he speaks of the honor, worth, and value given to men in a number of historical cases. The historical references are political or religious. In the two chapters which follow, Hobbes again repairs to political and religious history, even referring to recent events in France, Holland, and England. In all of these instances, however, he points to alternatives to history as a means of discovering the "invisble" causes of future events. The alternative to historical worth, he says, is merit, which is a legal right "due by promise: of which I shall say more hereafter, when I shall speak of Contracts."[21] The state of nature and the contractual origins of merit are alternatives to history, but behind these alternatives is science, the alternative to prophetic faith.

Hobbes's discussion of power, then, portrays men who think and act on "estimates," but this opinion does not shade into madness until he considers political power. In political and religious historical contexts, nonpolitical or "private" power-seeking cannot be "sensible," because the search for both protection and preferment necessarily shades into the felt reality of the power of political and religious office.[22]

But if the seed of religion is "natural," is not its irrational product also "natural"? If anxiety for future time cannot be abolished, how can religious and political invention be abolished? And if invention cannot be stopped, neither can periodic anarchy, civil war, and revolution. "As men abound in copiousness of language; so they become more wise, or more mad than ordinary." The history of human politics is a history of "copiousness of language" and a concomitant madness in power relationships. "Natural sense and imagination," on the other hand, "are not subject to absurdity,"[23] for nature is not absurd.

Science and reason supposedly provide an alternative means to produce "copiousness of language" in human society and thus to prevent natural anxiety from leading to absurdity. But in order for this to happen, the search for invisible power cannot begin with secret thoughts and unguided passions. The search for invisible power by reason must bypass anxiety; invisible power must be found "without thought of [our] fortune."

The acknowledging of one God Eternall, Infinite, and Omnipotent, may more easily be derived, from the desire men have to know the causes of naturall bodies, and their severall vertues, and operations; than from the feare of what was to befall them in time to come.[24]

This derivation of God's invisible power leads men to "choose to confess he is Incomprehensible, and above their understanding." To do otherwise is only to project and objectify things which appear in our dreams. These "apparitions are nothing else but creatures of Fancy."[25]

To derive a god by reason and confess him to be beyond understanding is also to confess that the "fancies" in ourselves are beyond natural understanding. The certainty of this knowledge of the limits of both self-understanding and "ultimate" understanding is the starting point for Hobbes's search for certainty in general. His search for "invisible power" through a study of the causes of natural bodies is a call to understand ourselves as if we, too, were natural bodies.[26] This is where Hobbes begins when he introduces the state of nature. This is also where he introduces us to liberal man and the possibility of impersonal political authority. Yet, the invisible power backing this order is not a "historical god" who acts providentially. The new political order will be timeless and will represent a victory over both history and those forms of personal anxiety which have led men to create gods from the perturbations of their own minds.

3

Rules in Nature

Up to this point, I have isolated those elements in the early chapters of *Leviathan* which tie Hobbes's psychology to religion and politics in history. In so doing, I have stressed those elements which point away from Hobbes's main enterprise in the first half of *Leviathan*, namely, to construct a reason-based civil philosophy. This enterprise begins with man in "meer Nature," not history, and ends with a stable commonwealth, not periodic chaos. Hobbes now considers the manners, passions, and powers of men in a nonhistorical context. Madness is gone; supernatural gods have been banished; priests, rituals, and codes of honor have disappeared. All power inequalities based on trust, loyalty, and opinion are gone. What remains the same is the psychological makeup of man. In the state of nature, however, this man learns different lessons from those taught in history. Whether these lessons alone are sufficient to transcend a history of irrationality, injustice, and conflict is an open question. Equally open is the question of whether Hobbes considers these lessons sufficient to create and sustain a Leviathan in history.

Manners in the State of Nature

At the very beginning of his discussion of the natural condition of mankind in "meer" nature, Hobbes deviates from his earlier discussion of power, manners, and religion in a crucial way, by "setting aside the arts grounded upon words."[1] He then demonstrates that men are roughly equal, because he has removed acquired wit from consideration altogether. In one stroke, the "gods of fear" are removed, "Government of Religion" vanishes, and the power relationships of historical politics are annihilated. In short, because of this initial deletion of the irrational products of men's capacity for "industry," men are left with their natural faculties of bodily strength and prudence and an uncorrupted (unused) capacity for reason and power acquisition. Hobbes does not remove men's "traynes of thought" or the desires which regulate those trains; he does, however, do away with words and powers which make the natural search for power after power until death sometimes mad. Within limits, Hobbes's discussion of power in Chapter 10 is still valid for the state of nature.

In this context Hobbes considers the "manners" of men, namely, their voluntary internal trains of thoughts and their voluntary external actions.[2] These thoughts and actions fall within the realm of "morals," or manners, because they occur in a social environment, albeit of a peculiar kind. To disassociate and equalize men is to establish a social context purged of anything men have built or invented: gods, modes of worship, legal systems, even relationships of trust. In this context Hobbes asks: what words do men invent; what do men learn? In a direct sense, Hobbesian man in the state of nature begins with a tabula rasa with regard to common names.[3] Thus, the common power built primarily on anxiety and secondarily on belief in other men is not present to "keep men in awe." The only god in this "society" is the god of nature, who leaves "the world, and the Philosophy thereof, to the disputation of men, for the exercising of their naturall Reason."[4]

Men in mere nature are roughly equal and "without a common Power to keep them all in awe";[5] any supposed "inequality of Power is not discerned, but by the event of Battell."[6] The state of nature is a state of actual or potential battle of every man against every other man because from equality "ariseth equality of hope in the attaining of our Ends." There are some men whose "ends" do not include means which require competition, but all men seek to defend their present gains and each man demands that other men value him at "the same rate he sets upon himselfe." Competition, diffidence, and glory in a state of equality "maketh men invade" one another. Men's manners, construed as actions, are described as a state of war: "every man, against every man," not always in actual fighting, but always in the "known disposition thereto."[7]

The search for instrumental power in history is profoundly shaped by belief in religious doctrine and rules. In nature, this search is unalloyed by such beliefs, but the fear of "invisible power" remains. In the state of nature, the operative fear is not the punishments of supernatural gods after death but rather fear of death itself. In the state of nature, the operative hope is not eternal felicity after death but continuous felicity in the only life which reason tells us we are to have. The search for instrumental power in the state of nature teaches rules of morality sanctioned ultimately by the common invisible power of the fear of death.

Instrumental power is chiefly "strengths united." The only mechanism that enables men who are equal to draw on the power of other men is that described by Hobbes in Chapter 10: "The Value or Worth of a man, is . . . his Price . . . but the buyer determines the Price." In the state of nature, contractual relationships are the only possible forms of human connection: without irrational religious-political power, these contracts would allocate to every man exactly what he deserved, because each partner is free to "estimate" the worth of another man's power, and all men begin with nature's given equality. Potentially at least, human relationships are a series of equal rights and duties.

But without any common power, "there is no Law: where no Law, No Injustice,"[8] so this potential justice of private contract is aborted. Contracts are not kept and legality cannot prevail. In this natural state, however, we cannot condemn men who continually break potential legality:

> The Desires, and other Passions of man, are in themselves no *Sin*. No more are the Actions, that proceed from those Passions, till they know a *Law* that forbids them: which till Laws be made they cannot know: nor can any Law be made till they have agreed upon the Person that shall make it.[9]

To make a contract is to bind future actions by words. Such bonds, however, "have their strength, not from their own Nature, but from Feare of some evill consequence upon the rupture."[10] Men may attempt contractual relationships in the state of nature, but the potential justice of deserved merit cannot prevail. The potential legal system of voluntarily constructed relationships is sought by men in the state of nature as a necessary part of their search for power, power required as a means for attaining or defending desired objects.

This seeking is what Hobbes means by the first law of nature: "That every man, ought to endeavor Peace, as farre as he has hope of obtaining it."[11] In the state of nature, what men "ought" to do and what men "want" to do are identical.

The second law, largely an articulation of the first, is that

> a man be willing, when others are so too, as farre-forth, as for Peace, and defense of himselfe he shall think it necessary, to lay down this right to all things; and be contented with so much liberty against other men, as he would allow other men against himselfe.[12]

This law is also a description of what men would actually endeavor to do in their search for power. Contractual relationships would in fact enforce this "equity" of liberty because "contract building," or the construction of peaceful relationships, is attempted among men who are equal.

Men "acquire wit" as they seek to acquire power; the state of nature is an ingenious environment for acting and learning since both are necessary and purely voluntary. Just as contractual relationships are deliberately and voluntarily constructed, so the endeavor to do so is always in men's minds. As learning and acting are merged, so is voluntarism and necessity. In the state of nature, men must do what they want to do.

Hobbes's long discussion of contracts, which follows the statement of the first two laws of nature, is not framed in terms of a "social compact" but of private contracts among two or more men.[13] Prior to a discussion of the problems involved in the third law of nature ("That men *performe* their covenants made. . . ."), consideration must be given to Hobbes's controversial and much disputed first "right" of nature. When a man who seeks peace cannot obtain it, "he may seek, and use, all the helps and advantages of Warre." The "summe of the Right of Nature . . . is, By all means we can, to defend ourselves." Peace is attempted contract-building and war is contract-breaking. The only motive for keeping a contract is the fear of retaliation by the other party to the contract. In the state of nature, however, the power of the other party cannot be known except by battle. In contrast, the good resulting from a breach of contract can be known in advance. Hobbes concludes from this that no man would want to perform his side of the bargain first, because the other party, having already received the benefit, would want to avoid the cost by not performing his side of the bargain. In "voluntary acts of every man, the object is some Good to himselfe."[14] Therefore, the first performer "does but betray himselfe to his enemy; contrary to the Right . . . of defending his life and means of living."[15]

In the first two laws of nature and the first (and only) right of nature, Hobbes establishes a profoundly unreal system of "rights and duties." The laws describe the intentions of men; the right describes their actions. Justice (contracts) can rarely, if ever, be created. Contracts as power acquisition and goods acquisition "exist" in intention only. The problem of the future, the problem of foresight of good and evil consequences, again plagues Hobbesian man.

In the state of nature, fear of the future does not lead to gods of fear and thence to provisionally stable relationships of inequality and dominance. After discussing the mechanism of contract and before introducing the third law of nature, Hobbes introduces again the god of reason as intimated in his earlier chapter on religion.

God and Justice in the State of Nature

The problem of invisible power begins with the difficulties involved in contractual bonds and foresight of the good and evil consequences of action. Men want to seek power through peaceful contractual relationships. These relationships would be truly just because, if contracts were performed, every man would get exactly what was "owed" him by right. All power acquired in this manner would be merited because "the value of all things contracted for, is measured by the Appetite of the Contractors: and therefore the just value is that which they be contented to give." All other justice "is rewarded of Grace [gift] onely."[16]

For men to perform their contractual obligations, either of two conditions must be met: "A feare of [evil] consequence . . . or a Glory or Pride in appearing not to need to breake it." Pride is "too rarely found to be presumed on," so fear of consequences is "the Passion to be reckoned upon." This fear must have as its object either the "Power of Spirits Invisible" or "The Power of those men they shall therein Offend." The power of men is roughly equal, while the power of invisible spirits is "in every man, his own Religion . . . [which] hath place in the nature of man before Civill Society."[17]

In the state of "meer" nature, the only help for the performance of contractual obligation could be "the feare of that Invisible Power, which . . . every one Worship as God; and Feare as a Revenger of their perfidy." But this help proves to be no help at all. The only form it can take "is to put one another to swear by the God he feareth: Which Swearing, or OATH, is a Forme of Speech, added to a Promise."[18] Because "there is no *naturall* knowledge of mans estate after death; much lesse of the reward that is then to be given to breach of Faith," the laws of nature cannot include "those Rules which conduce to . . . the attaining of an eternall felicity after death; to which [men] think the breach of Covenant may conduce."[19] Unlike historical gods, the god of nature does not preside over a kingdom beyond death. The problem of evil consequence and, therefore, the whole problem of foresight is insoluble in the state of nature. Men can only make covenants with God "by Mediation of such as God speaketh to, either by Revelation Supernatural, or by his Lieutenants that govern under him, and in his Name: For otherwise we know not whether our Covenants be accepted, or not."[20]

Miracles and thus revelation have ceased and we are left without historical signs. Justice can only be achieved by making invisible power visible. The "Fountain and Originall of Justice" is the third law of nature: "That men performe their Covenants made; without which, Covenants are in vain and but Empty words; and the Right of all men to all things remaining, wee are still in the condition of Warre." The only natural measure of justice is performance of external action. Conversely, "Injustice is no other than the not Performance of Covenant." Without a visible common power, "there is no *Own* . . . no Propriety . . . no Injustice."[21]

> So that the nature of Justice, consisteth in keeping of valid Covenants: but the Validity of Covenants begins not but with the Constitution of a Civill Power, sufficient to compell men to keep them: And then it is also that Propriety begins.[22]

In introducing the possibility of visible common power and, therefore, visible standards of justice, Hobbes's vocabulary shifts from morality and manners to civility and civil law. For example, to speak of a just man is to speak in the language of invisible intentions; therefore, a just man is really a righteous man.

> That which gives to humane Actions the relish of Justice, is a certain Nobleness or Gallantnesse of courage, (rarely found), by which a man scorns to be beholding for the contentment of his life, to fraud, or breach of promise. This Justice of the Manners, is that which is meant, where Justice is called a Vertue; and Injustice a Vice.[23]

Righteousness is not only rare but impossible to see. Hobbes speaks of the unrighteous man whose "Will is not framed by the Justice, but by the apparent benefit of what he is to do." Though this man "does not lose his character, for such Actions, as he does, or forbeares to do, for feare,"[24] how are we to judge him? We cannot judge of the 'Justice of Manners" or virtue of a man. In historical politics a justice of mannners is always assumed to operate behind overt acts. In a political order backed by the god of nature, no such motivations can be presumed.

Hobbes introduces justice, the science of "guilt or innocence," by the third law of nature. The rest of the laws of nature merely buttress this law.[25] Taken together, the laws of nature constitute "the true and onely Moral Philosophy . . . the Science of what is Good, and Evill. . . . Good and Evill, are names that signifie our Appetites, and Aversions." Hobbes's move from good and evil to justice and injustice thus constitutes a problem. Moral philosophy is the science of "laws" which bind *in foro interno*, that is, "to a desire they should take place." In the state of nature, these laws "are easie to be observed. For in that they require nothing but endeavor; he that endeavoreth their performance, fulfilleth them; and he that fulfilleth the Law, is Just."[26]

The laws of nature "tend to Natures preservation." To move from invisible endeavor to visible justice is to perform private contracts. For the latter to be valid, a common power must be erected. Invisible morality can become visible justice because men are internally motivated by fear of death to construct "a Feigned or artificiall" common power: the Leviathan. Instead of relying on the invisible common power of nature's god, Hobbes relies on the invisible aversion to simple death. But, are not these two "invisibles" the same?

> These dictates of Reason [reckoning of consequences], men use to call by the name of Lawes; but improperly: for they are but Conclusions, or Theoremes concerning what conduceth to the conservation and defence of themselves; whereas Law, properly is the word of him, that by right hath command over others. But yet if we consider the same Theoremes, as delivered, in the word of God, that by right commandeth all things; then are they properly called Lawes.[27]

This time around, Hobbes's god is derived from natural reckoning of consequences. In history, the passions to sustain common power are desire for ease *and* fear of death. But these commonwealths are also sustained by belief, loyalty, and trust, because of the invention, or feigning, of gods. After Hobbes constructs his civil commonwealth in Part II of *Leviathan*, he devotes the last chapter to a consideration of rewards and punishments (good and evil consequences) of the god discoverable by natural reason. He puts into legal language the old question of why evil men often prosper, and good men suffer, by asking "by what Right God dispenseth the Prosperities and Adversities of this life?" His answer is, by "right" of irresistible power.

From the perspective of natural knowledge, "the Right of afflicting men at his pleasure, belongeth Naturally to God Almighty; not as Creator, and Gracious; but as Omnipotent."[28] But punishment is due only for sin, for breaking God's "laws of nature." Hobbes shows why this right is "natural" by pointing to the lack of individual power among men in the state of nature. The punishment for sin is death. Men in the state of nature are naturally motivated to act in accordance with these laws of nature. Lacking a civil sword, men are led by reckoning on good and evil consequences to break the third law of nature. "The wages of sin is death." Natural men fear natural punishment. To strip men of historical ties is to reveal the "irresistible power" of the fear of death. War and death follow from breach of the third law of nature. The rest of God's natural punishments provide a glimpse of the secular hopes of Hobbes's natural man:

> There is no action of man in this life, that is not the beginning of so long a chayn of Consequences, as no human Providence, is high enough, to give a man a prospect to the end. And in this Chayn, there are linked together both pleasing and unpleasing events; in such manner, as he that will do any thing for his pleasure, must engage himselfe to suffer all the pains annexed to it; and these pains are the Naturall Punishments of those actions, which are the beginning of more Harme than Good.[29]

Men who are in and of a world without redeeming grace must be very careful indeed. In a world of natural depravity and equality, no one should get anything for nothing. Here Hobbes succeeds in substituting for the notion of historical time a notion of endless time. Rules obtaining in historical politics are built on systems of inequality and belief backed by gods who promise final judgments after death. The justice of private contracts blots out this conception of time in order to construe future time as the continuous fulfilling of specific obligations. At any given point in time, each man has any given number of pledged futures defined as what he contractually owes and is owed. But the larger time-frame within which these pledged futures take place is simply cosmic endlessness.

To construct a visible common power is to make certain that the specific pains to purchase our specific pleasures are known in advance. The actions of each man will be bound in the future by contract: each man will get in this life exactly what he merits. If all future time consisted of routinely enforced contractual pledges, the unknowable short-term "futures" could become known. If men could be chained in the future simply to those actions promised in the present, future time in those realms would be known in advance. Anxiety is thus transformed into continuous short-term industry.

The god of nature is the casual framework which assures this form of temporal certainty; visible common power is the guarantor of this certainty. From the standpoint of natural reason, fear of death is that which holds us to the performance of contracts. Such omnipresent and collective fear in the state of nature is the god of nature. In discussing the worship of the invisible god of nature, Hobbes argues that this "God has no Ends."[30] It remains to be seen whether that is also true of the Leviathan.

Outer Rules and Inner Discipline in Civil Society

Beyond death lies ultimate mystery which reason cannot penetrate. Within each man lies a realm of unguided passion, unregulated thought, fears without sensible objects: "Reason . . . so farre from teaching us any thing of God's nature . . . cannot teach us our own nature."[1] Hobbes's state of nature constitutes an attempt to "set aside" the problem of mystery and thus political history, in order to construct a comprehensible legal order. The state of nature provides the foundation of a fortress against mystery. The purpose of this chapter is to show that Hobbes's commonwealth is an attempt to construct a civil order on that foundation, which is designed to keep out political history.

In his argument with Bishop Bramhall, Hobbes asserts that "All the real good . . . is that which is not repugnant to the law . . . for the law is all the right reason we have, and. . .is the infallible rule of moral goodness."[2] At times Hobbes seems to imply a purely arbitrary relationship between law and "right reason."[3] In *Leviathan*, however, the connection between coercive power and natural reason is not arbitrary. The specific cause for war in the state of nature is the failure to perform private contracts binding the future actions of one or both parties. Without a common power (and, therefore, such fear), contracts demand trust. "Upon any reasonable suspicion," these contracts are voided. In a civil state, however, suspicion "is no more reasonable . . . he which by the Covenant is to perform first, is obliged so to do."[4] The cause of war and, therefore, the rise of "invisible power" in the form of fear of death is also the cause of sovereignty and stands as the invisible guarantor for the performance of the political contract. But the only way in which the potential justice in the state of nature can become visible justice in civil society is for the sovereign to resemble, in efficacy and purpose, the god of nature.

Hobbes's discussion of the use of sovereign power is a demonstration of how to keep men in a psychological condition resembling that posited in the state of nature. In contrast to past forms of rulership, the rule of Hobbes's sovereign constructs a barrier against the intrusion of opinion founded on feigned gods. In this way, Hobbes can be consistent when he claims that obedience to sovereign will is "really good."

Rights and Powers of the Visible God

If the unfortunate features of historical politics can be traced to fear of invisible gods, a commonwealth built to avoid this result must seek to quash the ties of historical politics. The state of nature as an "ideal" moral context abolishes such ties by definition. A civil war can also be viewed as a starting point for a new form of politics, a historical moment when most ties of trust have dissolved and men can be viewed as if "the arts grounded upon words" are absent. Viewed this way, civil war tends to reduce men to those natural bodies who could only rebuild relationships with each other by contract. The state of war, then, can be an event in history, as well as a deduction from the state of nature. As an event in history, this war is a crisis and an opportunity, for it destroys commonly held opinion. Man's collective slate is relatively clean: the task of Hobbes's sovereign is essentially to keep it that way.

The new civil discipline consists of both new restraints and new liberties. Anxiety for future time becomes channeled into private interest rather than into religious and institutional ties. Predictability now rests on contract enforcement rather than on the continued adherence to some shared belief. To enforce this new civil discipline entails unlearning the past as much as learning a new present and future. But the power to teach and enforce this new discipline rests on a decidedly new and rather strange creature: an artificially created "god" who has no will of his own.

Visible sovereign power is artificial and deliberately created by other men. The "rights" of the visible sovereign purportedly flow from the pact creating him, not from his natural power. Hobbes first establishes this fictional character of sovereignty during his discussion of representation in Part I of *Leviathan*[5] and then establishes potentially total "rights" for this sovereign near the beginning of Part II. And yet this feigned and artificial power is intended to become a factual power in history. Hobbes's discussion of the "rights" of sovereignty makes clear that the political power of the sovereign stands outside of the legal system; nothing he does as sovereign constitutes an "injury" to his subjects.[6] The de facto power needed to enforce civil law requires that the sovereign be able to defend his power against challengers. Actions in defense of sovereign power cannot be unjust, for the realm of justice is restricted to civil law as private contractual dealings among subjects.

To enforce civil law is to enforce the peaceful intentions of private men. In that sense, the internal standards of morality and the external standards of law merge: natural law and civil law "contain each other, and are of equall extent."[7]

Many commentators on Hobbes have accused him of "sleight of hand" in dealing out justice in this way.[8] In the state of nature, justice means equity, the result of the "appetites of the contracting parties"; in civil society it means obedience to sovereign will "whatsoever [it] be."[9] These commentators have accused Hobbes's sovereign of being an arbitrary dealer who can both name and change the trump. The players never know what their hands are worth. Those who accuse the dealer in this way also ask why the players, whom Hobbes describes so clearly, would want to stay in the game and how the dealer could maintain his power to call and change trump. Put most strongly, the charge is that any de facto theory of sovereignty necessarily means that civil law is arbitrary—that it is what the sovereign says it is. If simply true, this charge would condemn most of *Leviathan* to "insignificant speech."

Such accusations demand a logical answer and a psychological answer, both hinging on civil law, criminal law, and punishment. When Hobbes discusses the powers of sovereignty vis-à-vis civil law, he does so exclusively within the context of individual property:

> Rules, whereby every man may know, what Goods he may enjoy, and what Actions he may doe . . . men call Propriety. For before constitution of Sovereign Power . . . all men had right to all things; which necessarily causeth Warre: and therefore this Proprietie, being necessary to Peace, is the Act of that Power, in order to the publique peace. These Rules of Propriety (or Meum and Tuum) and of *Good, Evil, Lawfull,* and *Unlawfull* in the actions of Subjects, *are the Civill Lawes.*[10]

If one assumes that the sovereign does not assign specific property to every individual and that he does not command every exchange of property, then the sovereign "will" would seem to be quite divorced from the content of civil law. The sovereign grants no specific rights and commmands no specific duties.

The relationship between civil and natural law is that civil law is the enforcement of desire in the state of nature as expressed in contractual intentions. Political sovereignty turns morality into civil law. Sovereign power cannot define the content or value of the rights and duties exchanged in private contracts.

> But because Covenants of mutuall trust, where there is feare of not performance on either part . . . are invalid; *though the Original of Justice be the making of Covenants; yet Injustice actually there can be*

none, till the cause of such feare be taken away; which while men are in the natural condition of Warre, cannot be done. Therefore before the names of Just, and Unjust can have place, there must be some coercive Power, to compell men equally to the performance of their Covenants, by the terrour of some punishment, greater than the benefit they expect by the breach of their Covenant; and to make good that Propriety, which by mutuall Contract men acquire, in recompense of the universal Right they abandon; and such power there is none before the erection of a Commonwealth.[11]

The grounds of sovereign rights "have the need to be diligently, and truly taught; *because they cannot be maintained by any Civill Law, or terror of legal punishment.*"

For a Civil Law, that shall forbid Rebellion (and such is all resistance to the essentiall Rights of Soveraignty,) is not (as a Civill Law) any obligation, but by virtue onely of the Law of Nature, that forbiddeth the violation of Faith; which natural obligation if men know not, they cannot know the Right of any Law the Soveraign maketh.[12]

Men want their contractual rights and are compelled to meet their contractual obligations, but neither these rights nor obligations have any direct connection to the basis of political power.

The "rights" of sovereignty rest ultimately on opinion requiring the use of persuasion, not coercion.[13] Hobbes's discussion of how sovereignty can be maintained recalls his earlier discussion of historical politics. Subjects are to be taught not to love neighboring forms of government and not to admire "the vertue of any of their fellow Subjects, how high soever he stand, nor how conspicuously soever he shine in the Commonwealth."[14] The very features which distorted individual power-seeking in history and which necessarily led private men to contest the grounds of public power in history are to be absent in Hobbes's commonwealth.[15]

Hobbes quite consistently argues that, if whole nations can be taught "the great Mysteries of Christian Religion, which are above Reason . . . there is no difficulty (whilest a Soveraign has his Power entire)" in instructing subjects in natural reason.[16] To prevent ties of trust and belief is to make possible instruction in reason which would be equivalent to learning in the state of nature.

The instruction which the sovereign gives his subjects must be buttressed by his actions. Unlike holders of political power in the past, Hobbes's sovereign should never be seen as the font of "grace," All public reward should be for specific services rendered, as if the sovereign himself were merely another private subject.[17] Subjects should expect no favors and expect to give none: "the most common Souldier, may demand the wages of his warrefare, as a debt."[18] When Hobbes turns to punishments, however, his problem is more complex. Only when the sovereign simply enforces preex-isting private agreements can he appear to be acting impersonally and without a will of his own. To force a recalcitrant party to pay restitution or to perform a previously promised action, "is no more a punishment than is the paying of a Debt."[19] The party who receives restitution is, likewise, not being rewarded by the sovereign but merely receiving his due. The in-equalities resulting from the enforcement of contracts are not willed by the sovereign. The subject cannot properly blame the sovereign for his position in life so long as that position is a product of his own enforced intentions.

But the sovereign does more to his subjects than compel monetary res-titution or its equivalent. Criminal law surrounds civil law. The sovereign does in fact punish crimes and treasons: he causes men to be locked up, beaten, or destroyed. Physical forms of punishment are acts of hostility and revenge. Sovereign grace can be removed from Hobbes's rationally con-structed commonwealth, but sovereign vengeance cannot. The sovereign can choose whether or not to punish a subject for breach of criminal law and that choice radically affects a subject's position in life, indeed, affects whether he shall continue to live at all. Within the limits of Part II of *Leviathan*, Hobbes tries to avoid this logic, for it leads directly back to historical politics, mystery, and prophecy: "Revenge . . . belongs to God, and under God to the King, and none else."[20]

Crimes, Punishment, and the Limits of Reason

Hobbes's search for behavioral certainty in his commonwealth to match the intentions of men in the state of nature leads him consistently in the direction of limiting definitions of crime and of narrowing the scope and severity of physical punishments. Men uncorrupted by historical opinions and ties will rarely commit crimes and possibly never commit treasons: in neither case is it in their interests to do so. If the source of every crime "is some defect of the Understanding; or some errour in Reasoning; or some sudden force of the Passions,"[21] only the latter would remain as a persistent threat to peace. Moreover, with an effective system of detection and trial, fear of punishment largely replaces the need for its use and "of all passions, that which enclineth men *least* to break the laws, is Fear."[22]

Hobbes further limits the reach of physical punishments in his discussion of excuses and extentuations. Again, the intent is to confine the actions of the sovereign within the moral limits of the state of nature and the god of nature. "Where a man is captive, or in the power of the enemy . . . the Obligation of the law ceaseth; because he must obey the enemy, or dye."[23] Any man "by the terror of present death" is totally excused if he transgresses law. By Hobbes's own reasoning, furthermore, he is also absolved from sin in such cases, if sin is defined only as the intention to commit a crime.[24] In the state of nature no rewards and punishments beyond death exist, and no gods with power to reward and punish exist. There is no cause for martyr-dom or self-sacrifice and no motivation to break the law in the name of obedience to a higher law. These same features largely obtain in Hobbes's civil society.

A final context in which Hobbes suggests that his civil state is to maintain the psychological conditions of men in the state of nature is his discussion of the causes for the dissolution of his commonwealth. In past political orders, one of the chief causes of both crime and sedition was vainglory, a "presumption of strength, riches, or friends to resist those that are to execute the Law." This presumption of impunity "is a Root, from whence springeth . . . a contempt of all laws."[25] False religious beliefs and related moral opinions are prime contributors to this presumption. To keep out false teachings is to strike at the root of serious crimes and the need for drastic punishments. Two such doctrines are "that every private man is Judge of Good and Evill actions," and "that whatsoever a man does against his Conscience, is Sinne." Hobbes demolishes them by a restatement of the relationship of sins and laws.[26] A third doctrine, "That Faith and Sanctity, are not to be attained by Study and Reason but by Supernaturall Inspiration or Infusion,"[27] takes Hobbes right back to that mystery and history he sought to abolish in the state of nature.

Hobbes argues that to grant this doctrine would be to say that every Christian is a potential prophet. "Faith comes by hearing, and hearing by those accidents, which guide us into the presence of them that speak to us." What remains unobservable, "and yet . . . not supernaturall," are all of the natural causes which lead to this Christian faith.

> Faith, and Sanctity, are indeed not very frequent; but yet they are not Miracles, but brought to passe by *education, discipline, correction,* and other naturall ways, by which God worketh them in *his elect,* at such times as he thinketh fit.[28]

Even though Hobbes has clearly shifted away from the language of natural religion, he still seeks knowable causes of religious faith. Hobbes clearly attempts to make obedience to law the test of a good Christian even though divine "election" and life after death come from faith. The world of works, civil law, and sin exists within a framework of timeless reason; that of faith, grace, and the criminal punishment by death exists within a framework of history beginning with the Old Testament and ending with the second com-ing of Christ and the final judgment.

The purpose of public authority is to maintain the "psychological con-ditions" found in the state of nature. In Hobbes's civil society, desire and reason—or intention and action—are merged because sovereign power to punish makes possible systematic private reward for those who industriously acquire the means of their happiness. Both in the state of nature and in Hobbes's civil society, the problem is that man has certain knowledge that, despite everything, he will eventually die. In the societies Hobbes discusses before introducing the state of nature, such an ending was not the case. Politics based on "feigned gods" or false doctrine not only holds out hope of heavenly reward but is also based on the giving of public reward to those who most support order.[29] Indeed, seeking power through politics or through religion is exposed by Hobbes as one and the same thing. Both yield unjustified inequality, continuous disputes, and, eventually, war.

Hobbes's state of nature contains no grounds for expecting heavenly reward and Hobbes's civil society is constructed to provide only "merited" reward. Like the god known by natural reason, Hobbes's Leviathan "has no ends" which can be expressed in the certainty of civil rules. But the "seed of religion" is natural in man, Hobbes argues, because man's desires have no time limit, and, we might add, every man has a history.[30] Sovereign power to punish crime with death stands outside the limits of law and reason in the state of nature. Hobbes externalizes sin and conscience and, in discussing the "disease" of inspiration, seems to externalize faith into good behavior. Despite these translations—the most notable one is moral intentions becoming civil law—Hobbes could not bring the "seed of religion" and, therefore, the mystery of a final time or last judgment under the aegis of law and reason. The foundations of sovereign power and therefore the guarantor of reason and law are at stake. In his earlier *Elements of Law* Hobbes asks, "For why should a man incur the danger of a temporal death, by displeasing of his superior, if it were not for fear of eternal death hereafter?"[31] This question is crucial to an understanding both of Hobbes's enterprise in the last half of *Leviathan* and subsequent English philosophy.

Death, Eternity, and Political Power

In Part I of *Leviathan* discussions of the maintenance of politcal power shade into discussions of the mystery of man's fate after death and the effects of opinions in these matters on political order. These issues merge because the power of the sovereign rests on fear of death. The strength of this fear, however, is doubtful because beliefs concerning supernatural existence can more powerfully effect action than rational knowledge that all living things die. A man's consciousness necessarily encompasses two worlds simultaneously. The sovereign right to end a man's natural life cannot be grounded in the world of natural reason, even though that right is necessary for reason to prevail in man's temporal relationships.

Hobbes does not attempt to hide this logic, but he tries in a variety of ways to minimize its impact on sovereign power. His discussion of the natural causes of religious faith,[32] his limitations on the reach of criminal law and punishments,[33] his legal rendering of sin and conscience,[34] and his hopes for education in the utilities of peace, equity, and prosperity[35] all attest to this attempt. His boldest claim for the primacy of law and reason, however, is his promise that a commonwealth properly constructed might last an eternity. This vision, tendered with some important qualifications, suggests a kind of grandeur even within the natural world of passion, interest, and power. "Though nothing can be immortal, which mortals make," commonwealths can be built to last "as long as Mankind, or as the Lawes of Nature, or as Justice itself."[36] Hobbes does not ask whether men would willingly give the only lives they have for this vision. Indeed, rather than ending his discussion here—as if the alternative hope of individual life everlasting had disappeared from the earth—Hobbes asks whether the "principles of reason" on which an eternal commonwealth is built are in fact true. And having raised this question, Hobbes immmediately turns to the other world of prophecy: "yet I am sure they are Principles from Authority of Scripture."[37] Hobbes prepares us for entry into this world and its logic which constitutes the second half of *Leviathan*.

A host of new considerations now enter, almost all of which were first raised in the early chapters of Part I on power, manners, and religion. The first of these is the relationship of individual anxiety to the nature of public power. "The Maintenance of Civill Society," Hobbes states when considering the biblical promise of eternal life,

> depending on Justice; and Justice on the power of Life and Death, and other lesse Rewards and Punishments, residing in them that have a Soveraignty of the Common-wealth. *It is impossible a Common-wealth should stand, where any other than the Soveraign, hath a power of giving greater rewards than Life; and of inflicting greater punishments, than Death.*[38]

If the sovereign is an artificial creature of reason, representing the god of nature, how can he do more than that god? If he cannot, by what right can that sovereign punish criminals by death? Within limits of reason, the only sense in which one can use the word "man" is in terms of his body. Capital punishment is thus an irrevocable judgment of the man and not merely of his external acts. Legally authorized punishment by death is a logical and psychological impossibility. But if this be the case, the status of the subjects' promise to obey this killer of criminals becomes dubious. All Hobbes grants in Part II is that the subject may resist, if he can, when the Leviathan tries to kill him.

The issues at stake when Hobbes concludes Part II of *Leviathan* appear to be on the same order as those raised at the start of the book. The major difference, of course, is that by now Hobbes has constructed a civil philosophy not only without a time dimension but seemingly designed to nullify history altogether. Yet, at the conclusion of that enterprise, Hobbes not only reintroduces history, now as the record of Scripture, but argues that the kingdom of the biblical god rests on pact or covenant while the kingdom of reason's god rests on sheer power. At issue in this distinction is the precise nature of invisible power to ground obligation to the visible sovereign. Since no civil law can command general obedience, there are three ways to construe the motivation to obey. (1) De facto power: if the sovereign does have power greater than the individuals or groups who might want to disobey him, obedience is simply another way of putting this fact. "Invisible common power" becomes the fear of death which men universally feel. Criminal punishment by death is simply outside the limits of obligation. (2) De facto power justified by reasons of private interest: if the sovereign does have preponderant power, obedience is deserved because this power permits men to be moral and just in their private relationships. This construction more or less begs the question of "invisible common power" and the issue of general obligation. The reasonable tests for obligation consist of the legal system's ability to permit and enforce contractual justice. (3) Religious motivation: men who believe Christ's promise of a return and a final judgment, after which God's eternal kingdom will be established on earth, and who further believe that God commanded general obedience to de facto political power until that time will be motivated to obey from the long-range interests dictated by their faith.

The first and second alternatives would fly in the face of Hobbes's argument that it is impossible for justice to prevail without the power over life and death and that, therefore, a commonwealth cannot stand "where any *other than* the Soveraign, hath a power of giving greater rewards than Life; and of inflicting greater punishments, than Death."[39] Parts III and IV of *Leviathan* assume the problem is not resolved simply by the statement that the civil sovereign can teach whatever religion he wants, but that reason, justice, and political stability can only prevail if the sovereign and the subjects interpret written prophecy in a certain way.

Hobbes's own discussion of the kingdom of god known by reason suggests why natural religion is inadequate:

to call this Power of God which extendeth itselfe not onely to Man, but also to Beasts, and Plants, and Bodies inanimate, by the name of Kingdome, is but a metaphorical use of the word. For he onely is properly said to raign, that governs his Subjects, by his Word, and promise of Rewards to those that obey it, and . . . Punishment that obey it not.[40]

Not only is this argument in explicit contrast to the prophetic kingdom contained in the biblical Word, but Hobbes later takes pains to underline the distinction in his discussion of the Christian Commonwealth: "The

Kingdome . . . of God, is a reall, not a metaphoricall Kingdome [estab-
lished] by force of our Covenant, not by Right of God's Power."[41]

This is not to deny that Hobbes eschewed de facto argument—indeed,
he was one of its modern inventors—but it is to assert that Parts III and IV
of *Leviathan* reintroduce opinion, custom, imagination, experience, and
historical politics, all within the framework of the status and uses of faith.
In order to understand this enterprise and, indeed, many similar tensions
in later liberal thought, a slight historical detour is necessary.

Obligation in Two Worlds

Three of Hobbes's political writings were published during the English Civil
War. These writings share many elements with contemporary pamphlet literature, especially those written to attack traditional defenses of royal and
ecclesiastical power and, after the regicide of 1649, to defend the legitimacy
of the Commonwealth. A prominent feature of this literature is its thor-
oughgoing rejection of secular and institutional history as either a valid
source of political power or a repository of political knowledge. Just as
ecclesiastical power was seen by radical Puritans as a usurpation and a corruption of the polity of the primitive church, so the royal engines of prerogative and power were viewed as aberrant growths following the Norman
Conquest. This "Norman Yoke" argument and its appeal to a prehistoric
Saxon commonwealth was a powerful weapon in the weakening and destruction of the entire apparatus of prerogative courts and commissions by
the mid-1640s.[42] This same argument was used after the regicide to launch
a powerful movement for radical reform of the laws and procedures of the
common law and equity courts.[43]

In place of legitimation resting on institutional continuity, a new appeal
was made to private interest. Political institutions and public good should
serve the legitimate concerns of private safety and property. This appeal to
civil and secular interest necessarily results from the destruction of appeals
to history and tradition because that destruction unbinds men from institutional connections which merged or mediated public and private concerns.
The separation of public power and private interest, so vividly symbolized
in state-of-nature theory, was tied in the pamphlet literature to de facto
theories of politics. If the primary end of public power is to serve aggregate
private interest, the origins of those who wield that power are no longer
central to one's reasons for obedience. Whatever its history and origins,
private interest contains its own obligatory logic. Parts I and II of *Leviathan*
contain arguments quite familiar to defenders of Cromwell's Commonwealth.[44]

Another part of this new and ahistorical way of thinking about political
obligation is a theological perspective which located the appearance of this

kind of politics *in history.* Stress on eschatology and use of millennialist doctrine powered Puritan attempts to dismantle the institutional apparatus of church, courts, and crown.[45] Morality is reduced to individualist, secular, and universal standards, because salvation rests on faith, not works. In its most revolutionary formulation, millennialist doctrine urged the destruction of practically all institutional structures as idols born of blasphemy. Thus prepared, the world would witness a new thousand-year epoch of equality, harmony, and prosperity.[46] Even in its less radical forms, this mode of political thinking served the cause of secular and materialist perspectives on political life. The faithful are urged to live in this world on its own secular terms. The faith which earns eternal reward should not be jeopardized by believing that adherence to particular rituals, rules, and institutions is the same as faith. Secular history is the record of these "works" and of their corruption. The best one can do is to shape and adhere to legal and moral standards appropriate to this world under a system of public power and of private motivations that reflect man as he is. To attempt more is to tempt one's faith. One's political duties are to destroy institutional tributes to vainglory (they prevent the workings of faith), not to construct new ones.

Those who defended the Commonwealth under Cromwell best articulate the separate logics of works and faith. The Puritan defenders of the "Engagement" addressed two audiences: radical millennialists whose loyalty was weakened because reforms were not radical enough and moderate Puritans who had qualms of conscience taking an oath of allegiance to a new regime in light of their standing oath to the reformed regime as it stood immediately prior to the regicide. In this Engagement literature, the connection of *Leviathan's* two halves becomes readily apparent. Public power and political obligation are located in two distinct worlds: one defined by timeless reason and natural depravity, the other willed by a providential god who will ultimately judge every man's life. Reason and philosophy are appropriate to the first; faith and scriptural authority to the second. The world of works and its logic is wholly dependent upon the world of faith for its appearance and maintenance in history.

The starting point in this argument is the attempt to sever questions of the origins of particular governments from the reasons for obeying them. When the contests for political power are placed under the aegis of God's providence working in history, the question of origins is put outside the reach of reason.

> As for the Law of necessity which begetteth war, whereby God is immediately appealed unto, by those that pretend to have no Superiors on earth, that he may judge of their rights; whatsoever his hand doth determine in the event, is to be counted the right of those in favour, of whom the determination is made by his Judgement.[47]

Secular appeals to the legitimacy of traditions is a vain attempt to pretend otherwise. Unbiased reason tells us "That the Power of the Sword Is, and Ever Hath Been, the foundation of All Titles to Government."[48] Because "all Governments now extant had their foundations laid in the dirt, tho' time may have dried it up by Oblivion, or flattering Historians licked it off," conscience as a guide to civil obedience is "a stumbling-block."[49]

The results of civil war or invasion are determined by "the course of Divine Justice." No private man, therefore,

> can be counted guilty; whatever the intent of your promise was in the Covenant, because it was neither morally possible, nor lawfull to you in the way of your [private] calling, to hinder the cause or effect of that change.[50]

Providential change of government is the result of forces which overwhelm both individual action and individual responsibility. Both victors and vanquished operate on a plane of action beyond legal and moral tests: God presides over their battles. In answer to the argument that previous political ties were not "meerly civil and humane, but sacred and divine and above the absolution of any earthly power," one Puritan divine asserts that intelligent Christians have an obligation to consider "the expediency of a thing" before they engage their conscience.[51]

Christian liberty frees men from slavery "to any that will rule over them" because it makes of the Christian "a stranger, passenger and pilgrim" who "takes things as he finds them on his way . . . and meddles onely with his own matters, how to advance prosperously and easily towards his journies end."[52] Christian men do not change their characters with changes of government; they remain free to use their liberties "so far as they can lawfully and with expediency be referred unto [Christian] edification." The concluding link in this argument is that obligation is deserved if the government makes it possible for Christian men to be legally moral in their private affairs.[53]

Anthony Ascham, a lawyer and an agent for Parliament to Spain, articulates the most sophisticated defense for the Engagement. He casts the distinctions between politics, law, and conscience into a systematic legal language in order to make his case for obedience to the new regime. Political justice, by which public men achieve and maintain sovereignty, is of an entirely different order than legal justice, "whereby we maintain equality in private Contracts with other private men," and private justice, which is "virtue in its internall habits, and relates to God and ourselves only, and not to another."[54] These Hobbesian distinctions lead Ascham to Hobbes's conclusion: when political justice is infringed and "runs into a Ware, it disorders all other relations of Justice." In such suspension of political justice, the worst result is that ambitious and angry men forme subtilties and pretences, and afterwards the poore people (who understand them not) are taken out of their houses, as horses are out of Pastours, to fight and maintaine them at the perils of one anothers lives.[55]

Coming from an agent and supporter of the Commonwealth, such language clearly relies on a religious justification. Yet Ascham constructs a rational legal case solely on the basis of the guarantee of legal justice and private interest. Even significant and sudden changes in the distributions of public power mean little in comparison with that which gives government "its life and being, by the administration of Justice, whereby we are secured from suffering wrong, enjoy the communion of rights, and have punishments for Vice, and rewards for Virtue." That is what materially affects private men, and not the particular "figures" of monarchy, aristocracy, or democracy. Changes at this level are in "the Novelty and Opinion of it, to which if the circumstance of a Little time be added, all our wonder is gone."[56]

The scope of reason extends to our own actions and the actions of other private men. Private justice (morality) and legal justice (civil law), however, depend upon political justice or authority. "In *true Authority*, men must not be believed or obeyed for their reasons, but for their Votes [i.e., decisions]. Thus, when we know God hath said this or that, we conclude without any further examination, that is true."[57] Ascham separates these three realms both epistemologically and existentially.[58] His intent, like Hobbes's, is to separate questions of religious doctrine from law and obedience.

According to Ascham, what matters is not to prove that God established religion and justice in the world—that, "no man doubts"—but to ask how "both ought to be continued." To base evidence of religion and justice on those who happen to have authority in church or state plunges us into futile historical labyrinths. Even to grant the origins of justice and religion in God is of no use: no matter how much one claims congruity between the laws of heaven and the laws of this world, there is "no necessity of their Actually being such, and every book which is good, is not therefore of divine Revelation. For God made his Laws freely, and might have made them different from what they are, if he had so pleased."[59]

Political authority reflects the divine justice of a providential god, but our reason and our private religious beliefs offer no sure guidance. Ascham tantalizes the reader with a further possibility, one on which Hobbes ends the first half of *Leviathan*.

The dissatisfaction in Tradition, Authority, Miracles, and the Spirit, hath begot a strange Question concerning a Naturall Religion more Catholique and Universall than any other, viz. Whether Naturall Religion be a Part of Justice? Which Justice not depending immediately on Authority, Religion they say doth much less [i.e., because it rests on election and faith], and therefore reason may make it out, as it is a holy Virtue.

Ascham asks whether "the native and purest principles of Justice may be the best principles of Religion."[60] Ascham is at his Puritan best. Religion is a

> Doctrine of faith, as Faith relates to a principle out of the discovery of Nature, and is of things not seen, to be rendered to a Superiour not seen: Justice is the Doctrine of works, in the discovery of Nature, of things seen, and to be dispenc'd to those with whom we visibly converse.

In history, justice and taught religious doctrines are the "counterfeit" of each other: most men adopt the religion of their parents and country, "not having more choice of our religions, and divine Laws, than we had in what part of the World we would be borne."[61] Ascham concludes that "we cannot make a mixture of Reason and authority, yet we may make a mixture of reason and Obedience . . . [for] our reasons and our owne Obedience relate to the same persons, so that it is but reasonable, just, and Necessary, that we obey those, who in good and Convenient things, command and Plenarily possesse us."[62]

Ascham's *Confusions and Revolutions* was published in 1648 and republished a year later with additional chapters.[63] In these additions, he integrates long quotations from Hobbes's *De Cive* and adds a section on the relationship between the invention of money, the need for private contracts, and the necessity of inequality.[64] These latter arguments, so Lockean in their import, did not weaken the wall separating the timeless logic of "works" and the workings of faith and providence in history. Discounting the more radical social visions of millennialist doctrines, this separation put the status of political obligation on two distinct footings. Political power is established, maintained, and overthrown in accordance with purposes which men can only believe in and not know. From this perspective, the connection between subject and sovereign rests on faith. The power over life and death and the "necessities of state" which compel its use preclude the rational connections of interest and calculation. From another perspective, however, these rational connections do constitute a logic of obligation if men confine their actions and ideas "according to the virtues of their natures, which . . . will serve at least to condemne others."[65] To become private men within a natural world of works would yield coherent standards for civil law and morality. For this to happen, however, a new set of relationships between religious faith and public power must be established. Like the Puritan Revolution, the second half of *Leviathan* puts the timeless logic of civil law, morality, and liberal politics in history.

5

Liberal Politics
External Desire, Internal Faith

*But we are borne to two Worlds, and are made of matter proportionable
to both, and therefore cannot but naturally have some kind of affection
for both.*

ANTHONY ASCHAM, Confusions and Revolutions

In Parts III and IV of *Leviathan,* Hobbes once again confronts mystery and
its relationship to politics, this time in the form of biblical prophecy. The
foes Hobbes engages in Parts III and IV are often contemporary doctrines
and temporary foes—special cases of more general counterdoctrines he has
already dispensed with in Parts I and II. However, Parts III and IV are
essential to Hobbes's work, not only to take care of those elements of human
nature bracketed out of the state of nature, but also to address the problem
of the admitted deficiencies of the kingdom of god known by reason. These
tasks are crucial if reason and peace are to prevail in history.

Hobbes begins Part III of *Leviathan* by asking how one is to understand
"not only the Naturall Word of God, but also the Propheticall," the Bible.
In those things beyond rational understanding "wee are bidden to captivate
our understanding to the Words." The tests of logic and the laws of epistemology are set aside, for "Faith reposed in him that speaketh, though the
mind be incapable of any Notion at all from the words spoken."[1] Without
the "will to obedience," men who confront the results of their reckoning
until they can reckon no farther,

> must either take their owne Dreams, for the Prophecy they mean to
> bee governed by, and the tumour of their own hearts for the spirit of
> God; or they must suffer themselves to bee led by some strange Prince;
> or by some of their fellow subjects, that can bewitch them . . . into
> rebellion.

In short, Christians must take their "Christian Sovereign for Gods Prophet."
In confronting these sacred mysteries, men must choose either to have faith
in the sovereign or "destroy . . . all laws, both divine and humane, reduce
all Order, Government, and Society, to the first Chaos of Violence, and
Civill warre."[2]

The choice Hobbes gives to men is clearly not between a rational life of
enlightened self-interest along with natural religion and one guided by nonrational beliefs. And he is surely not giving the reader a choice between
Leviathan I and II and *Leviathan* III and IV. The choice Hobbes appears
to be offering is one between two forms of prophetic belief. One form,
described as "humane politiques" in Part I, systematically distorts standards
of justice by inserting elements of religious belief into areas of life which
can and should be judged on purely rational grounds. The other form, called
"divine politiques," which Hobbes urges men to accept in Part III of *Leviathan* , is firmly and irrevocably separated from standards of civil law. To
accept the latter form of belief is to forswear moral or logical connections
between events at the level of political power and events within the civil and
private sphere. Like Ascham and others, Hobbes maintains that the realm
of prophetic belief has the same status as political conquest and the power
to punish by death: none can be judged by the standards of reason which
discover natural and civil law.

What Hobbes has pictured as a "Feigned or Artificiall person" created
by men out of fear of death now becomes the sovereign as the voice of
prophecy in whom men must trust to attain "eternal life." The whole scheme
of legal responsibility for action developed in Parts I and II of *Leviathan*
is simply rejected in this prophetic context. In the discussion of doctrines
of prophecy found in the Bible, the subject becomes the artificial actor and
the sovereign becomes the responsible author.

> He [the sovereign] cannot oblige men to beleeve; though as a Civill
> Soveraign he may make Laws suitable to his Doctrine, which may
> oblige men to certain actions, and sometimes to such as they would not
> otherwise do, and which he ought not to command; and yet when they
> are commanded, they are Laws; and the externall actions done in
> obedience to them, without the inward approbation, *are the actions of
> the Soveraign,* and not of the Subject, which is in that case but as an
> instrument, without any motion of his owne at all; because God hath
> commanded to obey them.[3]

This "reversal of roles" is indicative of Hobbes's treatment of prophetic
history and provides a key to understanding the purpose of the "church
visible." Rules which establish churches and religious doctrine do not have
the same status as civil law, the content of which can be expressed in contracts. Prophecy, as rules governing religious observance, breaks the con-

nection between sovereign law and the subjects' intentions. The necessity of such rules of Scripture confuses the distinction between faith and works, for religious rules are sovereign opinion expressed as law. The giver of such personal opinion was previously pictured as a feigned and artificial person, the sovereign; the receivers of this opinion as law are now pictured by Hobbes as feigned and artificial actors.[4] The only bridge is what Hobbes terms a "will to obedience," which can only be expressed as faith in the sovereign, or, more broadly, faith that a prophetic God stands behind nature and history. The sovereign's de facto power becomes "Faith . . . in him that speaketh, though the mind be incapable of any Notion at all from the words spoken." To remember that the sovereign is only interpreting the words of Scripture is to be reminded that Hobbes is not simply plunging us back into the subjective morass of "humane politiques." Rather, he is suggesting that an interpretation of scriptural prophecy which does not contradict natural reason is "divine politiques."

Hobbes's interpretation of Scripture is an attempt to explain precisely why prophecy does not contradict civil certainty. Indeed, to have faith and trust in the interpreter is to lift political obligation from fear of de facto power to belief in the divine justice of sovereign punishment by death. This same belief transforms the de facto justice of external actions into a belief that obedience to civil law is righteousness. The belief which makes this transformation possible is biblical, but Hobbes attempts to show that it is actually grounded in the same Christian faith that is necessary for salvation.

The Bible as Cosmology and History

Hobbes's interpretation of Scripture is a theory of history. In the most general sense, this history is cosmology, embracing the entire world, from the beginning to the end of time. Because this form of history precedes nature and will succeed it, biblical interpretation, no matter how "reasonable," cannot subordinate Scripture to law, as if Scripture were particular and law universal. On the same logic, the revelation which marks the unfolding of this story cannot be subordinate to reason, any more than Christianity can be subordinate to natural religion. Of specific importance to Hobbes's politics is the second meaning of Scripture as history, namely, its periodization of political history. The Old and New Testaments contain a record and a prophecy of distinct political kingdoms with changing relationships between God, rulers, and subjects.[5] To have faith in the biblical word is to believe in this periodization of history and in the political obligations appropriate to the present age.

The Old Testament, according to Hobbes, is a record of the kingdom of God established on earth by covenant with a particular people—the Jews. This "peculiar Kingdom" merged works with faith, and politics with religion. In this prophetic kingdom on earth, God's commands were known by sense: miracles accompanied prophets and prophecy. With the election of Saul—"after the Israelites had rejected God"—this kingdom left the earth and the legitimacy of theocracy left with it. Later, prophets could only foretell the restitution of this kingdom on earth but not rule in its name. Christ as prophet is the last historical proof of this coming kingdom. The future kingdom now exists only in the faith of the Christian elect whose identity is known only to God.

Until the second coming of Christ, natural reason cannot tell men what their obligations to this kingdom are.[6] The eschatological emphasis in Hobbes puts men in the contemporary condition of a depravity which only inward faith and an act of grace can redeem. God intended this and gave men natural reason and motivation to construct rules of morality appropriate to their depravity—rules presupposing a natural desire for power after power until death. The state of mere nature symbolizes this moment in sacred history. Reliance on natural reason to construct a political and moral order is a religious obligation at this time in sacred history.

Political sovereigns should stand as physical guarantors of the second coming, having power "to make the Scriptures . . . Laws." Nonsovereign prophets should give counsel but not law. Since the kingdom of prophecy is a kingdom of faith, "The Office of Christs Ministers in this world, is to make men Beleeve, and have Faith in Christ: but Faith hath no relation to, nor dependence upon Compulsion, or Commandement."[7] As prophet, Hobbes's sovereign is in a peculiar situation. In early Old Testament history, some determinate person or persons had the sovereign right and the power to interpret religious doctrine.[8] This right was granted directly—and often dramatically—by God. After the election of Saul and until the Christian kings, the office of priests was "ministerial" and not "magisteriall."[9] Since Christ did not rule and "did . . . nothing against [Roman] laws,"[10] Christian men have only their inner faith and the Bible. And notwithstanding "blasphemous" Catholic kingdoms, Christian sovereigns still preside over a kingdom of works, even though they are confronted by the problem of biblically derived rules which can affect men's behavior toward each other and civil authority. Thus far, Hobbes's scriptural interpretation supports the paradigm suggested in the Engagement literature.

In his commonwealth, Hobbes constructs the state church and gives to its head power over scriptural interpretation, but he is forced to reject the moral result of obedience to these scriptural "works." If external obedience as to worship and particular doctrinal confession is exercised without belief, it is the act of a legal puppet who is not to be held responsible by God. Here Hobbes is consistent with his argument in Part I of *Leviathan:* since we cannot know, but only believe, Scripture, "worship amongst [Christian] men is Power."[11] The crucial difference between the human politics of the corrupt past and Hobbes's divine politics is that rules of worship in his commonwealth are made deliberately "artificial." Faith and election by "grace" lie outside of prescribed ritual. Hobbes is radically antinomian when discussing the "true" meaning of religion, even though he can appear quite legalistic—even authoritarian—in treating the "meaningless" but necessary outward forms of religion. As with Naaman, who was converted to the God of Israel but bowed down before pagan idols in obedience to his sovereign, "that action is not his, but his Soveraigns."[12]

Clearly, the distinction between the visible church of rules headed by the political sovereign and the invisible body of the faithful known only to God is not unique to Hobbes. From the mid-sixteenth century onward, the theology of the English Reformation developed many of these same perspectives into a complex mixture of radical theology and conservative church polity. In the early seventeenth century, for example, Bishop Joseph Hall viewed both prince and church in secular political terms: "Princes and Churches may make Lawes for the outward man; but they can no more bind the heart than they can make it." And Robert Sanderson, a vigorous defender of uniform public worship, added the proviso "that by requiring obedience to these ceremonial Constitutions," the church was seeking only "orderly uniformity in the outward worship of God; so far is she from seeking to draw any opinion either of divine necessity upon the Constitution, or of the effectual holiness upon the Ceremony." The English Reformation tradition insisted upon a political defense of Church polity, even to the extent of seeing each clergyman in a dual role. John Whitgift, the powerful champion of episcopacy, for example, held that hierarchy and subordination within the clergy are justified only *"quoad ordinem et politicam:* touching order and government," while a strict equality prevails among them—as indeed among all true Christians—*"quoad ministerium;* touching the ministry."[13]

Hobbes's dual image of religion not only reflects this tradition but complicates his task. The realm of certain knowledge teaches men natural law and leads them to the knowledge of death. The biblical realm of mystery and faith leads the faithful to believe in eternal life as a reward after death. In Hobbes, the fear of death leads to the feigned and artificial power of the Leviathan. The promise of eternal life leads to a Leviathan as an object of trust and faith, culminating in the sovereign as head of the institutional church. But this same church teaches that no man can be saved by works, for the whole order of works assumes natural self-interest ending in death, while Hobbes has stressed that only faith in Christ's second coming earns eternal salvation. Faith is not law and cannot be commanded. In trusting and obeying this artificial prophet, then, men cannot be guaranteed the reward of eternal life. All they can believe is that it is right for the Leviathan to punish those who disobey the law. No matter how far Hobbes goes in "legalizing" Scripture, in urging external obedience in worship and public expressions of belief, the faith required for eternal reward is uncertain.

Felicity Here and Hereafter

From the perspective of Christian men the sovereign rules by right of covenant: "we should not violate our *Faith,* that is a commandment to obey our Civill Soveraigns, which we constituted over us, by mutuall pact one with another."[14] A willingness to obey civil law—not simply out of fear of punishment but by reason of keeping faith in a covenant, backed by a covenant with the prophetic god—constitutes the necessary obedience required for eternal reward. Whereas the intention to obey natural law in the state of nature is easy, willingness to obey civil law in civil society is difficult. With enforced civil rules, one "sins" not only by intention to break the law but by every actual breach of it. Obedience to the civil laws simply out of fear of punishment will not lead to salvation. This obedience is simply natural: any depraved man with an ounce of sense can calculate the difference between paying a debt of five dollars as against being hauled to court and ordered to pay five dollars plus a fine and court costs.

The only point at which reason and faith are thoroughly integrated is in Hobbes's discussion of the future kingdom. His picture of the millennium and then heaven itself most strongly resembles that of the radical Puritan sects of his own time.[15] This eschatological integration, however, does not bridge the ambiguities of Hobbes's solution for his own commonwealth. To say that "doctrine concerning the Kingdome [of] God, have so great influence on the Kingdome of Man, as not to be determined, but by them, that under God have the Soveraign Power,"[16] does not in itself clarify the status of that doctrine nor the status of church governance. Indeed, Hobbes deprecates the specifically religious rules of the sovereign by stressing that such rules cannot reach to the "inner realm" of true faith.

When discussing regular civil law, Hobbes has no difficulty reaching the inner "will" of men, because his picture of natural man is such that desire and power-seeking take the form of enforceable contractural rights and duties. But the realm of doctrine and belief regarding the promise of ultimate reward cannot be embraced by categories of external rights and duties or internal appetite and aversion. In terms of time as personal history, a will to obedience is motivated by the personal hope of eternal felicity following a final judgment. Natural reason teaches us nothing about "the nature of any living thing." The laws flowing from this reason only reach to that portion of a person's will which can be expressed contractually; they cannot reach what Locke and Bentham are later to call a man's "consciousness" of himself as a distinct person. Only a prophetic judgment at some final time guarantees that one's entire way of life is judged.

Hobbes can only rely on sovereign power to keep men's thoughts of "ultimate good" either totally internal or wholly objective. If doctrines of saving "faith" were ever translated by private men into moral opinion, faith would affect manners in such a way as to plunge men back into the "madness" of history. If individual belief becomes translated into collective guides for action, it signals that men have allowed

> themselves to bee lead . . . by some of their fellow subjects, that can bewitch them, by slaunder of the government, into rebellion, without other miracle to confirm their calling, then sometimes an extraordinary successe, and Impunity; and by this means destroying *all laws, both divine, and humane,* reduce all Order, Government, and Society, to the first Chaos of Violence, and Civill warre.[17]

The connection between the inner discipline of rational appetite and the one who is the systematic enforcer of contracts is pictured by Hobbes as so fragile that the least injection of other loyalties would plunge the world into chaos. According to Locke, one must choose "either law or force," and law demands a very special kind of self-discipline and self-denial. But Hobbes, who seeks to construct an order which does not rest on the maintenance of the virtue of ministers or on networks of trust among private men, is compelled to make his sovereign an object of religious veneration.

Church Authority and Religious Freedom

Hobbes's discussion of the faith requirement for salvation is a discussion of an "inner realm." This locus of belief is seemingly immune to all of the necessity and regularity which characterize man's inner trains of thought. Indeed, Hobbes appears to make Christian faith absolutely inviolable and protected from earthly powers, "For internall Faith is in its own nature invisible, and consequently exempted from all humane jurisdiction." But this faith can lead to "words and actions . . . as breaches of our Civil obedience," and thus faith can cause "injustice both before God and Man."[18] Opinion is the medium of the transformation of inner faith into outward injustice.

In Hobbes's commonwealth the church is admittedly powerless to control invisible faith, for its power is no greater than the power of civil law—in fact, its rules bear no necessary relationship to men's motivations in the state of nature. Like "human politics," its specific doctrinal rules are one man's interpretation, even though the sources of all possible interpretation derive from the Bible. Through the sovereign the church can prevent private men from teaching moral doctrines based on particular doctrines of faith or on biblical passages. Civil law and punishment can also enforce outward forms of worship and demand of the subjects public assent to prescribed religious doctrine. But in Hobbes's commonwealth the church partakes of the same limitations as the state; it is as unable to judge a "true and unfeigned Christian" as the state is of judging a just man. Both the just man and the true Christian can only be judged and punished by reason of external actions, that is,

> till his Hypocrisy appear in his Manners . . . till his behaviour bee contrary to the Law of his Soveraign, which is the rule of Manners, and which Christ and his Apostles have commanded us to be subject to. For the Church cannot judge of Manners but by externall Actions, which Actions can never bee unlawfull, but when they are against the Law of the Common-wealth.[19]

In Hobbes's commonwealth the church is very tolerant of differing beliefs but very intolerant of dissenting actions. The status of rules governing church polity and discipline, however, is quite arbitrary. Any particular rule of Scripture made law is not universally valid moral philosophy and not strictly a part of the rational authorization process which establishes sovereign authority. Like the death penalty or a general's command to a soldier, the power over the church is derived from necessity and not right. Indeed, Hobbes builds a powerful case against church authority and the power of the clergy precisely because religious belief should not penetrate everyday moral and legal relationships. The longest and one of the most powerfully argued chapters in *Leviathan* denies autonomous ecclesiastical authority.[20]

Hobbes's denial of independent authority to the church, however, does not resolve the deep ambiguities in his own position. Viewed from one perspective, his church looks like a reincarnation of Old Testament theocracy—but without continuing miracles to prove its legitimacy. This purely Erastian result is undermined by Hobbes, however, when he grants all Christians a perfect freedom to "dispute the doctrine of our pastors." Thus, a second possible model is one which entrusts the purity of doctrine not to sovereigns as legal prophets but to the ministerial role of the clergy—implying a shared informal obligation of all members, including sovereigns, to uphold the true faith. This solution confronts another difficulty, namely, the suggestion of an implied contractual limitation on the sovereign's power over the legal church: no exercise of legal powers by the king may violate the central teachings of the faith as defined by the informal body of the faithful. Other models are possible within Hobbes's framework, but the one that is clearly the most extreme is that of complete religious freedom. This possibility requires that certain historical and sociological preconditions be met, but the end result is that the category of "church" dissolves into Hobbes's state, leaving no religious content whatsoever, except the bare injunction to obey the sovereign. Religion would then become an entirely personal affair, its only institutional marks being a multitude of ever-shifting voluntary sects, each headed by ministers with no legal authority. Hobbes's sovereign would continue to control these ministers and their churches only in the sense of having residual power, inherent in sovereignty, to punish any manifestation of political claims arising from religious belief. In short, the church headed by the sovereign becomes transmuted and reduced to laws against blasphemy and treason that would provide a minimal framework within which the "sects" could conduct their respective redemptive missions.

Given Hobbes's interpretation of biblical history and its succession of "kingdoms," this last solution is most consistent with his own understanding of the appropriate sources of knowledge about religious duties. The Bible, for Hobbes, is the only repository of revealed knowledge. After Christ, miracles ceased, so all later claims of revelation made by the institutional church and its leaders are without foundation. The primitive church, then, is the ideal solution for Hobbes in two senses: first, this solution constitutes his expressed hope at the end of *Leviathan* and, second, the model of the primitive church provides the standard he uses to judge the purposes and reach of his own less than ideal alternative.

In the conversion of the Gentiles, Hobbes begins, the disciples and apostles could only suggest conditions for becoming a Christian. These conditions could not include

> alledging the Scriptures, which they beleeved not. The Apostles . . .
> laboured by Reason to confute their idolatry; and that done, to
> perswade them to the faith of Christ, by their testimony of his Life,
> and Resurrection. So that there could not yet bee any controversie
> concerning the authority to Interpret Scripture; seeing no man was
> Obliged during his infidelity, to follow any man's Interpretation of any
> Scripture, except his Soveraigns Interpretation of the Law of his
> countrey.[21]

Thus, any church rules established by the primitive church were counsels given by the disciples and apostles. "[T]he Faith of the Hearer caused him to receive it" as canon or law for himself "which he might again reject, by the same right he received it."[22] In the same manner, financial support for the early churches was by "benevolence" of the believers. Excommunication, too, occurred in the context of a "voluntary group" and had nothing to do with laws.

Once he has shown that both the early ministry and the early congregations had no legal powers over rules derived from scriptural interpretation, Hobbes comes close to destroying the validity of all such rules, except as they are derived from power granted to sovereigns by virtue of natural law and by the example of the early Christians. But having shown that the sovereign and law generally are impotent in the realm of belief and that ecclesiastical claims of a legal right to interpret Scripture are spurious,

Hobbes makes the sovereign the head of the church. At the same time he admits that this "prophet" is powerless to command faith, just as all prophets after the election of Saul were powerless.

In the realm of faith required for salvation, "wee may dispute the Doctrine of our Pastors; but no man can dispute a Law."[23] Salvation by faith is unalterably personal—even selfish—and should have nothing directly to do with manners, since visible manners are controlled by law.

> For the reason of our Obedience, is not drawn from the will and command of our Pastors, but from our own benefit, as being the Salvation of our Souls they watch for, and not for the Exaltation of their own Power, and Authority.[24]

Shared faith cannot be a means to hold men together; only when such faith is expressed as de facto political power can it create dependency and therefore unity. Hobbes makes this abundantly clear in his discussion of the biblical requirements for salvation by faith in the last chapter of Part III of *Leviathan*. There he argues that "conversion" in the Bible stipulated that the only requirement of faith for becoming a Christian was a belief that "Jesus is the Christ."[25] This single belief necessary for salvation is no more than belief in Christ's return to earth as he promised. The second coming will establish an eternal political kingdom of saints ruled directly by God. The content of Christian faith is eschatology, and its power is that of reward and punishment after death. This belief anchors political loyalty.

The power of the sovereign is not to teach true doctrines of faith—such truth no man can know—but to prevent the teaching of false ones by others in order to protect secular order. This secular order, in turn, is a period in sacred history. "Christian Soveraignes . . . are [now] the Supreme Pastors" not because they are in fact prophets but because they protect the possibility of saving faith among the elect. Until the end of history, no real prophets can appear with power to rule other men. No man can claim earthly pre-ferment or power by claiming to be among the elect, for "he that pretends to [grace], pretends to be a Prophet and is subject to the examination of the Church."[26]

Only with sovereign power over the church can "government of religion" be transcended. Only then can the objects of power-seeking remain secular and private and the link between the sovereign's power and subject's inner discipline be preserved. In the face of Hobbes's "faith requirement" for salvation, the state church exists as an empty container, sustained only by the meaningless external acts of its members. It can never again be the repository of the private power-seeking which had historically distorted rational appetite. The main function of the institutional church, then, would be to prevent both the traditional Catholic influence over standards of "works" and the inspired claims of lone prophets in the realm of opinion and obligation. Disciplined in this way, each individual has a truly "free" conscience; in Hobbes's commonwealth neither the state nor the church interferes with a person's freedom to believe simply that "Christ is the Messiah." The realm of faith viewed this way is the true realm of freedom in Hobbes's polity, for it is unaffected by natural fear, swords, laws, and even the compulsions of reason. This faith can also generate the power to affect human history at those revolutionary moments which mark new epochs in sacred history. But neither the institutional church nor its sovereign head can import that freedom into law and morality. Religion may be the realm of freedom, but the church remains a negative instrument to preserve the de facto power necessary for sovereignty—power which is right only by an act of faith in prophetic history.

That Hobbes intended this purpose for the church is evident in his attack on traditional moral philosophy and in his vision of toleration as an "ideal" solution to the problem of inner man—provided that every man viewed faith as a Puritan. Both of these themes are discussed in the last part of *Leviathan*, "Of the Kingdome of Darkness."[27] At the end of Part IV, Hobbes recalls the first Christian churches and suggests that the ideal solution to the problem of religious motivations and political stability is toleration. As if to recognize that the church he has suggested in Part III is indeed an empty vessel having no more redemptive capacities than the secular state, he launches into an analysis of the institutional Christian church from its earliest formation to the English Civil War and into a prophetic future.

Recalling his discussion of religion in Part I of *Leviathan*, Hobbes asserts that the "first Elements of Power" in the Christian church were the "Wisdome, Humility, Sincerity, and other vertues of the Apostles" whom the early Christians obeyed "out of Reverence, not by Obligation."[28] Their consciences were free because their external words and actions were controlled only by civil laws. But these first elements of power became the "first knot upon their Liberty," with the establishment of "Presbyters" who, when assembled together, invented rules for the church, disobedience to which entailed the punishment of excommunication as well as the threat of damnation. Presbyters in chief cities became bishops, and the chief bishop became the pope, "the third and last knot."[29] Just as the process of the erosion of Christian liberty ended with "Pontificall Power," so the rebirth of this liberty was historically accomplished by the civil war:

> First, the Power of the Popes was dissolved totally by Queen
> Elizabeth. . . . After this, the Presbyterians lately in England obtained
> the putting down of Episcopacy: and so was the second knot dissolved:
> And almost at the same time, the Power was taken also from the
> Presbyterians: And so we are reduced to the Independancy of the
> Primitive Christians to follow Paul, or Cephas, or Apollos, every man
> as he liketh best.[30]

Unlike the primitive Christian leaders, however, contemporary ministers are not prophets. Independence "if it be without contention, and *without measuring the Doctrine of Christ, by our affection to the Person of his Minister,* is perhaps the best." The only power over the consciences of men ought to be "the Word it selfe, working Faith in every one, not always according to the purpose of them that Plant and Water, but of God himselfe."[31]

Coming at the end of an extensive critique of Catholic theology, his discussion of the English Civil War can be seen as Hobbes's assertion of a historical as well as a philosophical defeat of the "kingdom of darkness." The English Civil War broke the grip of religious doctrine and institutional church power over moral opinion, creating a historical moment when morality could become reduced to natural law and religion to inward faith. There is in *Leviathan,* then, an incredible coincidence between the possibility of the reappearance of true Christian liberty and the historical possibility of establishing a political order based on reason and justice. This moment in history anticipates the millennium in joining reason and revelation, works and faith, true philosophy and true religion. *Leviathan* is a single book whose halves are held together by hope in this prophetic moment. In the first half, Hobbes says that word-bonds without the sword are powerless; in the last half he shows that without the Word the sword is without power. This paradox has haunted the tradition of English liberal political philosophy ever since.

6

Leviathan *and the Structure of Liberal Political Philosophy*

In the introduction, I suggested that Hobbes's *Leviathan* defined the structure within which the ideas of subsequent English liberalism developed. I want to be more specific about this structure by summarizing the ways in which elements of "time" and "history" shape Hobbes's discussion of law, morality, and religion.

1. *Hobbes's attack on historical politics.* Historically known political associations are all based on moral opinions tied to religious doctrines, and ultimately to fear of gods who promise rewards and punishments after death. The fear backs the laws of men, who "invent" explanations of these gods.

2. *"Seed of religion" and historical politics.* The reason men have been held together politically can be explained psychologically. As men anticipate the future in order to attain present desires, their calculations naturally become more indeterminate the farther into the future their chains of cause and effect extend. Indeterminateness, in turn, produces a generalized anxiety about the future, an anxiety assuaged only by belief in invisible powers.

3. *State of nature.* To view men as they universally are and not as historical opinion and political power have distorted them, one needs to strip away all verbal artifacts constructed in history and all authority tied to these artifacts. The psychological knowledge gained differs significantly from the knowledge we have of men trapped by historical politics and by invented moral-religious doctrines. The new knowledge exists within a timeless context and without the specific historical artifact which was built on invented religious doctrines.

4. *True moral philosophy and civil law.* To pit the intentions of men in the state of nature against the beliefs and actions of men in history is to construct a theory of law which is independent of traditional moral opinion and authority. This theory of law depends upon an equally nonhistorical necessity: de facto power to sanction contractual word-bonds.

67

5. *Political obligation and natural invisible power.* In the past, political obligation, common moral opinion, religious belief, and actual power-seeking tended to constitute a relatively coherent body of thought—all of which Hobbes "exposes" as the work of particular men who seek power by inventing gods and religions. These gods and doctrines threaten disobedient acts and thoughts with divine punishment. In Hobbes's politics the invisible power standing behind the sovereign is neither a historically specific "invention" nor a god who judges the person at some final time. Rather, the god of nature is timeless necessity and has no relationship to political history or to any man's personal hopes and fears.[1]

6. *Political obligation and prophetic invisible power.* Hobbes reintroduces historical features into his politics when he shifts from the invisible power of the kingdom of god known by reason to a god known through sacred history as recorded by the Bible. His interpretation of sacred history denigrates the rules of the Old Testament and demonstrates a lack of rules after Christ's coming. Thereby he makes it religiously appropriate to define rules by natural reason and secular civil law. This restoration of a time element is both politically and psychologically necessary, given the defects of natural religion, but it does not threaten the timeless logic of his civil philosophy. At the same time, the state of nature—and, indeed, Parts I and II of *Leviathan*—attain historical location and historical relevance.

7. *Sovereign power over external religious acts.* Sovereign power over institutional churches and specific religious doctrines serves only the negative purpose of preventing the reappearance of moral opinion which counters true moral philosophy. Under a regime of toleration, multiple religious sects serve this negative function as well. In either case, history as eschatology and inviolable faith is not compromised—even though the former solution introduces significant elements of arbitrary sovereign will, elements not present in a body of civil law reflecting true moral philosophy.

8. *Political history and sacred history.* Past political history is inseparable from biblical and church history. The history of the Christian church has been impelled by the mingling of works, faith, and the passion to dominate other men. The medium of this mingling was the false moral philosophy and opinions held by men: the past has been both unjust and blasphemous. When discussing toleration and recent political events in England, Hobbes suggests a parallel defeat of false moral philosophy. The historical victory of Independent sects over the last remaining bond on Christian liberty and his own philosophical victory provide the evidence.

This summary in terms of the element of "time" ends on a note of incredibly fortuitous congruence between political-religious history and true civil philosophy. As if a corrupted and earthly form of sacred history had finally culminated in the Puritan Revolution, Hobbes suggests a future and lasting congruence between the sacred history of the Bible and his own true civil philosophy. Is not this the congruence which Hobbes requires when he combines the god of nature with the god of prophecy? Is not this same congruence necessary to explain the relationship between the two halves of *Leviathan*? Hobbes promises the reader this congruence toward the end of Part II, when he says:

> So, long time after men have begun to constitute Common-wealths, imperfect and apt to relapse into disorder, there may, Principles of Reason be found out, by industrious meditation, to make their constitution . . . everlasting. And such are those which I have in this discourse set forth: Which whether they come not into sight of those that have Power to make use of them, . . . or not, concerneth my particular interest, at this day, very little. But supposing that these of mine are not such Principles of Reason; yet I am sure they are Principles from Authority of Scripture; as I shall make it appear when I shall come to speak of the Kingdome of God.[2]

Immediately following this passage, Hobbes condemns "the Rich, and Potent Subjects of a Kingdome" who, in conjunction with "the most Learned," corrupt the common man for their own vain purposes. The obstructions to Hobbes's doctrine "proceed . . . from the interest of them that are to learn." Both "Potent men" and "Learned men" resist this learning, but hope lies in those whom Hobbes calls the "Common-peoples."[3] If common men are privatized and insulated from the powers and ideas which moved historical politics, they remain alone with their interests, their everyday prudence, and their faith in a final judgment. This combination is only insured by political power which can overawe the pretensions of the learned and the powerful as well as guarantee strict contractual justice for the remainder of men.[4] The timid (and perhaps envious) common man should welcome the bargain.

Hobbes, to repeat, is a secure skeptic. His skepticism shares many elements with Calvinist skepticism. Both forms support a politics forcing all men to recognize their natural depravity and to find hope in an incommunicable but common faith. Hobbes describes past philosophy as "more a Dream than a Science," and his politics seeks to abolish the public expression of dreams. To institute Hobbes's regime would be to compel a *de jure* puritanism though not necessarily a real community of saints. In secular terms, however, the crucial element is the brute necessity for *de facto* power: unless fear of death motivates men to create their own executioner, the requirements for instituting a just order lie quite beyond Hobbes's epistemology and philosophy.

Hobbesian politics is a precarious equilibrium among manners, laws, and gods created and sustained (if sustained at all) by sovereign power. I have stressed that Hobbes's path from individual men driven irrevocably to seeking their own good to a civil order which is intended to embrace moral good and reflect common good, requires one to place heavy burdens on the person of the sovereign. This artificial construct becomes the incongruous figure of the de jure prophet—as if to say that this transformation was the only way to make sovereignty powerful enough to be noncompetitive. Hobbes places these burdens on the sovereign because his radical distinctions between the timeless logic of law and the workings of divine providence in history require it. Hobbes's sovereign stands firmly in the two worlds of liberalism.

The subjects of the sovereign also stand in two worlds. Hobbes pictures state-of-nature men as devoid of personal ties and therefore as driven by universal, simple, and "legal" intentions, even if those intentions, frustrated, lead to conflict and violence. These intentions, or natural laws, articulate a new set of relationships among men, relationships based on impersonal ties and enforced by a contractually created sovereign power presumed to have no ends of its own. Success rests on maintaining this contraction of human purpose by keeping the effects of religious faith and therefore historical forms of language and human connection out of political and legal relationships.

If Hobbes's skepticism is reflected in a politics based on systematized depravity and fear of death, his faith is reflected in his treatment of sacred history. The sovereign must be believed to offer punishments greater than death and rewards greater than life. He is de jure Vicar of Christ. This is the only element of faith that enters Hobbes's politics. All else, doctrinal and church rules, the power of the clergy, and even speculation about heaven and hell, seem subservient to the rules appropriate for men living after Christ but before the final judgment. The result is a political order designed expressly for men seeking temporal and natural ends held together by a prophetic sovereign.

Hobbes's *Leviathan* contains two separate languages, logics, psychologies, and politics. On one hand the sovereign looks suspiciously like a liberal constitution: stern but impersonal enforcer of the principle of ownership and voluntary exchange; grantor of no special favors; source of no duties save those defined clearly by law or marketplace. On the other hand, this same sovereign is the one person acting within the time frame of sacred history, whether he came to power by conquest or by deliberate institution. He is the only man in the society who can judge other men outside of legal categories: when he is executioner, he judges not only the specific actions of a man, he represents God's vengeance by pronouncing a final judgment on another's natural life. When the sovereign pardons a man for a capital crime, he represents God's mercy. These powers cannot be authorized by natural men nor can they be justified by appeals to moral philosophy. To integrate this split language and logic into one sovereign and one body politic requires of the citizen an act of faith, the belief that willing adherence to the law of "works" is part of a larger plan of redemption for the individual and for mankind. Without this act of political faith, a leap of faith without the light of reason, the private man lives in a regime of endless necessity. His own passions drive him to make endless contractual bargains and the constant threat of punishment guarantees that he will keep them. He can be freed from the regime of necessity only in death.

Hobbes bequeathed to liberalism a systematic structure, but one replete with paradox. Men are born to liberty and from "Principles of Reason" can be shown the necessity of sovereign power. Men are born to servitude and from "Authority of Scripture" can be shown that following the dictates of reason is an act which transcends necessity. Reason proves that perpetual anxiety and fear of death are inseparable parts of the mechanisms of legal liberty; the regime of law and liberty is absolutely essential in this stage of sacred history. Under the proper conditions most men will obey the Leviathan because he protects their bodies and goods. But both the Leviathan and those few who fight to establish him must act on different principles in order to create and sustain the proper conditions. Presumably, all other men will share in these principles and actions only to the extent of accepting them on faith. For the average man, properly construed religious belief is not an opiate but a means of convincing him to act on principles of self-interest and to believe that it is a religious obligation to be bound by voluntary word-bonds spelling out private desires. Hobbes's hope is that most men would exchange their past servitudes and sacrifices for a safer but more constricted world of contractual liberty. In giving up their past servitudes, however, men also relinquish a capacity for significant political action. Only the few men of faith might consistently be motivated by different principles, but these men are only seen when a liberal regime is threatened and some men rise to defend it with their lives. How the Leviathan might seek to ensure such men is an abiding problem, for the very principles of reason which animate a liberal regime ensure its fragility in history—a history which can be understood only dimly from the authority of Scripture.

Part Two

John Locke

The cold clarity of Hobbes's politics is often contrasted with the warmer but somewhat muddled political doctrines of John Locke. Hobbes's devastating reason is not only cold comfort but quite removed from many familiar notions of liberal politics: revolution in defense of liberty, legislative protection of personal rights, and, most important, a political executive bounded by law, institutions, and morality. Moreover, Locke's *Second Treatise* suggests something of a constitutional order with the attendant play of political roles, permitting us to see signs of political conflict and political life. But the warmth of familiarity often includes some contempt: so much of Locke's politics is indeterminate, inchoate, and simply confusing. Interpretations of Locke's writing, therefore, span a spectrum of possibilities from radical democratic to authoritarian and even absolutist.[1] The examination of Locke's political philosophy which follows will neither begin with the *Second Treatise* nor attempt to weigh Locke on an ideological scale. My intention is first to make explicit the larger structure of his politics by reference to a variety of his writings and then to locate the *Second Treatise* within that structure.[2] In this way, I think that the reasons for the variety of interpretive possibilities can be explained and the relationship to Hobbes's politics can be specified.

Major elements in Locke's thought—his periodization of sacred history, his psychological theories, and his epistemology—are extremely close to those of Hobbes. Despite these similarities, however, the locus and operation of political power cannot be found in some definite person or institution. But all of Locke's writings begin with the assumption that man is born to two worlds and that politics must somehow mediate between them. From his earliest concern with the relationship of morality to revealed religion to his last writings on reasonable Christianity, Locke saw political life as requiring both reason and faith.

73

In gaining access to Locke from this perspective, we find that two tasks are foremost. We must seek to understand how he portrays each of these worlds and then try to see how he relates them to each other. The world that Locke creates by reasoning as if men were "born to freedom" is more complex and changing than that found in Parts I and II of *Leviathan*. Conversely, the logic of a world of men born to servitude includes norms and practices which signal much closer relationships between religious faith and ordinary motives than granted in Hobbes. Because the boundaries between these worlds are much less distinct than in *Leviathan*, the task of mediating between them differs. No single man or action or institution constitutes the political linkage point connecting liberty and servitude. Indeed, a difficulty one faces with this approach is to know when Locke is writing clearly within one world or the other and when he is attempting to build another bridge between them. And he does build many bridges. The radical skepticism in Hobbes leaves a systematically split view of man and his moral, legal, and religious relationships. Hobbes's *Leviathan* carries these divisions to their farthest point and codifies them in the structure of the book. Locke begins with these divisions and seeks to bridge practically every one of them. Thus, where Hobbes radically distinguishes the entirely personal status of saving faith from the brute necessity of an institutional state church, Locke urges the acceptance of voluntarist sects as a bridge between individual faith and collective acts of worship. Hobbes distinguishes firmly between actions motivated by natural desires and those prompted by belief in supernatural rewards and punishments. Locke begins with this distinction and then shows that most actions and opinions relevant to politics fall somewhere in between. Both Hobbes and Locke recognize two distinct notions of time, one a sacred history reflecting revelation, the other a timeless dimension of material cause and effect discovered by reason. Locke alone, however, outlines a natural history of mankind which explains dramatic change and distinct epochs in history by reference to natural causes and effects. Both writers firmly reject theories of political authority grounded in Old Testament examples and paternal analogies. Locke, however, locates political authority in a particular stage of man's development, showing that political power has its origins in paternal authority. Hobbes and Locke each stress the radical difference between a natural condition without authority and a political one with punishments and law. Locke, however, appears to have two states of nature, one of which contains features distinctly belonging neither to natural nor to political society. Finally, both Hobbes and Locke stress the absolute necessity that sovereignty rest on the physical power to punish with death. This power and the need for one final voice in its use forever distinguishes the ruler from the subject. Locke at once accepts this sine qua non of political order and maintains that the legislature—a body which commands no army and has no sword—is sovereign in a legitimate political order.[3]

Locke's writings affirm and articulate the two distinct worlds of thought contained in *Leviathan*, even as they explicate a series of political doctrines which contain theories of religion, history, morals, and government expressly mediating between those worlds and blurring their distinct features. This combination has always left room for interpreters of Locke's politics to place him both very close to and very far from Hobbes—especially a Hobbes known only from the first half of *Leviathan*.[4] By maintaining that Locke is both, I am not splitting the differences dividing interpretive schools, but broadening the framework within which Locke's explicitly "liberal" political teachings are located.

Another feature of Locke's entire enterprise which distinguishes it from Hobbes's is the difficulty of deciding which of Locke's many writings define his political thought. Earlier, I insisted that Hobbes's politics must include the second half of *Leviathan*. This insistence has strong surface plausibility no matter how convincing the other reasons are that I have given. To ask the student of Locke's politics to range across more than the *Two Treatises* is hardly novel in recent Locke scholarship.[5] In joining this call, I add—indeed, I begin with—Locke's writings on religion. The persistence and volume of these writings already distinguish him from Hobbes. Insofar as these writings have relevance to his politics, they shift the location of political life away from rulers exercising state power and toward men in society examining their own rights, duties, and motives. The *Second Treatise* also implies this shift in its stress on the preconditions which must be met before consent can be presumed. This idea is carried further in his other writings. Standards for judging the quality of popular moral opinions, tests of religious belief conducive both to morality and political legitimacy, and the many calls for rigorous self-examination all suggest that a major location for bridging the two worlds of liberalism and therefore a major location of political life is within the psyche of man himself. This psychological focus is a counterpart to Locke's concern with popular forms of religious belief and represents as important an element in his politics as the *Second Treatise*. And in his *Essay Concerning Human Understanding*, the psychological explorations—especially the problem of personal identity—lead Locke to confront the possibility that freedom itself cannot be located exclusively in a realm accessible to reason and thus measurable by rules of law and morality. Locke's periodic resort to religion, then, is less an act of piety (or failure of analytic nerve) than an integral part of his philosophical and political enterprise. In this last feature, Locke most clearly reflects the structure set forth in *Leviathan*.

7

Toleration and Reasonable Opinion

Locke's writings on religion and politics span his entire intellectual career.[1] He wrote his first "Letter Concerning Toleration" about the time he wrote the *Two Treatises of Government*. The English version was published just a year before publication of the *Two Treatises*.[2] In this letter and in the replies to its critics, Locke clearly states the relationship between religious and political obligation, outlines the difference between religious belief and natural motivations, and ties both of these arguments to a formal theory of knowledge. Locke's discussion of the reach of magisterial authority is more comprehensive and philosophically defended in these letters than in the *Second Treatise*.[3] And his conclusions regarding the limits of toleration forcefully demonstrate Locke's understanding of the sources of obligation and loyalty in a liberal regime.

Magistrate and Minister

The last chapter of Hobbes's *Leviathan* is entitled "Of the Benefit proceeding from [the kingdom of] Darknesse, and to Whom it Accreweth." In that chapter, Hobbes catalogues with scathing wit the purposes served by "vain philosophy, and fabulous traditions."[4] In the more somber "Review and Conclusion" which follows, he suggests that "the contrariety of mens Opinions and Manners in generall. . . by Education, and Discipline may be, and are sometimes reconciled."[5]

Throughout Locke's first letter on toleration, he reminds those who would "call in the magistrate's authority to the aid of their eloquence and learning" that "whilst they pretend only love for the truth . . . [they] betray their ambition, and show that what they desire is temporal dominion."[6] But Locke, unlike Hobbes, would construct no civil church, no legal prophet, no required public mode of worship, no legally enforced articles of faith.

76

This letter strikes a clear antinomian note: "The inventions of men in religion need the force of men to support them. A religion that is of God wants not the assistance of human authority to make it prevail."[7] Instead of invoking the need for civil power in aid of religion, Locke argues, in a manner anticipating the plea for tolerance in John Stuart Mill's *On Liberty*, that "speculative" religious truth

> certainly would do well enough, if she were once left to shift for herself. She seldom hath received, and . . . I fear never will receive much assistance from the power of great men, to whom she is but rarely known, and more rarely welcome. She is not taught by laws, nor has she any need of force to procure her entrance into the minds of men.[8]

Locke begins his plea for toleration within the framework of prophetic or revealed religion. His starting point is the Word, not the historical church. Speculative religious articles of faith are those which do not affect men's will to act. Things we cannot truly know cannot be part of the causal chain used to explain the origins of ideas. Locke simply asserts, with Hobbes, that laws and coercion cannot reach speculative belief, because the only appropriate content of religious belief is eschatological. "True and saving religion," Locke argues, "consists in the inward persuasion of the mind. . . . And such is the nature of understanding, that it cannot be compelled to the belief of any thing by outward force."[9]

In most of Locke's arguments for toleration, he pictures two separate worlds. One is based on outer command, the other on inner belief. One rests on the external dominion of man's external actions to protect his tangible interests: "life, liberty, health, and indolency of body" and "the possession of outward things, such as money, lands, houses, furniture, and the like." The other world is based on dominion by an invisible power over men's "inward and full persuasion of the mind" with an end to the "salvation of [men's] souls."[10] The realm of civil power is built by men working in common and results in public laws binding on the actions of all subjects. The world of religion concerns that salvation after death which is beyond human knowledge and control. As with Hobbes, care of the soul for Locke is entirely an unshared personal concern.

This distinction between civil and religious "interests," as Locke puts it, is reflected in the distinction between knowledge and belief. This distinction, discussed in his third letter on toleration, provides the philosophical basis for those utilized in his direct argument. Speculative truth is

> faith . . . and not knowledge, persuasion, and not certainty. This is the highest the nature of the thing will permit us to go in matters of revealed religion, which are therefore called matters of faith: a persuasion of our own minds, short of knowledge, is the last result that

determines us in such truths. . . . Knowledge, then, properly so called [is] not . . . to be had of the truths necessary to salvation. . . . If therefore it be the magistrate's duty to use force to bring men to the true religion, it can be only to that religion which he believes to be the truth.[11]

The distinction between church and state parallels those between religious and natural interests and between faith and knowledge.

The church itself is a thing absolutely separate and distinct from the commonwealth. . . . He jumbles heaven and earth together, and things most remote and opposite, who mixes these societies, which are in their original, end, business, and in every thing, perfectly distinct, and infinitely different from each other.[12]

Works, Faith, and Practical Opinions

The status of faith, the causes of salvation, and the motivations for worship all dictate great latitude for institutional freedom within each voluntary gathering of believers.[13] After Locke applies this reasoning to a variety of specific issues, however, he shifts the direction of his argument. Having asserted and defended a set of irrevocable distinctions, he presents a category of ideas, called "practical moral opinions," and a pattern of actions, motivated neither by speculative faith nor by direct material interest, called "moral actions." Locke here introduces an important bridge to span the separate worlds of faith and works, belief and knowledge, religion and politics. "Moral actions belong to the jurisdiction both of the outward and inward court; both of the civil and domestic governor, . . . both of the magistrate and conscience." Moral actions are more than good behavior, they are the constituent of "a good life . . . and in it lies the safety both of men's souls and of the commonwealth." Unless one knows the proper limits of the magistrate and minister, the realm of dual jurisdiction constitutes "a grave danger."[14]

Articles and doctrines of faith, of course, lie wholly outside the power of the law and of the magistrate. Acts of worship are equally exempt from legal regulation. Except for clearly illegal actions outside of the church, all acts of worship, whether thought by the worshippers to be divinely ordained or to be quite irrelevant for salvation, are "in their own nature indifferent" to the magistrate. Consequently, this entire category of actions cannot "by any human authority, be made part of the worship of God." For the magistrate to interfere in this area would be to "destroy the church itself; the end of whose institution is only to worship God with freedom, after its own manner."[15]

Because speculative opinions "are required only to be believed . . . and to believe this or that to be true *does not depend upon our will*," the legal imposition of beliefs is "absurd"; they *"are not in men's power to perform."*[16] Men's actions on earth which affect others flow from causal chains having nothing to do with grace. Legally to require that men profess certain articles of belief would be to oblige "men to dissemble, and tell lies both to God and man, for the salvation of their souls! If the magistrate thinks to save men thus, he seems to understand little of the way of salvation."[17] The isolation of the status of faith yields an absolutely inviolable area of individual right:

> [S]eeing one man does not violate the *right* of another, by his erroneous opinions, and undue manner of worship, nor is his perdition any *prejudice* to another man's affairs; therefore the care of each man's salvation belongs only to himself. Nobody is obliged . . . to yield unto the admonitions or injunctions of another, farther than he himself is persuaded. Every man, in that, has the supreme and absolute authority of judging for himself; and the reason is, because *nobody else is concerned in it,* nor can receive any prejudice from his conduct therein.[18]

Although these conclusions of Locke would seem properly to conclude his discussion of toleration, they only begin it. All legal acts of worship must be tolerated, but not all professed articles of belief fall within Locke's "speculative" category. Some doctrines and beliefs are "practical" or moral; they are beliefs concerning good and evil in everyday social relationships. They motivate legal and illegal actions outside of church. Once Locke introduces this realm of practical moral opinion, his vocabulary shifts from "faith" to "works," from mercy to justice.

> Every man has an immortal soul, capable of eternal happiness or misery; whose happiness depending upon his believing and doing those things in this life, which are necessary to the obtaining of God's favour, and are prescribed by God to that end: It follows from thence, first, that the observance of these things is the highest obligation that lies upon mankind, and that our utmost care, application, and diligence, ought to be exercised in the search and performance of them; because there is nothing in this world that is any consideration in comparison with eternity.[19]

The realm of practical moral opinion yields legal authority for the magistrate and legal duties for the citizen. Social acts express moral opinion. Both action and opinion can be subject to laws because together they can violate "those moral rules which are necessary to the preservation of civil society."[20] As moral rules they also determine the actions necessary to achieve the "works" required for salvation. But what should these moral rules be? How

[handwritten margin note: arg. for pol. intervention in relign. or exceptns to tolerat.]

can they be known with certainty? What are the criteria for correctness and for judging church support of them?

Locke's answers begin with an articulation of an integrated theory of natural religion, natural law, and political authority which bypasses the entire realm of prophetic religion and historical forms of political rulership. In so doing, he gives us a beautifully clear version of the postmonetary state of nature as articulated in the *Second Treatise.* The works required for salvation are discovered by philosophy.

> 1. Men in their temporal lives "have need of several outward conveniences to the support thereof, which are to be procured or preserved by pains and industry," because nature does not "offer [them] fit and prepared for our use."
> 2. The comforts purchased by this pain and industry are threatened because the "pravity of mankind [is] such that they had rather injuriously prey upon the fruits of other men's labours than take pains to provide for themselves."
> 3. "The necessity of preserving men in the possession of what honest industry has already acquired, and also of preserving their liberty and strength, whereby they may acquire what they farther want, obliges men to enter into society with one another; that by mutual assistance and joint force, they may secure unto each other their properties, in the things that contribute to the comforts and happiness of this life."
> 4. The society thus formed "for the defence of [men's] temporal goods," must have means to protect men in those goods both from "the rapine and fraud of their fellow citizens" and from "the hostile violence of foreigners: the remedy of this evil consists in arms, riches, and multitudes of citizens: the remedy of others in laws: and the care of things relating both to the one and the other is committed by the society to the civil magistrate. This is the original, this is the use, and these are the bounds of the legislative, which is the supreme power in every commonwealth."[21]

Unlike the complex discussion of nature's bounty, the benign light of nature, and universal obedience in the *Second Treatise,* Locke's state-of-nature conclusion is clear: left uncontrolled, most men prefer stealing to working. Given this clear statement of the means and purposes of morality, practical moral opinion falls within the ambit of law and punishment. As a general principle, Locke maintains that civil authority can proscribe all "opinions contrary to human society."[22]

Locke's application of this principle yields some rather paradoxical results—results that are not uncommon in the history of toleration. Professed beliefs by individuals are perfectly protected; outward acts of worship, whether thought important or indifferent by the individual worshipper, are outside the ambit of civil authority. Entire churches, however, can be outlawed. Unless they meet both organizational and doctrinal tests congruent

with the maintenance of true practical moral opinion, they have no right to
exist. In his examples, Locke is not entirely clear whether bad doctrine or
bad polity would justify prohibiting a church to exist at all, but his contrast
of independent sects to established or national churches strongly implies
that the two issues cannot be separated.

Independent Protestant sects would rarely reach "such a degree of madness" to teach doctrines which "manifestly undermine the foundations of
society . . . because their own interest, peace, reputation, everything would
be thereby endangered."[23] Of more probable and immediate danger are those
doctrines (more typical of Anglican and Catholic tradition) which are "in
effect, opposite to the civil rights of the community," but only indirectly.
Doctrines such as "faith is not to be kept with heretics," or "dominion
is founded in grace," are in effect claims for "peculiar privilege or power
above other mortals, in civil concernments"; as such, these doctrines have
no right to be tolerated by civil authority. More generally, *"those that will
not own and teach the duty of tolerating all men in matters of mere religion"*
have no right to toleration, "for what do all these and the like doctrines
signify, but that they may, and are ready upon any occasion to seize the
government, and possess themselves of the estates and fortunes of their
fellow subjects."[24]

One example of doctrine pernicious to civil authority is expressly formulated to apply to national churches: "That church can have no right to
be tolerated by the magistrate, which is constituted upon such a bottom,
that all those who enter into it, do thereby, *ipso facto*, deliver themselves
up to the protection and services of another prince."[25] Though Locke chooses
the example of the "Mohometan" who yields blind obedience to a Mufti
who, in turn, is entirely subservient to the Ottoman emperor, the principle
could most certainly apply to Catholicism. The last legitimate case for civil
intervention in religion concerns those who "deny the being of God." Because societal bonds consisting of "promises, covenants, and oaths . . . can
have no hold upon an atheist," to deny God, "even in thought, dissolves
all."[26]

Many Sects, One Opinion

As suggested by Locke's exceptions to toleration, the protection of proper
moral opinion is a central purpose of the types of toleration he advocates.
Locke's view of appropriate forms of church polity is also central to this
protection. His discussion of the relationship between church and member
is deeply antinomian. Having shown how limited are the political and social
effects of "saving" faith, Locke can picture the church as needing no legally
enforced rules of internal discipline. Men join churches voluntarily for the
sole purpose of salvation; thus, "No member of a religious society can be

tied with any other bonds but what proceed from the certain expectation of eternal life."[27] This "certain expectation" is each individual's faith. For example, Locke's discussion of excommunication is based on the church as a voluntary association: the break between member and congregation injures no one, so no legal rights are affected. "For there is no civil injury done unto the excommunicated person by the church minister's refusing him that bread and wine, in the celebration of the Lord's Supper, which was not bought with his but other men's money."[28] Dissenting sects are the most appropriate organizational model for protecting moral opinion. Locke's doctrine of toleration is uniquely fitted for the sects and for an answer to those who urged civil punishment for dissenting sects as "conventicles, and nursuries of factions and seditions."[29]

Locke's doctrine of toleration not only uniquely parallels the claims of conscience found in dissenting congregations; it suggests that under proper circumstances, dissenting sects will prove a boon to proper civic education. By tracing past disorders from dissenting congregations to arbitrary actions by magistrates and national churches, Locke can argue that members of dissenting congregations appear to be more solicitous of their "natural rights" than those of other churches. Dissenters demand equity, not preferment.

> Take away the partiality that is used towards them in matters of common right; change the laws, take away the penalties unto which they are subjected, and all things will immediately become safe and peaceable: nay those that are averse to the religion of the magistrate, will think themselves so much the more bound to maintain the peace of the commonwealth, as their condition is better in that place than elsewhere; and all the several separate congregations, *like so many guardians of the public peace, will watch one another,* that nothing may be innovated or changed in the form of government: because they can hope for nothing better than what they already enjoy; that is, an equal condition with their fellow-subjects, under a just and moderate government.[30]

In my discussion of Hobbes, I suggested that in his commonwealth the function of the church was to keep men in the same psychological condition found in the state of nature. Locke's doctrine of toleration suggests a more sophisticated formulation of a similar function. Locke obviates the need for faith in the person of the magistrate and seems to rid the political order of the necessity to make rules out of prophecy—even empty Hobbesian rules.[31] Given toleration, churches will spontaneously educate their members in "good citizenship" by teaching that political claims cannot be made on the basis of man's "inner life" as symbolized by faith. Free churches teach and practice public distrust in the name of men's private search for the highest and most intensely personal good. The possibilities inherent in this form of toleration go beyond religious organizations:

> How much greater will be the security of a government, where all the good subjects . . . enjoying the same favour of the prince, and the same benefit of the laws, shall become the common support and guard of it; and where none will have any occasion to fear the severity of the laws, but those that do injuries to their neighbors, and offend against the civil peace.[32]

The distinctions Locke uses to justify his doctrine of toleration do not necessarily support that doctrine. Hobbes constructed a case for a national church on those distinctions, and Locke's earlier *Two Tracts* justified the proscription of the sects precisely on the grounds that saving faith was independent of external signs. Locke's developed doctrine reflects these possibilities, for it is at once incredibly generous and almost cynically narrow.[33] This combination reflects Locke's difficulty in mediating between the political claims of natural and religious motivations. Independent sects necessarily teach what philosophy recommends. To protect them is to protect the proper spheres of law, manners, and gods.

Locke urges wide toleration whenever he discusses the "true" purposes of religion within the framework of prophetic purpose and prophetic judgment. He demands narrow toleration whenever he broaches the subject of moral rules which might be challenged by churches or beliefs which engender strong loyalties among men, loyalties which would necessarily counter the individualism implicit in Locke's natural law and his view of prophetic religion.

Locke's views of human nature reveal this same combination of wideness and narrowness. Whenever men are thought to be thoroughly anchored to the pursuit of "conveniences" in this world, their "inner lives" are thought safe from harmful consequences; these men are "free," rational, and industrious. When, however, men's external actions are thought to flow directly from this inner freedom and therefore cannot be traced to the lawful pursuit of material happiness, these men are often pictured either as under the insidious power of other men or in the helpless grip of "the ungrounded fancies of [their own minds]." Such men are not truly "free" but they are dangerous and require both the discipline of law and a restructuring of their faith. This enterprise, in turn, requires knowledge in two distinct areas, human psychology and Christian theology. A recent study of Locke suggests that the place to find Hobbesian logic in Locke's writings is not in the contorted explication of the *Second Treatise* but in the more obvious psychology of the *Essay on Human Understanding*.[34] That suggestion is sound, but it requires an addendum: the place to find Hobbesian periodization of sacred history and theology is in Locke's *Reasonableness of Christianity*.

8

Faith in the History of Freedom

God when he makes the prophet does not unmake the man. He leaves all his faculties in their natural state, to enable him to judge of his inspirations, whether they be of divine origin or no.

JOHN LOCKE, *An Essay Concerning Human Understanding*

Locke's voluminous writings on religious toleration are almost equalled by his writings on theology.[1] Locke's major work of scriptural interpretation, written in 1695, is entitled *On the Reasonableness of Christianity, as delivered in the Scriptures.* As with his first letter on toleration, this work provoked the ire of more traditional theologians and required two long "Vindications."[2]

Locke's attempt to reconcile natural law, psychological empiricism, and religious faith was continuous. His purposes in writing the *Reasonableness* and its vindications confirm this larger task. These works are efforts to convince deists and other "skeptics" that Scripture does not stand in the way of constructing a coherent world on the basis of reason.[3] Locke, however, has another purpose as well, that of relating both moral knowledge and religious faith to history and to political life. To put it as strongly as possible, Locke concludes that belief in a final judgment makes the rational construction of a moral world historically possible. In a series of poignant statements toward the close of *Reasonableness*, Locke acknowledges the impotence of reason and morality in history. "Philosophy seemed to have spent its strength." "It is plain . . . that human reason unassisted failed men in its great and proper business of morality." "It should seem by the little that has hitherto been done in it that it is too hard a task for unassisted reason to establish morality in all its parts upon its true foundation with a clear and convincing light."[4]

This weakness of philosophy and reason is relative, for their product, rules of morality, was always in competition with religion. Historically, "religion was everywhere distinguished from and preferred to virtue." Empty rituals were easier for men to practice than were the rigors of "a clean conscience . . . a steady course of virtue . . . a strict and holy life."[5]

Locke does not make clear exactly when or whether such competition ceased. He does explain, however, why religious rules had always been more psychologically compelling: they were perceived as decreed by a law giver capable of rewards and punishments. By contrast, moral virtue was urged by "this or that philosopher [who] was of no authority."[6] Only when the truth of morality is seen as part of a system of divine rewards and punishments will it attain both psychological force and historical reality. Only under these conditions will morality provide the basis for a civil law with teeth in it. Historically, politics and religion, not politics and morality, are inseparable.

Both Hobbes and Locke face the same difficulty of establishing when it was historically possible for the truths of moral philosophy to appear compatible with religious belief. Both damn polytheism and pagan religious ritual for preventing true morality. Both date compatibility of morality and religion with the coming of Christ and the teachings of the primitive Christian churches: the New Testament contains no standard of works. The point in time at which the Bible stops and miracles cease—and the institutional history of Christianity begins—is that point at which the pre-Christian and baleful effects of religion on morality are reintroduced.[7]

Corruption and wars are the external marks of a long historical period of conflict between religion and reason, priest and philosopher. In this struggle, the priest always wins in the battle of defining man's highest duties. Hobbes called this period the kingdom of darkness. This same conclusion is clear throughout the *Reasonableness* and is articulated earlier in Locke's *Letters*. It is not, however, the final word in either *Leviathan* or *Reasonableness*. The contemporary battle is not simply between philosopher and priest but between priest and minister, between false religion and true religion, between human invention in religious practice and the simple power of the Word. Philosophers in the past did little "to establish morality in all its parts . . . with a clear and convincing light," because it was impossible to do so.[8]

The contemporary situation collapses the time difference of more than one and a half millennia. Christ's coming and the teachings of the New Testament have made it theoretically possible for philosophy to define "works"; the battle for toleration and biblical religion makes it historically possible:

[O]ur Savior found mankind under a corruption of manners and principles, which ages after ages had prevailed, and must be confessed, was not in a way or tendency to be mended. The rules of morality were in different countries and sects different. And natural reason nowhere had cured, nor was likely to cure, the defects and errors in them. Those just measures of right and wrong, which *necessity* had anywhere introduced, the *civil laws* prescribed, or *philosophy* recommended, stood on their true foundations. They were looked on as bonds of society, and conveniences of common life, and laudable practices. But where was it that their obligation was thoroughly known and allowed, and they received as precepts of a law—of the highest law, the law of nature? That could not be, without a clear knowledge and acknowledgement of the law maker, and the great rewards and punishments for those that would or would not obey him.[9]

Christ's coming and his teachings in the New Testament did not introduce natural law. What Christ's appearance did do was simultaneously to release some men (Jews) from the direct legislative power of God and place all men under the dictates of natural law, now backed by eternal rewards and punishments. Following Christ's appearance, prophetic rule in the world stopped. Miracles ceased; the kingdom of God now becomes a promise for the future and exists in faith, not on earth. In this situation, a "state of nature" prevails at least in the sense that natural reason must now define the moral virtues. The intervening period of false doctrines and church corruption fulfills the biblical prophecy but establishes nothing obligatory for Christians. Christ's coming makes natural law alone obligatory and sets the true task for the philosopher. Locke uses the past tense for all statements referring to the weakness of unaided reason. The same is true, a fortiori, regarding motivation to obey. But for men to feel religiously obliged to natural law, they must come to share Locke's interpretation of the consequences of Christ's coming. For his logic to have efficacy, false theology and false principles of religious organization must be defeated. Unaided, philosophy can never achieve this defeat; only an alliance of reason and true faith is adequate to this possibility. The burden of the *Reasonableness* is to establish this alliance, and the chief theological conclusion is identical with Locke's definition of "saving" religion in his earlier *Letters:* To become a Christian is to believe in a final judgment followed by rewards and punishments—to believe, in short, that "Christ is the Messiah." Locke claims that this test is exactly the one used when Christ first appeared, and before churches became political institutions.

Two Kingdoms

The theology of the *Reasonableness* is consistent with Locke's defense of independent churches. The central argument of the *Reasonableness* transforms Christian faith into a rejection of the institutional history of the church and of the moral and political theories of which it was a part. In a reply to a critic, he makes plain the association of reasonable faith with the primitive church:

> He [Edwards] does not observe the difference there is between what is necessary to be believed by every man to *make* him a Christian, and what is *required to be believed* by every Christian. The first of these is what, by the covenant of the Gospel, is necessary to be known, and consequently to be proposed to *every* man, to make him a Christian: the latter is no less than the whole revelation of God, all the divine truths contained in holy Scripture: which every Christian man is under upon his serious and constant endeavours, to enlighten his mind to understand them.[10]

Any middle ground, any construction of creeds by any human authority "required to be believed by every Christian" will plunge man and society into the same condition that has prevailed

> these thousand years and upwards; schisms, separations, contentions, animosities, quarrels, blood and butchery, and all that train of mischiefs which have so long harassed and defamed Christianity.[11]

His antagonist, who attempted to set up a series of fundamental beliefs necessary for every Christian to accept, would, according to Locke, "erect [himself] presently into God's throne, and bestow on him the title *Dominus Deusque noster*, whereby offences against him come to be irreligious acts.[12] Any creed asserted as necessary for salvation by any human authority is ipso facto a claim for temporal dominion, when these creeds are in fact only "interpretation or opinion" which "no man . . . has a right to prescribe,"[13] and no one has an obligation to heed.

From the distinction between making and being a Christian it follows that each private individual is alone responsible for the content of other beliefs. The standards outlined in Locke's *Letters* come into play regarding these other Christian beliefs: "in effect, almost every particular man . . . has, or may have, a distinct catalogue of fundaments, each whereof it is necessary for him explicitly to believe"; thus, "nobody can tell what is fundamental to another." Because this "explicit assent cannot go any farther than his understanding, who is to assent," these creedal fundamentals constitute, in Locke's terminology, speculative articles of faith.[14]

Such a position means that only with Christ's coming do two complementary kingdoms come into being:

> As men, we have God for our King, and are under the law of reason: as Christians, we have Jesus the Messiah for our King, and are under the law revealed by him in the Gospel. . . . [He] that believes one

eternal, invisible God, his Lord and King, ceases thereby to be an atheist; and he that believes Jesus to be the Messiah, his King, ordained by God, thereby becomes a Christian, is delivered from the power of darkness . . . ; is actually within the covenant of grace, and has that faith, which shall be imputed to him for righteousness; and, if he continues in his allegiance to this his King, shall receive the reward, eternal life. [15]

The Old Testament consisted of the promise of a Messiah and the record of a historically unique kingdom, one in which the prophetic God was temporal sovereign:

The laws established there concerning the worship of one invisible Deity, were the civil laws of that people, and a part of their political government, in which God himself was the legislator. [16]

Since "no positive law whatsoever can oblige any people, but to those to whom it is given,"[17] rules of the Old Testament were no longer obligatory once the Messiah appeared. In Locke's treatment of the New Testament, the Gospels quite overshadow the more historical Epistles, a record of "being" Christians in organized churches. So despite Locke's claim that "Christians . . . are under the law revealed by him in the gospel"[18] there can be no publicly known and enforced rules permissibly derived from the New Testament.

In this periodization, Christ's coming destroyed the only prophetic kingdom on earth, recorded in the Old Testament, and made obligatory the rules derived from the natural motivations of depraved men. A belief in this logic of history radically secularizes man's view of the world. A belief in Christ's second coming makes acceptance of this natural world both obligatory and an act of faith. This interpretation also unmasks the relationship between political injustice and Christian history. Without a true understanding of the Bible, the history of Christians is necessarily a record of idolatry and corruption.

Christ's coming could redeem both Jew and pagan; the former from God's direct commands, the latter from the grip of false gods. Christ's coming makes it possible for the first time for men to want to obey rules derived from the state of nature. The present reformation of the church on its original principles puts the logic of Christ's appearance into the present day. In this collapse of time, the appearance of Christ and the state of nature together signal a new beginning in the contemporary period. The state of nature becomes relevant now only from its location in prophetic history; moral knowledge and faith stand or fall together. [19]

Philosophy, by itself, is as impotent as the law of nature so long as supernatural religion defines men's moral opinions. Exactly paralleling Hobbes's argument, Locke argues that Christ's coming divorced religion from this history even though Christ's followers soon made the church an engine of earthly advantage and morality a servant of priestly and despotic interest. Locke explicitly places both himself and the task of philosophy within the time frame of sacred history. When mankind was under the sway of false religious doctrine, philosophers were shouting to the winds. Only *now*, when religious reformation is ushering in a new age does it become the task of the philosopher to outline the entire set of duties appropriate for men. Only *now* is a willing audience assembled to listen, for only now does reformed religion support the conclusions of true moral philosophy.[20]

Toleration rescues men from the grip of false religion and therefore from rules taught and enforced in history; philosophy powered by true and saving faith can teach men the elements of "a clean conscience . . . a steady course of virtue . . . a strict and holy life."[21] The state of nature is the medium of instruction. The end of instruction is obedience to those who enforce proper rules. The means of instruction for natural men can only be pain.

Philosophy, Punishment, and Pain

The distinction between faith and reason is central to Locke's argument for toleration; the distinction between faith and works is crucial to his theology. And in both sets of writings the contrast between religion and philosophy in the domination of men is central to his reading of the past. In the future it might be possible to make operative in the world both religious toleration and true Christian faith. When proper distinctions between religious faith and moral knowledge are established, the one-sided contest between philosophy and religion will be overcome and philosophy might define what religion impels. Faith and reason will complement each other to yield a "practical moral opinion" both powerful and true. A major task of philosophy is to outline the entire range of man's moral obligations. Moral opinion is the bridge between belief and knowledge; moral philosophy reconciles man's interests in two separate worlds.

In his *Essay Concerning Human Understanding*, Locke discusses how men come to learn rules which define good and evil. In that discussion, he makes no distinction in principle between the processes of learning pure or corrupt sets of rules, or between learning rules in a traditional society or in a state of nature. What his discussion does show, however, is that learning in a state of nature would yield far different rules and opinions than learning as it has taken place heretofore in history.

When Locke had discussed speculative religious faith in his argument for toleration, he had argued that faith promising eternal reward terminated simply in the understanding. This termination meant that belief concerning life after death could not directly affect specific actions and thus could not be the cause of any other man's injury. This is simply a fact. True or not, however, past societies generated and enforced rules concerning professions of belief even though belief itself could motivate no "injurious" consequences. Thus, absurd and unjust rules can teach absurd and unjust morality. Locke's epistemology rests on pleasure and pain.[22] He who has power to enforce rules defines good and evil. Opinions of good and evil determine our wills and our actions.

Will is the power to act or to refrain from action. Action, in turn, is motivated by a desire to seek pleasure or avoid pain.

> A power to direct the operative faculties to motion or rest in particular instances is that which we call the will. That which in the train of our voluntary actions determines the will to any change of operation is some present uneasiness, which is, or at least is always accompanied with, that of desire.[23]

In contrast to the desire to seek pleasure, desire to avoid pain is always a motivating factor and always causes "uneasiness," because "a total freedom from pain always makes a *necessary* part of our happiness."[24] It is inappropriate in this context to speak of freedom of the will, for so long as man has the capacity to move and to desire he *must* will. Not freedom, but power, is the appropriate term: "For desire being nothing but an uneasiness in the want of an absent good, in reference to any pain felt, ease is that absent good."[25] "Uneasiness of desire" is that which "immediately determines the will."[26] Since power is always relational, he who, "has the power or not the power to operate is that alone which is or is not free."[27]

To move from this general theory of human action to Locke's theory of how men learn definitions of what is good and evil depends on an understanding of that most slippery of concepts, "uneasiness." Men will desire what they "think" is a good. But in Locke's definition, will can only be known by the act, the only proof that a person has willed. Thus, to say that "the will operates on the understanding," or that the understanding operates on the will, is not to speak properly.[28] A proper formulation of the relationship between acting (willing) and learning takes us into the language of pain and pleasure, punishment and reward, misery and happiness.

> Now, because pleasure and pain are produced in us by the operation of certain objects either on our minds or our bodies and in different degrees, therefore, what has an aptness to produce pleasure in us is that we call *good*, and what is apt to produce pain in us we call *evil*.[29]

Since Locke has already shown that not "all good, even seen and confessed to be so, necessarily move[s] every particular man's desire" but only that "taken to make a necessary part of his happiness,"[30] punishment in some form is a necessary part of the efficacy of teaching rules that define moral good and evil. In Locke's formulation, punishment is necessary both in learning the rules and then in being "willing" to adhere to them. Good and evil generally "are nothing but pleasure or pain, or that which occasions pleasure or pain to us." Moral good or evil, therefore,

> [is] only the conformity or disagreement of our voluntary actions to some law, whereby good or evil is drawn on us from the *will and power of the law-maker;* which good and evil, pleasure or pain, attending our observance or breach of the law by the decree of the law-maker, is that we call reward and punishment.[31]

For Locke—and only here does he differ significantly from Hobbes—moral rules are taught in a diffused set of contexts which mete out punishment. Locke's perception of rules and rule learning is at once central to his system and notoriously lacking a determinate source. For Locke, rules of good and evil are simultaneously articulated by divine law, the civil law, and the "law of opinion"; therefore, they are "taught" respectively by revelation, by government, and by public opinion. Here again, Locke has built a bridge spanning the separate jurisdictions of church and state and of faith and reason.

In the *Essay* Locke sees moral good and evil as being defined and enforced by church, government, and society; each realm possesses a unique set of rewards and punishments. His primary purpose in making these distinctions is to explain the origin in men of ideas of moral relationships, given the sensible reality of uneasiness in the mind or pain in the body when the rules are violated. On the purely descriptive level, Locke argues that the knowledge of moral realtionships and, therefore, of good and evil is "taught" to men through these three mechanisms.

Such a description does not raise the problem of reasonable assent or reasonable tests for assent to these rules. Nor does such a description raise the possibility of conflict among rules. The important element is the power to punish their breach. The source of power behind civil law is the physical power of the magistrate; in most cases that source is easily known. The source of power behind the law of opinion is the power of the "public" to distribute reputations and thus affect the distribution of wealth, power, and happiness. This source is somewhat indeterminate because opinion is segmented and often divided, even though its effects are palpable. The source of power behind the divine law is God. This source is most powerful and most indeterminate, because the use of this power cannot be proven. Only belief in a future judgment, and opinion regarding the standards for judgment, stand behind divine law.

In the *Essay* Locke makes no attempt to rank either these three sets of rules or the relative efficacy of their sanctions. Both in the *Letters* and in *Reasonableness,* however, he strongly suggests that political life in history merges rule-sets and sanctioning power into the power of the despotic king. The king and his priestly allies enforce divine law through the agency of an intolerant church; he and his dependents distribute reputations and rewards, thus dominating opinion and manners; he and his hangman sanction civil law—indeed, sanction all laws, for despotism claims power over faith, reason, opinion, and interest. And no matter how harshly the despot metes out pain, he is obeyed so long as religious belief supports his power: "The view of heaven and hell will cast a slight upon the short pleasures and pains of the present state."[32] The historical success of despotism proves that men are enslaved by their own false religious beliefs, not that the despot's physical power is unchallengeable. Because the power backing divine law is not of this world, the causes of despotic power are also the source of its overthrow. The claim by civil authority or dominant opinion that certain rules are direct commands of God is a claim always open to challenge. And if men believe that politically enforced rules are contrary to divine law and that obedience to the former is breach of the latter, civil war and political revolution result.

The *Essay* contains no discussion of despotism, no guarantee that men will learn the right moral relationships, and no promise that correct knowledge of right moral relationships is discoverable through reason alone. The *Essay* claims only that faith and reason have "distinct provinces" which bar the right of magistrates to command faith.[33] An enormous gap exists between man's history and the teachings of philosophy. This gap reflects the paradox that divine punishment is the most powerful and the least determinate sanction and that divine law is the most obligatory and the least known. The Bible as written revelation contains evidence from the past of determinate divine punishment and positive divine law. But God does not act supernaturally in the present epoch; Christ's coming demands that reason search out the laws of God as they operate in a world without visible signs of grace: a state of nature. This is the historical setting of the *Second Treatise* and the justification for Locke's hope that law, moral opinion, and religion can be integrated by reason and not by the despot. Natural law taught by the pains and pleasures in a state of nature is at once divine command, the sum of individual desires, and, ultimately, the model for civil law.

Seen solely through the lens of Locke's formal epistemology, the search for natural laws in a state of nature is an exercise in futility: all men are born entrapped in webs of extant powers and are taught good and evil by self-interested men. Locke's exercise would seem as futile as the first half of Hobbes's *Leviathan:* the discussion of toleration by Locke and his interpretation of Scripture would suggest that his discoveries from state-of-nature reasoning—like Hobbes's civil philosophy—is dependent on prophecy for relevance in history. This conclusion is not fully warranted. The *Second Treatise* is not only an account of man's natural faculties played out in a timeless natural environment. Locke's state of nature has its own history—albeit a natural history—and the obligations learned in the state of nature are also learned in this history. Even in the *Essay* Locke suggests that adopted as well as natural desires and acquired habits, and also natural wants, inexorably teach man in history lessons which run counter to the disutilities sanctioned by prevailing laws, opinion, and religious belief.[34] The *Second Treatise* contains a history of this acquisition, a history culminating in the present age.

The fact that the *Second Treatise* contains two somewhat contradictory states of nature has often been remarked.[35] The logical tensions between the two are treated here as more properly viewed as tensions between a logic of nature and a logic of materialist history. Viewed this way, Locke's discussion of punishment—especially the right of every man in the state of nature to punish crime with death—takes on new meaning. Locke asserts that this natural right is given to men by nature's God and then shows why man would never exercise that right until a particular stage was reached in his history. The political import of this tension is that Locke's natural history includes a history of political sovereignty and despotism. The right to kill thieves includes the right to destroy rulers who wrongfully take property by force. To ask of the *Second Treatise* when in history the need to kill despots arose is to ask also when men in history began to question the legitimacy of paternalistic and theocratic political authority. The answer in the *Second Treatise* is not "when Christ appeared," but perhaps when property and markets and inequality did. Answers to questions of this type can never be entirely satisfactory, if only because the *Second Treatise* is such a limited production in the repertoire of Locke. No understanding of either these questions or their possible answers can be gained, however, if we begin with some "light of nature" sparked by the wand of a benevolent deity—unless we are to believe that this treatise is Locke's only published fairy tale.

Natural Obligation and Historical Learning in the State of Nature

Experience shows that the knowledge of morality by mere natural light (how agreeable soever it be to it) makes but a slow progress and little advance in the world. And the reason of it is not hard to be found in men's necessities, passions, vices, and mistaken interests, which turn their thoughts another way, and the designing leaders, as well as the following herd, find it not to their purpose to employ much of their meditations this way.

JOHN LOCKE, *The Reasonableness of Christianity*

True morality must be implanted against the two forms of human depravity: its natural form as simple laziness or selfishness and the far more complex institutional form of creeds, churches, and despots. The theological answer to this condition in the *Reasonableness* differs from the philosophical answer in the *Second Treatise*.

In the *Reasonableness* Locke shows that both pagan history and Old Testament history cannot be sources of knowledge about morality. Paganism is a "state of darkness . . . vice and superstition." Because of "ignorance of the true God, . . . sense and lust . . . and fearful apprehensions" ruled men's opinions and actions. Christ's coming "made the 'one invisible God' known to the world . . . with such evidence and energy that polytheism and idolatry have no where been able to withstand it."[1] In both the *Reasonableness* and the *First Treatise of Government,* Locke rejects Old Testament history as authority not because of the imperfections of that theocratic order but because Christ's coming ended the epoch when God ruled directly through his chosen agents. Christ's appearance did not institute a state of nature, but it made obligatory the use of natural reason to discover obligatory rules of good and evil. In the *Second Treatise,* Locke's discovery is that man learns true morality naturally and over time despite the teachings and punishments of pagan, Jewish, and Christian history. At a certain point in history, this counter-learning process makes it possible for men to be truly receptive to the moral obligations commanded by true Christianity. Natural history reverses the cause-effect chain in prophetic history. Material causes teach true morality; the acceptance of these teachings as divinely ordained precludes any view of Christianity except the reasonable one.[2]

The following analysis does not suggest that Locke's natural history supercedes either his state-of-nature logic or sacred history. Locke's natural history can be seen more properly as a bridge spanning the chasm that divides both *Leviathan* and Locke's own discussion of reason and faith in the *Essay*.[3] Natural history only joins these two worlds at certain points, it does not merge them. That these bridges can be built at all may be testament more to Locke's belief in a future kingdom of God on earth than to confidence in the power of unaided reason.[4]

He Called a Crime, but Nobody Came

In contrast to the cogent statement of the origins of civil society found in the first *Letter on Toleration,* Locke's *Second Treatise* introduces the state of nature in three stages. The first three chapters are a discussion of the right of men to punish other men who have violated the laws of nature. Locke calls this right of executive power a "strange doctrine," an appellation appropriate for a variety of reasons. Traditional doctrine asserts that in the beginning God directly appointed particular fathers to be governors over other men. Locke's state of nature, however, is introduced as a state in which "the right of punishing is in everybody."[5]

Without specifying either the particular content of the "law of nature" or how men come to learn it, Locke begins by showing how men, subservient to no human authority, have the right to punish. Since every man has a right to punish crime and every injured man the right to seek reparation for civil injury,[6] an impersonal and even "natural" punishment mechanism is established at the very start. The stage would seem to be set for men to begin teaching each other. The problem is one of finding pupils or teachers; i.e., men who want to commit crimes and those who would want to punish them.

The second stage of Locke's discussion of rule-learning concerns property. Locke argues that mankind collectively was given rights by God over the "earth and all inferior creatures." By the exertion of labor, individual men can therefore acquire individual rights over articles in this common store. These individual rights to ownership, however, are resricted to as many goods as each man can use. Private possession is earned by the pain of labor and extended to "fruits of the earth," "beasts that subsist on it," and "the earth itself." Land is not left for men to enjoy in common, because God commanded man "to labor, and the penury of his condition required it of him." The right to land was granted by God for use by "the industrious and rational—and labor was to be his title to it." The "fancy or covetousness of quarrelsome and contentious men" who "desired the benefit of another's pains" constituted a threat to natural rights of land ownership and was a breach of natural law. By giving rights of land only to industrious men, God did not thereby "injure" others, because there "was still enough and as good left, and more than the yet unprovided could use."[7] As a general condition in this picture of the state of nature, then, "God, by commanding to subdue, gave authority so far as to appropriate; and the condition of human life which requires labor and material to work on necessarily introduces private possessions."[8]

If we stop at this second stage of Locke's discussion of the state of nature, we can see the outline of rights and duties in relation to property earned by the pain of labor; the rights of all men to punish breaches of these rights; and the rights of injured parties to seek reparation for damage done by others. This environment is deficient as a context of "learning" on two counts. First, Locke has not shown, without introducing additional factors, why land cultivation and appropriation would begin at all. Second, he has not shown why "quarrelsome and contentious" men would invade the property of "rational and industrious" men.

"God has given [men] all things richly," Locke argues, but the cultivation of land is required to increase nature's "common stock."[9] If we assume a condition of nature's plenty, "right and convenience" would "[go] together."[10] Since the goods of nature are appropriated for consumption, no man of any sense would take more than he could use before it spoiled or more than he would make use of even if it would not spoil. God's "duty" regarding the quantity of appropriation would be honored. Men desire to do what God commands them to do. Even if one grants that land cultivation is required in these circumstances, one can argue that no individual would cultivate more land than was necessary to supply his wants, and no one else would be in a position to want to consume cultivated surplus goods. The "strange doctrine" of executive power in the state of nature would seem to be largely superfluous. Also superfluous would be any recognition of an invisible source of "law," such as God. Nature's god gave nature's man the faculties and the plenty for nature's preservation.

The gap between Locke's opening discussion of the right to punish—even to kill—and his picture of men's use of that right in the state of nature is enormous. Despite this gap, Locke continues to insist on the presence of crime and the need for punishment. Some men are pictured as "beasts of prey," "dangerous and noxious creatures that will be sure to destroy [others] whenever [they] fall into their power." This model of conflict between men of law and men with "no other rule but that of force and violence" is a state of war. To take property from another is to place the victim's life in the control of another man. "[H]e who would get me into his power without my consent would use me as he pleased when he got me there, and destroy me, too, when he had a fancy to it." The use of force against another man is taken by Locke to mean an attempt to put him in slavery. Thus, Locke concludes,

> This makes it lawful for a man to kill a thief who has not in the least hurt him, nor declared any design upon his life, any farther than, by the use of force, so to get him in his power as to take away his money, or what he pleases, from him.[11]

How and why Locke can transform simple theft into a form of de facto attempted enslavement and de jure attempted murder adds a psychological gap to the logical one. Under what conditions would men want to kill thieves and under what conditions would a man want to steal, if his life were thereby endangered?

The third stage of Locke's discussion of the state of nature introduces a history of changing economic and moral relationships.

> [I]n the beginning, before the desire of having more than man needed had altered the intrinsic value of things which depends only on their usefulness to the life of man, or had agreed that a little piece of yellow metal which would keep without wasting or decay should be worth a great piece of flesh or a whole heap of corn, though men had a right to appropriate, by their labor, each one to himself as much of the things of nature as he could use, yet this could not be much, nor to the prejudice of others, where the same plenty was still left to those who would use the same industry. To which, let me add that he who appropriates land to himself by his labor does not lessen but increases the common stock of mankind.[12]

The invention of money symbolizes a transformation of the notions of quantity and sufficiency in the state of nature, just as it alters the quality of men's actions enough to justify killing a simple thief. By altering the "intrinsic value of things," money also creates a situation in which some men are in want vis-à-vis nature while other men hold legal right to the most productive parts of the common stock.

A Natural History of Uneasiness

When Locke introduces money and transforms intrinsic (use) value into economic value, he introduces both scarcity and distributive inequality. These dynamic elements in the state of nature propel man and Locke's own analysis into artifice and history. For example, Locke speaks of land values in Spain where the "extent of ground is of so little value without labor that

. . . a man may be permitted to plough, sow, and reap, without being disturbed," with no other title to this land than "his making use of it." Turning from historical example to the natural or universal causes of money, Locke can assert that unimproved nature is qualitatively deficient: "ninety-nine hundreths" of all goods "as they come to our use . . . are *wholly* to be put on account of labor."[13]

With the invention of money, land held in common "is called 'waste;' and we shall find the benefit of it amount to little more than nothing."[14] In Rousseau's language, "everything begins to change its appearance."[15] Locke pictures savage Americans as "rich in land and poor in all the comforts of life," not having a "one-hundredth part of the conveniences we enjoy."[16] Their idyllic life is also impoverished. Scarcity of money and land necessitates systematic labor and, therefore, the systematic production of "conveniences" which can only be purchased because they cannot be found in nature. The reach of desire is vastly extended, and the distance between men increases. The rich become "vulnerable in every part of their goods."[17]

The foundation for money value and the origins of scarcity and inequality are not to be found directly in God's gifts and God's "laws" but rather in man "being master of himself and proprietor of his own person and the actions or labor of it." In short, money and scarcity—human inventions—make possible the buying and selling of individual labor "power," and the accumulation of the labor value of other men.

> [L]abor, in the beginning, gave a right of property wherever anyone was pleased to employ it upon what was common. . . . Men, at first, . . . contented themselves with what unassisted nature offered to their necessities . . . though afterwards, in some parts of the world—where the increase of people and stock, with the use of money, had made land scarce and so of some value—the several communities settled the bounds of their distinct territories. . . .[18]

Scarcity and inequality, however, are not construed by Locke to be "artificial" with historically unique patterns of politically created inequality. Money is introduced by tacit, informal use "outside of the bounds of society and without a compact"[19] and, one might add, outside the bounds of historically variable political determination. No determinate human society created money, inequality, and scarcity. No historically determinate human power or set of punishments can, therefore, be held responsible for the introduction of economic value. Though Locke often speaks in terms of *labor* "that put the difference of value on everything,"[20] he makes clear that the value he is speaking of is money value. Without money and the availability of goods not found in nature, the motivation for labor would be as limited as in the wilderness of America.

Given the processes which began with money, accumulated land "stands" for accumulated money, just as accumulated labor and humanly created objects have a money equivalent. Both land and money are in short supply, some men having appropriated "larger possessions and a right to them." Men without land, now become scarce, still require money (correspondingly scarce) to purchase even those goods "unassisted nature" used to provide. Thus, while "a man may fairly possess more land than he himself can use the product of," other men must labor for money to purchase that product. Locke concludes by recognizing the inadequacy of his "idyllic" earlier picture as an environment for rule-learning:

> And thus, I think, it is very easy to conceive how labor could at first begin a title of property in the common things of nature, and how the spending it upon our uses bounded it. So that there could *then* be no reason of quarreling about title, nor any doubt about the largeness of possession it gave. *Right and convenience went together;* for as a man had a right to all he could employ his labor upon, so he had no temptation to labor for more than he could make use of. This left no room for controversy about the title, nor for encroachment on the right of others; what portion a man carved to himself was easily seen, and it was useless, as well as dishonest, to carve himself too much or take more than he needed.[21]

In an environment of unbounded acquisition, both of the "common things of nature" and of the created products of labor and industry, right and convenience do not go together: rational apprehension of "right" and the facts of human behavior do not merge. Discounting direct revelation from God or the existence of innate ideas which might reflect some coherent legal and moral order, Locke must merge right and convenience by reliance on punishment. "It would be vain," Locke argues,

> for one intelligent being to set a rule to the actions of another if he had it not in his power to reward the compliance with and punish deviation from his rule by some good and evil that is not a natural product and consequence of the action itself. For that, being a natural convenience or inconvenience, would operate of itself without a law.[22]

Locke begins the *Second Treatise* with a discussion of "executive power" in the state of nature but provides little possibility for its exercise.[23] In an environment of money, markets, and scarcity, those who possess property and those without property would be motivated: the former to protect their possessions, the latter to seize them.[24] Theft, as the forcible seizure of a man's "labor," which is then used as the thief wishes, is now perceived as a threat to life itself. So poignant is Locke's identification of personality and possession that he could indeed describe the thief as if he were "one of those wild savage beasts with whom men can have no society nor security."[25] To take and use another man's goods is to "devour" that man as a moral person. If the acquisition and defense of worldly goods can teach morality, Locke can arrive at what he terms in the *Letters* "civil interests" and "practical moral opinion" without resort to heavens and hells and without the distortions of political beliefs and rulers.

Locke's state of war, discussed in conjunction with executive power in the state of nature, now attains relevance. Those who acquire large possessions do so "freely," without determinate human authority; indeed, the pre-civil legal order and the "citizens" of that order are literally defined by rights and duties regarding possession. Any breach of this order by theft is the use of force to hinder another man's freedom. As Locke maintains later, theft is a micro-version of tyrannical and arbitrary government. Locke's clear distinction between the rule of law and the rule of force means, then, that those who defend their possessions in the state of nature are defending man's moral personality and are, by definition, "innocent." Therefore, in a state of war "the safety of the innocent is to be preferred; and one may destroy a man who makes war upon him."[26]

Both in the state of nature and in a tyrannical civil society, "where there is no common superior on earth to appeal to for relief," the first use of force, in fact or by clear design, creates a state of war. This state of war, "once begun continues with a right to the innocent party to destroy the other whenever he can, until the aggressor offers peace and desires reconciliation on such terms as may repair any wrongs he has already done and secure his innocence for the future."[27] To avoid this particular condition, Locke concludes that men are motivated to quit the state of nature which lacks a settled law of title to possessions and a disinterested executor of this law. By this point all men have learned the right rules.

To stop at this point and ask of the *Second Treatise*, "What happens next?" is to pose a difficult question. It is quite inadequate to say that the obvious and correct answer is "civil society" and that it, along with the state of nature, constitute the outer limits of Locke's political thought. To view the *Second Treatise* as confined within these limits is to say that Locke sought to avoid precisely those issues which formed the lifelong core of his intellectual life. The very nature of these limits would belie all Locke had written concerning the impotence of unaided reason, the historical struggle between moral behavior and religious ritual, and the decisive changes which men and society would undergo if permeated with a saving Christian faith. How these latter issues are approached and mediated or resolved in the *Second Treatise* must be left to later consideration. The more immediate task is to follow the path from state of nature to civil society to see why it takes us so short a distance, and why it cannot even serve as the major route to the attainment of a just and moral order as defined by Locke.

Possessors and Possessed in Civil Society

In civil society, the liberty of man is "to be under no other legislative power but that established by consent in the commonwealth, nor under the dominion of any will or restraint of any law but what that legislative shall enact according to the trust put in it."[28] Given Locke's description of the state of war and the assumption that only possessors of property would be motivated to protect their "liberty" in the form of valuable possessions, Locke's civil society vis-à-vis these men is quite consistent. Legislative power, "the supreme power of the commonwealth . . . sacred and unalterable in the hands where the community have once placed it," would readily turn "natural law" into civil law, if the "community" and its delegated legislative agents consisted of men of property. Executive power—in Locke's sense the judiciary and executor(s) of judicial decision—is "to be considered as the image, phantom, or representative of the commonwealth, acted by the will of the society, declared in its laws." Those men who learned the moral rules while acquiring property in the state of nature become the real legislators and have the real power in civil society "to direct how the force of the commonwealth shall be employed for the preserving of the community and the members of it." Executive power in civil society is transformed by Locke into an impersonal, seemingly shadowy force, judging and executing judgments without a determinate will of its own.[29] Propertyless men in the state of nature would presumably have difficulty "remembering" the right rules even in civil society, for continuous labor is more painful than stealing—unless one is caught.

The hierarchy of subordination, then, is pictured by Locke as very exact. At the lowest level is "everyone," for everyone is subordinate to "the laws." Within the governmental structure, "ministerial and subordinate powers . . . have no manner of authority, any of them, beyond what is by positive grant and commission delegated to them and are all of them accountable to some other power in the commonwealth."[30] Above these offices lies executive power, usually in the hands of one man. This man shares in legislative power and has discretionary power in military and foreign affairs. Above the physical power of the executive lies the legislature, directing through positive legal enactment his coercive powers. The legislature, in turn, holds its position by trust of the community; its power to act is limited "morally" by "natural law" which delineates the purposes of civil society and "physically" by the dominant forces of the community or those who presumably have learned natural law.[31]

In the beginning stages of the establishment of civil society, "it being necessary to that which is one body [the community prior to establishment of government] to move one way, it is necessary the body should move that way whither the greater force carries it." Since the "whole power of the community [is] *naturally* in . . . the majority,"[32] this preponderant strength determines the particular forms of "constitutional mechanism." When the legislature "rebels" against the community by violating this constituion, the legislature, much like the thief in the state of nature, creates a state of war between itself and the community.[33]

The legislature would not normally "rebel" against the community, however, both because the members of the legislative body must periodically stand for elections and because they do not command armies. The legislature, in Locke's view, is largely a negative body protecting the community from the misuse of executive power. Only if the legislature allies itself with the physical power of the executive to plunder the community would it be in a position to "rebel." The community represents the aggregate of rights against government, represented by the executive. The best summary statement ever written of this hierarchy and mechanism is James Mill's *Essay on Government*, which was published in 1820. People protect their property by creating a punisher who possesses the organized physical power of the community. This makes of the executive a great danger—the biggest thief of all if he uses that power for his own ends. The counter to that real power is a legislature which represents the community. But what constitutes the real power of the legislature? Surely not the paper on which its laws are printed. James Mill's answer is clear: the legislature represents the standing threat of the larger community physically to challenge the government in war. A relatively broad franchise of property-owners is required for this purpose, and a legislature which serves them is the only real proof that political power is exercised legitimately.[34]

Unlike Mill's *Essay on Government*, Locke's *Second Treatise* is not a utilitarian set piece with all of the dogmatic arrogance so common to that kind of writing and so vulnerable to ridicule and dismissal.[35] Neither could Locke's state of nature be viewed simply as an oblique anticipation of James Mill's picture of political and moral purpose in a purely utilitarian world.

> The means of insuring labor must be provided for as the foundation of all. The means for the insuring of labor are of two sorts. . . . The first sort is commonly denominated "force," . . . and the laborers are slaves. . . . This mode of procuring labor we need not consider. . . . The other mode of obtaining labor is by allurement, or the advantage which it brings. . . . The object, it is plain, can best be attained when a great number of men combine and delegate to a small number the power necessary for protecting them all. This is government.[36]

Locke's politics cannot be built on James Mill's simple foundation, even though the argument is one Locke formulated. Neither could his politics be sustained by James Mill's complacent faith that English gentlemen of a middling sort would be willing to take instruction from their betters and, in turn, would instruct a properly deferential propertyless class—even though this is an argument both partially formulated and surely assumed by Locke.[37] The foundations Locke utilized and the forms of sustenance he discovered should be sought in his own writings and not in interpretations of the *Second Treatise* written by later utilitarians and by Marxist critics. Locke's foundation is best seen in terms of the differences between legislation and execution in the state of nature and in civil society.

The relationship between Locke's "strange doctrine" of the right to kill in the state of nature and the transformation of men in nature has been stressed above. What requires elaboration before looking at Locke's natural history of man's political relationships in the *Two Treatises* is his treatment of the problem of the right to kill in his earlier *Two Tracts of Government*. Elaboration is required because the *Treatises* discuss the natural evolution of political authority from paternal authority and the *Tracts* discuss the origins of the right to kill in paternal authority. The paternal origins of "executive power" are identified in the *Tracts* as religious origins as well. Paternal authority and its history connects the *First Treatise* to the *Second Treatise* and his political writings generally to prophetic history and toleration. In symbolic contrast to James Mill, Locke's legislature is only a recently cleared patch of ground letting in a thin ray of light which in no way penetrates the surrounding forest that contains the mysteries of death and political obligation.

Paternal Power and Natural Right

Locke's *Two Tracts* are his first extensive writings on politics. Both *Tracts* begin with the same question: "Whether the Civil Magistrate may lawfully impose and determine the use of indifferent things in reference to Religious Worship."[38] His answer—a much more authoritarian one than in the later *Letters on Toleration*[39]—is less important than his discussion of the origins of magistracy. In the Latin *Tract* Locke directly ties the origins of civil authority to the right to kill. There are two foundations for civil power: "some suppose men to be born in servitude, others to liberty." The latter "assert an equality between men founded on the law of nature . . . the former maintain a paternal right over children and claim that government originates thence." The paternal theory entails a right to kill other men to enforce the law:

> he is the sole ruler of the land and its inhabitants without contract or condition and . . . he may do whatever is not forbidden by God, to whom alone he is subjected and from whom alone he received his title to *live* and to rule.[40]

A paternally derived civil executive has discretion over "the liberty, fortunes and the life itself of every subject."

A theory of civil authority derived from a prior condition of natural liberty meets with some difficulties regarding capital punishment. Clearly, men cannot remain in a natural condition; they must have law and a "sovereign which has no superior on earth to which it is bound to give an account of its actions." Such power can only be created by every man's giving up "the whole of this natural liberty of his . . . to a legislator, granting it to him who with the authority of all, empowered by the general consent of each, makes valid laws for them. Whence it follows that whatever any individual is permitted to do, that, too, the magistrate is permitted to command."[41]

Locke then concludes that both theories are deficient. It is not easy to derive "a right to govern . . . from the paternal right, nor a right of life and death from the popular." Suspended between two incomplete theories—a paternal one which claims power and a natural one which claims right—Locke tenders a qualified and hypothetical solution: "all authority is held to come from God but the nomination and appointment of the person bearing that power is thought to be made by the people."[42] Hypothetical consent joins hypothetical title to create de facto power to kill. It is not enough to suggest that Locke resolves this problem in the *Second Treatise* by introducing executive power in the state of nature.

The attempt to solve the problem within the philosophical limits of a civil society established from the state of nature appears quite hopeless for the following reasons.

1. Private thieves only appear as a problem in a premonetary state of nature—precisely when there is no reason for their presence. The "natural" right of executive power is based on a total fiction: there are no thieves, there is no crime.

2. Precisely when private thieves *would* constitute a problem and therefore a reason for exercising a right to executive power, they disappear from Locke's discussion. When money and inequality prevail in large-scale societies, men without property have three choices: work for others on their terms, starve, or steal. Instead of this logic and these thieves, Locke raises only the marginal problems of settling titles to possessions and the need for impartial judges in civil disputes. In short, the foundation for executive power is criminal law, but Locke says that the motivation for creating civil power is the need for civil law and civil sanctions—hardly a deterrent to thieves.

3. Once Locke has established civil society, its purposes and limits, the only theft problem is that of the despotic executive or the legislature in unholy alliance with him. The struggle of moral men in civil society, according to Locke, is not to sustain a political order which protects them

against thieves in the night but one which protects them against executive plunder in broad daylight.[43] How the executive—"the image, phantom or representative of the commonwealth"—could acquire the political power to become so dangerous is unanswered within the logic of natural law.

If one overlooks the thinly disguised and contradictory solution of problem 2, above, how might one establish a connection between private thieves and problem 1 and public thieves in problem 3? Logically, this is simply impossible. Logically, private thieves disappear; they were moral fictions used to convince us that present executives have a right to kill to sanction certain kinds of rules. However civil society came to be, these moral fictions were necessary characters in a philosopher's play. Because of this, we need not worry about how men came to form civil societies or why men without property would want to; we only need to worry about the real problems of arbitrary and despotic executive power.

If one views this same question of the connection between problems 1 and 3 in terms of Locke's natural history of political authority found in the *Second Treatise,* one attains quite different results. Private thieves do not miraculously disappear or become a docile working class, they become the political support for paternal power and false religious belief in history, yielding an executive with solid popular power for his God-given right to kill. Once this side of Locke's natural history is taken into account, all sorts of connections between these two kinds of thieves begin to take shape. "Political theft" in the past was justified largely by religious belief in a paternal theory of politics. Men without substantial property were less beasts of prey and private thieves than unwitting prey to religious superstition and personal political loyalty. This connection is pictured by Locke as familiar and warm before money was introduced. After money, it is called the engine of despotism. In Locke's own time, despotism assumed the form of intolerance enforced by property confiscation of those who worshipped outside of established churches. But in all cases the men who supported this policy were not beasts of prey but more like innocent children, too trusting to feel gulled, too full of loyalty to betray a king for mere material gain.

Viewed in this way, the *Second Treatise* is both a more political and a more revolutionary document than is commonly perceived.[44] The problem of despotism, crime, and punishment all point to the larger context of religion and history, thereby transforming these concepts from a philosopher's abstractions into key elements of an actor's praxis.

Natural History and Sacred History

Locke's two worlds have become very complex. The thief in a world of interest and reason shares many resemblances to the father-king-despot in the world of history and belief. Conversely, the legitimate political executive, as trustee of civil society, appears without historical origins, a pure product of calculation by men who have been taught the values of property, exchange, and merited inequality outside the bounds of political authority. These different possibilities symbolize the difficulty confronting private men: when they view a political executive, what do they see? Hobbes's answer was that men see double: in Part II of *Leviathan* they see their own construct, and in Part III they see a Vicar of Christ. In the *Second Treatise*, the subject can see a public thief, a loving father-king, a victorious general, or an agent of a legislature which, in turn, was instituted by the body of citizens. In his other writings a further possibility is a Vicar of Christ. In an examination of Locke's natural history, the various guises in which political executives can appear is clarified. In the process of clarification, however, the problem of consent and political obligation becomes more muddied. No longer can obligation be confined to the hypothetical world of interest and reason, for men in history are altered over time and become receptive to changing beliefs, commitments, and loyalties.

The natural history of the *Second Treatise* is not simply a restatement of a shift from premonetary to postmonetary states of nature or a summary study of the changing relationships between rulership and social/economic organization. These features are dwarfed by the central problem of the relationship among families, monarchs, and despots. As this central problem is discussed, a number of important implications appear. The first is that "moral men" suitable for sustaining legitimate political order appear only at a particular time in history. Second, with the appearance of these moral men, some historical manifestations of religion, superstition, and affective ties not only become superfluous as a basis of "political" order but might constitute a positive threat to morality. These two implications will be considered in turn, for both tend to supplant Locke's earlier arguments in the *Second Treatise*. In his discussion of natural history, Locke attempts to restate a secular version of sacred history. Natural history lends the support of reason to what really moves men in history. Natural history only seeks to support what Locke explicitly said he believed: the God of nature and the God of prophecy are one; reason and revelation lead to the same ends.

The Shaping of Moral Men in History

By the term "natural history," I mean the charting of those moral relationships among men which are not directly determined by the centralized power of political orders in history.[1] Natural history seeks universal and uniform causes in history, in order to explain the variety of men's manners, political orders, and beliefs.

According to Locke, social organization in the misty beginnings of time must have been paternal family organization: "the natural fathers of families by an insensible change became the political monarchs of them too." Though Locke maintains that paternal and political power "are . . . perfectly distinct and separate, [and] are built upon so different foundations," this distinction had no meaning to men at that time. Obligation to paternal power and obligation to paternal-political power are generally found combined in the earliest of times.[2] This combination arose for two major reasons. First, "absolute monarchy" was favored in the beginnings of human society because "the equality of a simple, poor way of living, confining their desires within the narrow bounds of each man's small property, made few controversies, and so no need of many laws . . . where there were but few trespassers and offenders." Second, the people in this early period were "less vicious subjects" and the governors more virtuous.[3] With equality of possession, kings resemble more a combination of benign father, general, and priest than a union of impartial judge and executor of judgment under law. The political ties and the foundation for "political" power consist of mutual trust, acquaintance, and friendship among subjects and between subject and king.[4] Rulership consists of the wise and virtuous use of prerogative rather than the impersonal execution of justice, for without great inequalities of possession and the attendant vice of ambition and luxury neither ruler nor subject is motivated to invade the meager possessions of another.[5]

The political executive in history is hardly an impersonal phantom constructed by knowledgeably consenting adults, and his task is not primarily the protection of "civil interests." But the one feature that "fathers" have which made the transition so obvious, but which Locke fails to mention, is the assumed right to kill. If maintained, such power is not dependent upon the leader's good will, virtue, and trust. But the source is dependent upon popular belief in his right of magistracy.

In early history, executive prerogative is, in fact, "power to act according to discretion for the public good, without the prescription of the law and sometimes even against it,"[6] because there is so little need of law or motivation to use prerogative against law. The growth of impersonal law against personal prerogative is attributed by Locke to defensive measures by the "people" against rulers who began to utilize prerogative against property for selfish ends. In this sense, the tyrant in political history is the thief in the state of nature: both become problems with the introduction of money and attendant temptations. Locke's state of war provides the conceptual link between the "moral fiction" of the state of nature (men are born to liberty) and political history (men are born in servitude); in each case war is caused by the use of force against property.

By patterning a natural history of politics on the two stages of his state of nature, Locke has also combined learning in the state of nature with learning in history—a history of changing economic relationships. Locke's description of men's "feelings" are descriptions of only some men at a particular stage in history.

> But whatever flatterers may talk to amuse people's understanding, it hinders not men from feeling; and when they perceive that any man, *in what station soever*, is out of the bounds of the civil society which they are of, and that they have no appeal on earth against any harm they may receive from him, they are apt to think themselves in the state of nature in respect of him whom they find to be so, and to take care, as soon as they can, to have that safety and security in civil society for which it was instituted, and for which only they entered into it.[7]

Civil society, properly so called, is one based on law and property. Though Locke speaks of paternal power become political in the earliest stages of history, this political order was not properly a civil society, for there was little need for law. The interesting feature of the paternal leader as first monarch is that he would possess the full range of punishing power prior to the need to defend property and distributive inequality. This punishing power helped to yield obedience to his commands, but these commands were expressions of prerogative, not law. In this sense, despotism is paternal power in a developed economic environment. Based on traditions of trust, friendship, acquaintance, virtue, and religion, despotism is the use of political power against law.

Locke's formal distinctions among paternal, despotic, and political power are not historical descriptions but rather a delineation of three sources of force in relation to property:

Paternal power is only where minority makes the child incapable to manage his property; political, where men have property in their own disposal; and despotical, over such as have no property at all.[8]

In earlier times, without the lessons of property, few men except philosophers were capable of discovering true moral principles. With the lessons of property, some men's "manners" become a fulfilling of the moral law, and these men are motivated to oppose tyranny and establish legitimate civil order. The morality of this community of men is literally in its possessions, its shared "civil interests." In that sense, natural history can fulfill what philosophers could only seek painfully to discover. These same men reject claims for political rule based on written prophecy, superstition, custom, and even the "virtue" of the ruler, in the same way that Locke's "philosophy"—his *Essay on Human Understanding*—explodes those claims. And since religion in the past was so much a part of prior paternal/political connection and constituted such an effective vehicle by which to acquire and sustain secular power among men, the "moral men" emergent in Locke's natural history will oppose much of past religious teaching and practice.

Thus one solution to the problem of "philosopher versus priest" consists in the natural emergence of systematic economic activity resulting in a sizable body of men demanding "justice." If, as Locke only briefly suggests, this need for justice arose by a combination of money, ambition, luxury, and those "necessary arts, provid[ing] for . . . safety, ease and plenty,"[9] then the possibility arises for bypassing sole reliance on rational consent or on prophetic belief as sources of political obligation. And a decisive individual choice need not be made between these sources. Nature's God works in reasonable ways to insure the eventual victory of true morality.

Natural history is a theory of necessity; the political order appropriate for a market society is one with legislative supremacy and law. Property holders who institute the legislature thereby institute true political authority. Law transforms despotism or potential despotism by hedging royal prerogative. This model shifts the issue of political obligation from a philosophical problem to a sociological and a psychological one. Many objections to this resolution follow. Distributive inequality and economic classes might make of the state a coercive holding company for the rich. Political loyalty might become merely a function of perceived threats to private interests; the origins and intergenerational transfer of wealth might negate the connection between labor and reward. These material objections, however, obscure more important difficulties with this reading of Locke's theory. Legislatures and the rule of law do not supplant executives and the paternally grounded right of life and death. The power of life and death which belonged to early father-kings and later despots is still a property of executive power and not of legislative or popular will. As the historical product of interest and reason, the legislature cannot transcend the limits of either—no matter how popularly supported.

Under these conditions, what happens to the status of consent and political obligation? Within the limits of interest and reason, standards constituting political legitimacy become evident in history. Unfortunately, the power required to enforce those standards exceeds what consent can grant. To put it differently, elements of paternal or despotic authority must be carried over into a liberal regime. Note Locke's dramatic contrast in the *Second Treatise* between the protections of civil law and the necessity of martial law:

> [T]he general . . . with all his absolute power of life and death [cannot] dispose of one farthing of that soldier's estate or seize one jot of his goods, whom yet he can command anything and hang for the least disobedience.[10]

What is true for martial law is also true for the entire range of criminal law and punishments. The magistrate inhabits two separate worlds: he can "remit the punishment of criminal offenses by his own authority, but yet cannot remit the satisfaction due to any private man for the damage he has received."[11] Neither consent nor interest can explain the circumstances under which a magistrate can give and take lives at will so long as no one gains or loses a farthing. As Rousseau posed the question in *Emile*, "Does a man go to death from self-interest?"[12] Rational obligation must be supplemented by loyalties and beliefs which transcend it.

Some more definite conclusions can now be reached. The legislature can only become sovereign in history if it already has an executioner to back its commands. Men can be born to liberty only if they have had a prior birth in servitude. The power of the executioner can rest on a variety of grounds—religion, custom, habit, inheritance—but it cannot be a product of unaided reason or the creature of aggregate individual interest. Locke's natural history in the *Second Treatise* appears distinct from the sacred history found in his other writings, but the "paternal" element is common to both. While natural history might seem an attractive alternative to sacred history (especially because it somewhat blurs the problem of power over life and death), for Locke it also constitutes the means of understanding the moral import of sacred history. In contrast to state-of-nature reasoning, both natural and sacred history assume that man is born in servitude to authoritative ends quite apart from and more significant than civil interests. Knowledge of this servitude from either or both histories can serve us in understanding our own duties to the political order and the proper limits of a ruler's power. In neither history, however, can our obligations and the ruler's limits be the product of individual and voluntary consent.

At the start of this analysis of Locke's writings, I suggested that the *Second Treatise* is best viewed as a series of bridges or mediations between two worlds. In contrast to the first half of *Leviathan*, the *Second Treatise* does not so much clarify the logic of one world as it points to connections to the other. Especially in his discussion of the history of political authority and its materialist dynamic, Locke never fully commits the *Second Treatise* to a self-contained civil philosophy. Neither, however, does the *Second Treatise* contain any equivalent to the second half of *Leviathan*. Rather, the discussion of paternal and despotic authority in history suggests that state-of-nature logic intrudes itself into an ongoing history only as much as legislative power intrudes itself into divine-right monarchy.[13] To state it more broadly, the reach and accomplishment of the *Second Treatise* is quite congruent with the lesson of Locke's *Essay Concerning Human Understanding:* our knowledge of political obligations, like our knowledge of moral duties, lies in a gray area between clear knowledge and blind faith.

Unlike in *Leviathan*, the political executive in the *Second Treatise* is neither pure artifact on one page nor legal prophet on another, but an ambiguous figure who predates civil society and yet is bound to serve its ends. Locke's executive, not the legislature, has a real history and serves to mediate between the state of nature and the motivations of historical men. His status and legitimacy, however, are much less clear than his obvious utility. Insofar as he faithfully executes the civil law, his power would appear to flow from the same sources which give legitimacy to the legislature. Insofar as he represents political power by enforcing criminal and military law, the lean and legal language of political obligation is quite inappropriate to describe the sources of his legitimacy and power. Indeed, if masses of men on the receiving end of criminal and martial law were to think in the language of consent, they would soon become rebellious. On the other hand, those who are the clear beneficiaries of this use of executive power would be ill-advised to inquire too closely into its origins, lest the inquiry destroy confidence in the legitimacy of the regime and their own favored standing in it.

The "strange doctrine" of executive power introduced in the early paragraphs of the *Second Treatise* does not clarify the status of the executive in history, but it does alert us to Locke's own consciousness of his enterprise. Resort to the logic of natural history rather than to a state of nature and consent only mediates but does not resolve the problem that was originally formulated in the *Two Tracts* and is obvious in the very structure of Hobbes's *Leviathan*. The fundamental problem is simply whether the foundations of political authority assume either that man is born in servitude or born in liberty. In the *Two Tracts*, Locke refuses to make a choice of these foundations because of the problem of death. Locke's refusal to choose can be explained on broader grounds than this, however. To place man in the framework of sacred history is to assume that he is "born in servitude" to prophetic purpose and therefore to obligations which vastly transcend his interests and calculation and his natural reason. These duties grounded in belief are capable of freeing men from enslavement to physical needs, worldly goods, and, most crucially, de facto political power. And because these duties change with the epoch, some men in particular periods of history are obliged to make revolutions in the name of divine purpose. Their freedom to act makes history and establishes liberty.

To assume that man is born to liberty places him in the state of nature where he acts according to his perceived self-interest. For men to live peacefully and rationally in this environment, they must fear physical pain and death above all else.[14] To establish a regime of liberty and defend it demands actions which risk and take lives. Were that not the case, political obligation and fear of death would be the same thing and de facto power would wholly dominate law and right. Birth out of the state of nature—in some form of history and servitude—teaches obligations to ends beyond the value of nature's incessant calls for self-preservation. Thus, paternal power, religious belief, and even habit and custom can constitute a form of liberation both from natural necessity and from the power of de facto political rulers.

Affection for both worlds is required for all politics, including liberal forms. Both worlds have their appropriate kind of freedom. The voluntary actions of men in a society grounded on natural right must reveal material interest and become expressed in contractual duties to others. Freedom is the ability to take on obligations, to pledge one's future actions in exchange for receiving the actions of another in return. This liberty to maximize one's interests yields actions which are so predictable that markets are formed and prices established on the aggregate results. Locke carries this a step further and suggests that men operating on this plane of action are so tied to their interests that they become agents of necessity in history, unwittingly serving collective ends which none of them understands or intends. The invisible hand making this possible takes on some of the attributes of a providential god.

Even if it might be said that men act according to their self-interest in both worlds, the notions of self in these worlds are so radically different that the quality of actions differ accordingly. Neither Hobbes nor Locke chooses finally between these two worlds and the interests in them because political life requires recognition of both. Natural reason and the state of nature promise accessible standards by which to condemn the actions of *other* men, but they do not and cannot establish a mark by which we could ever measure the value of our own life and the extent of our obligations. Locke's early *Tracts* and the two halves of *Leviathan* are clear recognition of this fact, but even Locke's natural history in the *Second Treatise* attests to a dual notion of freedom. Hobbes and Locke use the language of prophetic belief and millennialist hope to express this same idea, but, however expressed, their own views of the limits of freedom in their philosophical creations are clear. Toward the end of *Reasonableness of Christianity*, Locke seems to place both himself and his philosophy within this larger framework of obligation and freedom.

Mankind [was] under a corruption of manners and [moral] principles, which ages after ages had prevailed, and must be confessed, was not in a way or tendency to be mended. The rules of morality were in different countries and sects different. And natural reason nowhere had cured, nor was like to cure, the defects and errors in them. Those measures of right and wrong, *which necessity had anywhere introduced, the civil laws prescribed, or philosophy recommended*, stood on their true foundations. They were looked on as bonds of society, and conveniences of common life, and laudable practices. But where was it that their obligation was thoroughly known and allowed, and they received as precepts of law—of the highest law, the law of nature? That could not be, without a clear knowledge and acknowledgement of the law-maker, and the great rewards and punishments for those that would or would not obey him. [15]

Part Three

Utility and History

*If we are asked . . . where the state of nature is to be found? We may
answer, It is here. . . . While this active being is on the train of employing
his talents, and of operating on the subjects around him all situations are
equally natural. . . . In the condition of the savage, as well as that of the
citizen, are many proofs of human inventions; and in either it is not any
permanent station, but a mere stage through which this travelling being is
destined to pass.*

ADAM FERGUSON, *An Essay on the History of Civil Society* (1793)

Thomas Hobbes compares the state of nature to a primitve society. In
both "there is no place for Industry; because the fruit thereof is uncertain
and consequently . . . no Commodious Building . . . no Knowledge of
the face of the earth; no account of Time; no Arts; no Letters; no Society." Without industry, "the life of man [is] solitary, poore, nasty, brutish, and short."[1] The account of time which Locke only tentatively begins
to outline in the *Second Treatise* incorporates many features of his
states(s) of nature. David Hume and Adam Smith carry this process even
farther. Natural history becomes the framework within which many features previously attributed to natural man and the state of nature finally
come to be true. Within the processes of history, men do in fact come to
be as earlier philosophy had pictured them.

Utilitarianism in the early nineteenth century is grounded on the assumption that history reaches a culmination in which interest and reason
are the only significant realities remaining. Natural history represents a
victory of the timeless mechanisms of nature. Man himself, now purged
of his history, is finally capable of acting in ways which earlier state-of-
nature philosophers could only hope would come about. Perhaps man is
not born to liberty, but natural history documents the achievement of lib-

erty to a degree that economics, jurisprudence, morals, and psychology can now be placed on a purely empirical footing. Deductions from a hypothetical state of nature are transformed into the factual basis of a new social science. By the early nineteenth century, liberal political philosophy seems to have settled finally for only one world. All memory and affection for the other must be banished from systematic political and social thought.

The shift from hypothetical to more empirical modes of thought tends to dominate our thinking about the changes from Lockean liberalism to utilitarianism.[2] This reading assumes that the two poles of liberal thought are interests and passions on the one hand and reason on the other. The change from Locke to Bentham consists of the increasing substitution of the former for the latter. The analysis to follow differs from this reading. To this point, I have tried to show that in both Hobbes and Locke reason and interest are almost inseparably tied together when one begins with the assumption that man is born free. The state of nature is a learning environment beginning with the interdependence of reason and interest, and the resulting rational-legal notions of contractual obligation are always a direct outgrowth of calculation powered by desire. Even in Locke's natural history, reason and interest have parallel developments, so that the knowledge of legal rights and the standards for political legitimacy are "unthinkable" until industry powered by passion has created a society requiring a government of law. The prominence given to the passions and the centrality of psychological empiricism in Scottish Enlightenment and utilitarian thought is important but not innovative. What is new is the utilitarian claim of building a wholly self-contained intellectual world by combining interest and reason—of creating an entire theory of man, society, and politics within the confines of the first half of *Leviathan*. No more succinct expression of this promise can be found than in John Austin's jurisprudence: "we cannot be obliged to that which depends not upon our desires."[3]

The promise proved difficult to honor. Hume, Smith, and other luminaries of the Scottish Enlightenment wrote much of their political theory in conscious opposition to state-of-nature theory. And yet their use of natural history to account for changes in law, moral opinion, and government included many elements from the other world of liberalism. The supposedly vanquished irrational "past" seems always to intrude in the rational present and future. The more exacting their discussions of the psychological mechanisms behind the notions of justice versus benevolence, calculated versus spontaneous action, and legal obligations versus political loyalty, the more apparent it becomes that their view of contemporary man and society remains a dual one. The imperatives of interest, industry, and individualism charted by natural history appear in their writings to require the motives and assistance of historically particular and collectively inherited bonds of human connection.

Smith and Hume did not so much fail to recognize the importance of these latter elements as they failed to know how to accommodate them in their theories of man and society. The artifacts of institutions and language built on interest appear public, scientific, and timeless. The content of sentiments which constitute men's sympathetic bonds is consigned to the private and particularistic realm of "culture" consisting of and sustained by memory, myth, and illusion. Natural history formulations tend always to lend prestige and importance to the former features while banishing the other elements into the unseemly world of subjectivity. On this view, then "rationalism" did not gradually become subservient to "empiricism" in liberal political thought. Rather, rigorously rational theories of jurisprudence, morals, economics, and government held out the hope of channeling individual passions into predictable and productive directions. The rational institutions and coercive mechanisms required for this task were to be very selective of the appropriate interests and passions to admit to public view. All others were to be banished to a nether world—there perhaps to haunt the objective and public one.

Nineteenth-century critics of utilitarianism clearly saw this weakness and based their critical enterprise and their attempted reconstructions on it. These liberal critics accuse the utilitarians and their Scottish predecessors of a blindness to "history," by which they mean a failure to see the ways in which the "truths" of psychology, economics, law, and government are in fact contingent truths. As Leslie Stephen framed it, this supposedly universal knowledge in fact rests upon "the entire mass of its historical antecedents . . . the whole enormous aggregate of opinions, sentiments, beliefs . . . of ideas of all kinds." Even jurisprudence—next to economics and the proudest scientific achievement of late eighteenth- and early nineteenth-century liberalism—is subordinated by Stephen to the imperatives of the other world of liberalism, now defined as historic culture rather than religion: "The law itself, in fact, ultimately rests upon 'custom,' upon the whole system of instincts, beliefs, and passions which induce a people to obey government, and are, so to speak, the substance out of which loyalty and respect for the law is framed."[4]

Whatever the justice of Stephen's account, it remains true that natural-history formulations are inseparable from utilitarian attempts to create objective sciences of society and politics, as free from human subjectivity as they are from the contingencies of religion and history. The ways in which liberal theory was transformed by natural-history formulations and the utility principle is charted here in three contexts. The first context is law, especially the natural history of civil law on the one hand and criminal law and capital punishment on the other. A natural history of both

kinds of law suggests a paradox: a society dominated by economic calculation and market scarcity requires much more criminal law than earlier
societies bound by ties of affection and privilege that blunted the expression of self-interest. The march of utility is accompanied by its
opposite—the growth of spontaneous demands for vengeance on those
who commit crimes. The avenging God of an earlier liberalism disappears
only to reappear in a different guise: Locke's strange doctrine of executive
power in the state of nature becomes the central postulate of an empirical
psychology.

The second context in which natural-history assumptions will be explored is that of moral sentiments, that is, opinions and motives for action. Both Hume and Smith suggest that the liberal man of jurisprudence,
civil law, and economics did not fight his way into history powered by
his own qualities and in opposition to progressively weaker competitors.
Far from being robust and creative, this man as engine of natural history
is often pictured as imbecile, requiring qualities and motives quite foreign
to his nature in order to act in history. This same conclusion is found in
utilitarian writings which contain the corollary that the psychological and
normative foundations for liberal politics are subverted by its very success.

The last context is political loyalty and obligation. Utilitarian theory in
law, economics, and psychology is accompanied by an almost Hobbesian
insistence on coercion as the center of a theory of government. While
civil society is defined by individual action, personal interest, and voluntary exchange, the political order protecting it is defined by necessity and
physical coercion. And, as in the first half of *Leviathan*, the necessities
coerced are effective only with men presumed to have no consciousness
of a self beyond the consciousness needed for acquiring the means of self-
preservation. As John Stuart Mill was to remark later, such men literally
have no "power over [their] own character" and thus no "consciousness
of freedom."[5] The utilitarian resuscitation of a de facto theory of political
obligation is perhaps the inevitable price paid for attempting to create a
theory of politics entirely within the assumption that man is born to liberty. Another price paid is a theory which grounds political power on a
most fragile basis. Hobbes ends the first half of *Leviathan* with the vain
hope that "one time or other, this writing of mine, may fall into the
hands of a Sovereign" who might convert this "Truth of Speculation, into
the Utility of Practice."[6] The utilitarians, with no counterpart to the second half of *Leviathan* and therefore no book known to all, had an overwhelming faith in the truth of their political science but little hope at all
that the mass of men would either understand or willingly accept that
truth as the basis of their political life. The necessities of power alone
must demonstrate the truths of their science. It is in this last context—

that of political obligation and political authority—that the weakness of this form of liberalism is most obvious. But it is this context, too, which is both philosophically and historically required to sustain the rest.

The analysis that follows is restricted to isolating the changes in the major areas of liberal political philosophy after Locke and prior to John Stuart Mill. Natural history alters the nature of man's social relationships, his opinions of good and evil, and, most significantly, his view of himself. The celebration of the development of civil society and rational values is accompanied by a dread that man himself is diminished and perhaps even depraved by the process. This countertheme is an important one to consider for it is a primary means by which the "other world" from Hobbes and Locke was recognized as important—especially regarding the problem of political loyalty—and it becomes the point at which John Stuart Mill begins his critique of utilitarianism.

11

Law

Adam Ferguson, a Scottish contemporary of Hume and Smith, distinguishes between the chaotic events of political history and the inexorable logic of natural history by two archetypical acts. "He who first said 'I will appropriate this field; I will leave it to my heirs' " unwittingly laid the "foundation of civil laws and [legitimate] political establishment." This man was born to liberty. In contrast, "he who first ranged himself under a leader . . . [set] the example of a permanent subordination" wherein "the rapacious were to seize [men's] possessions, and the arrogant to lay claim to [their] service."[1] This man was born to servitude. Because Ferguson's *Essay on the History of Civil Society* charts the growth of governments from "seeds . . . lodged in human nature," the second actor quickly disappears from his analysis.[2]

Adam Smith's early lectures point to the analogous contrast between "projectors" who view government as "a sort of political mechanics" and wiser men who see governmental forms as flowing from and serving the needs of nature "in the course of her operations in human affairs." Governments which seek to "thwart this natural course . . . are obliged to be oppressive and tyrannical."[3] The proper knowledge of politics teaches men to shape themselves and their governments in accordance with the dictates of natural processes. Smith combines the image of speculator and speculative philosophy when he warns that man's place is a modest one, "suitable to the weakness of his powers and to the narrowness of his comprehension." His duties begin with himself, his family, friends, and country. Nature teaches that "the most sublime speculation of the contemplative philosopher can scarce compensate the neglect of the smallest active duty."[4] Political commitments, like philosophical speculation and religion, says Hume, should "only [enforce] the motives of morality and justice." To locate justice and morality in natural history is to see in autonomous religious and political principles "only a cover to faction and ambition."[5] Like the state of nature, natural history is clearly intended as an alternative source of ideas for understanding and guiding political life.

Civil Law and the Lockean Connection

The moral philosophy in Hume's *Treatise of Human Nature* can fairly be read as a skeptical exegesis on Locke's *Second Treatise*. By rejecting those elements in Locke's analysis suggesting the "rational" apprehension of moral rules, the deliberate construction of civil power, and the requirement of rational assent to political order, Hume's analysis consistently stresses the historical relationship between economic development, the passions, and the invention of "justice." Reason follows in the train of passion and invents the artifacts of civilization.

Hume's refutation of Locke's rational theory of the origin of property amidst nature's abundance is brief and compelling: "Why give rise to property, where there cannot possibly be any injury? Why call this object mine, when, upon the seizing of it by another, I need but stretch out my hand to possess myself of what is equally valuable?"[6] The growth of justice is as gradual as the growth of inequality, and both justice and inequality are by-products of man's continuous industry and acquisition. The inconveniences of Humean man are specific and continuous. The rational response to these inconveniences is cumulative legal invention.

> Mankind is an inventive species; and where an invention is obvious and absolutely necessary, it may as properly be said to be natural as anything that precedes immediately from original principles, without the intervention of thought or reflection. Though the rules of justice be artificial, they are not arbitrary.[7]

Three factors explain the necessity for inventing rules of justice: (1) "the scanty provision nature has made for [man's] wants"; (2) "the selfishness and confined generosity of man"; and (3) some impulse which drives man to some rudimentary form of society in order that he may come to know the advantages of society over the inconveniences resulting from the "numberless wants and . . . slender means" which nature has given solitary man.[8] This impulse, says Hume, is "the natural appetite betwixt the sexes" which first unites people "and preserves their union till a new tie takes place in their concern for their common offspring."[9]

Hume reworks Locke's distinction between paternal and political authority in such a way that paternal authority is never at issue. The moral and economic bonds of the family are quickly transcended by the rules of rudimentary civil society. Family society merely facilitates enough social intercourse to make possible the rudimentary construction of an external environment conducive to the shaping of self-interest into the civil virtues of impartiality and indifference toward others. In Hume's natural history, fathers are fathers and do not become kings. The history of justice is a record of man's external goods and impersonal relationships. Natural history cannot be concerned with "the internal satisfaction of our minds" or the "external advantages of our body," for neither good is of use to anyone else. This history looks only to that "species of goods . . . as we have acquired by our industry and good fortune."[10]

The invention of justice proceeds in three states. Each man finds it in his interest, in this early period, to establish a rule "for the stability of possession."[11] The first rule creates property ownership. The simplest mental abstraction required to "objectify" property in this manner is de facto possession. Later, prescription, accession, and succession come equally to be regarded as bestowing rights to property. Unfortunately, these now stable forms of property often "prove contradictory to both men's wants and desires; and persons and possessions [are] often very ill-adjusted." Free exchange of property is invented as the next rule.[12] Inconveniences arise even with this second invention, however, because men are naturally loathe to exchange goods with strangers except in situations of mutual performance and only "with regard to such objects as are present and individual [moveable]."[13] Having thus far avoided some of Locke's difficulties[14] Hume comes face to face with Hobbes: how can a self-interested man be held to a contract binding future actions, having already been rewarded by performance on the part of another?

Hume's easy answer is that "society" invents a form of words called a "promise," thereby subjecting the user of those words "to the penalty of never being trusted again in case of failure."[15] This third and last invention only appears after "self-interested commerce . . . begins to take place and to predominate in society." Contracts, then, distinguish this form of exchange from "the more generous and noble intercourse of friendship and good offices." Binding agreements "give a new direction to . . . natural passions," teaching men that they "can better satisfy [their] appetites in an oblique and artificial manner than by their headlong and impetuous motion."[16]

Hume concludes by stressing the absolute necessity of these rules as the foundation for morality and happiness.

> It is on the strict observance of those three laws that the peace and security of human society entirely depend. . . . Society is absolutely necessary for the well-being of men; and these [laws] are as necessary to the support of society. Whatever restraint they may impose on the passions of men, they are the real offspring of those passions, and are only a more artful and more refined way of satisfying them.[17]

In contrast to other rules of morality, rules of justice "admit of no . . . insensible gradation. . . . [A] man either has a full and perfect property or none at all; and is either entirely obliged to perform any action, or lies under no manner of obligation."[18]

Hume's analysis of the origins of civil society is almost exactly paralleled by Smith's. In both formulations, the sequential development of civil law is outlined without reference to crime on the one hand or to competing views of morality on the other. Left at this stage, a natural history of justice is a game of marginal utility in which all players win. Nature's god is indeed a benevolent deity.[19]

Jeremy Bentham's discussion of civil law in his *Theory of Legislation* begins where natural history ends and constitutes a psychological and economic counterpart to Hume's natural history of justice. Despite all that Bentham wrote about government being a "tissue of sacrifice," his view of civil law protecting contractual acquisition of goods approaches the value of a godly gift. If the possibility of crime is set aside, the pains of the obligation to abstain from another's goods are incomparably less than the benefits conferred by the corresponding rights acquired. "[E]ven under a bad government, there is no proportion between the acquisition [rights] and the sacrifice [obligation]." This protection of rights and obligations by law maximizes "good," or pleasure, and minimizes "evil," or pain, because obligation is exchanged for "a benefit of a clearly greater value."[20] Put in terms of utility theory, this contractual creation and exchange of rights and obligations is not at all problematic. Every reasonably prudent exchange maximizes economic value for both participants. This value can be easily assessed within reasonable limits by judges in cases of dispute. Civil law makes these agreements binding.

Bentham calculates the unalloyed benefits of civil law in two different ways. First, he weighs an individual's pains of involuntarily losing rights to some object against the pleasures gained by another. Since pain avoidance constitutes a necessary part of our happiness, security of possessions is a value. Thus, on a purely individual reckoning and in static terms, Bentham maintains that in cases of two equally rich competitors for rights to some object "the arrangement productive of the greatest sum of good will be, that which favors the old possessor to the exclusion of the new demandant."[21] But would not the involuntary loss of one-fourth of a large fortune by one man for the hundredfold gain of another who had very little result in a net gain of happiness? Bentham's answer is necessarily yes.[22] But this is only the beginning of his calculations. Happiness must be produced and reproduced in time through systematic and painful labor. Men must be motivated to produce happiness.

Bentham shifts his perspective on the pleasures of security from simple protection of present goods to security against pains of future loss. The calculation of pleasures versus pains bestowed by civil law now becomes infinitely unbalanced in favor of the benefits of civil law. Bentham maintains that the general purpose of civil-law rights and obligations is *"to prolong the idea of [man's] security through all the perspective [of time] which his imagination is capable of measuring."*[23] This form of security, which Bentham calls expectation, is central to happiness production.

The first sense in which security of expectation is important is that it makes it possible to talk about "persons" capable of rational action. Civil law creates expectation by creating stable rights to property; these rights make it possible to calculate from the immediate future into the distant future.

> It is hence that we have the power of forming a general plan of conduct; it is hence, that the successive instants which compose the duration of life, are not like isolated and independent points, but become continuous parts of a whole.[24]

Future time gives "being" to men, because expectation makes possible a merging of pain avoidance (man), industry (action), and external objects. Property lost outside of contractual exchange is not simply economic or quantifiable loss. Viewed in terms of time, property is integral to personality.

> Every thing about it, represents to my eye that part of myself which I have put into it;—those cares, that industry, that economy, which denied itself present pleasures to make provision for the future. Thus our property becomes a part of our being, and cannot be torn from us without rending us to the quick.[25]

To guarantee security of expectation and, therefore, the motivation to produce pleasure, is the primary purpose of law. The "sum of social happiness" or utility which depends upon civil law consists in the particular ends of "subsistence, abundance, [distributive] equality, and security." Subsistence and abundance do not require the artificial motivations of law: to provide security for those who labor and security in the proceeds from labor automatically guarantees both subsistence and abundance. Viewed in static terms, distributive equality would seem to maximize aggregate happiness, but equality must give way to security and the protection of prevailing inequalities. Indeed, in attempts to promote distributive equality by law, "a single error may overturn social order."[26] This danger exists because of the calculus built into men, whose laws create "security of expectation." To use power to take from one man to give to another creates insecurity of expectation. "When insecurity reaches a certain point, the fear of losing prevents us from enjoying what we possess already." If this enjoyment ceases, a "deadening of industry" follows.[27] The sum of social happiness would soon reduce to subsistence. Without industry, the life of every man would be nasty, brutish, and short.

John Austin's theory of law represents an even more decisive shift in this direction. In his jurisprudence, desires and interests become codified into a self-contained system of civil law. But the voluntary creation of law is translated into obedience only because of the overarching necessity represented by threat of punishment. Every contractual creation of rights and duties is motivated by the "involuntary suffering"—hunger, cold, or any relative deprivation—we avoid by making the exchange. Every contractual obligation thereby incurred is incurred voluntarily. We fulfill our resulting obligations even after we have received the benefits to avoid a second kind of involuntary suffering, namely, the threat of enforcement by the state. Thus, we always want to fulfill our obligations. John Locke says that, before money and inequality, right and convenience went together in the state of nature. David Hume says that the invention of civil law followed logically from men's desires over time. John Austin formally merges civil law and psychology: "we cannot be obliged to that which depends not upon our desires, or which we cannot fulfill by desiring or wishing to desire it."[28] In the world bounded by civil law, consent and obligation are the same thing.

In all of these discussions of rules, morality and civil law are almost identical. Desires are intentions, intentions become promises, and promises become legal obligations. This identification, however, is also a denial that morality can mean more than legal innocence and enlightened self-interest. Hume begins his discussion of justice claiming that

> the question . . . concerning the wickedness or goodness of human nature enters not in the least into that other question concerning the origins of society. . . . For whether the passion of self-interest be esteemed vicious or virtuous, it is all a case, since itself alone restrains it; so that if it be virtuous, men become social by their virtue; if vicious, their vice has the same effect.[29]

Austin carries Hume's view into the center of his jurisprudence. He maintains that legal obligation is what we desire and what we will, but that neither will nor desire has much to do with our character: "The dominion of the will extends not to the mind." The logic of civil law presumes that voluntary actions do not change the state of a man's mind. We cannot change the general "state of ideas and desires" simply by "desiring those changes."[30] Civil law and the government which enforces it has nothing to say regarding human character or larger freedom. An illustration of this is Austin's discussion of legal culpability.

Intention or inadvertence "is of the essence of injury or wrong; is of the essence of breach of duty; is a necessary condition precedent to . . . guilt.[31] Inadvertence (e.g., negligence, heedlessness, rashness) can only be imputed from some overt action or omission. Intention is a more difficult concept, because we often use it to mean not simply "present intentions" imputed directly from an act or omission, but "future intentions" which concern a settled design to pursue a long-range course of conduct or way of life. Can we be under a legal obligaton "to forbear from intentions, which regard future acts, or future forbearances from action?" Austin raises this possibility but concludes that it is logically impossible. All strictly legal obligations are relative, not absolute. A relative duty "corresponds . . . to a right . . . it is a duty to be fulfilled towards a determinate [private] person or . . . persons."[32] We have no legal obligations, strictly speaking, to the state, to the sovereign, to the public at large, or to any particular way of life.

Another illustration is the notion of culpability found in Bentham's writings on civil procedure.[33] Most civil disputes result from "meddling" with "things as are of value." In criminal acts it is clear who has the exclusive rights to meddle and who does not, but in civil disputes this is not clear. And whereas intention may "be presumed from the nature of the act itself" in a criminal case, in civil matters the entire question of intention and therefore culpability does not immediately arise at all.

> The general rule is, that there is always some one person at least who has a right to meddle with [things of value]: and the only question is who is it that has that right: who is it that is in such manner favoured by the law, as to have the right conferred upon him?[34]

In a civil suit the plaintiff seeks to obtain a right. If the judge decides in his favor "he gives a judgement investing [the plaintiff] with this conclusive right." Since the possession of the right is not decided until the suit, there could be no legal injury until then. "Previous therefore to the judgement there neither is nor can have been any offense whatever in the case."[35] All conflicts which can be placed within the rubric of civil injury can be settled without judging or punishing the moral intentions or character of the "guilty" party. Even in cases where evil intention—Bentham terms it "criminal consciousness"—is clear, one should not raise the issue or bring criminal suit if restitution is certain. The category of "business crimes" such as embezzlement or fraud furnishes examples of this kind of suit. Bentham's attempt to expand the reach of civil law and monetary compensation to the farthest extent possible is complemented by his attempt to reduce to a minimum the need for criminal judgments and physical punishment. In broader terms, the history of civil society is a history of restricting the use of public power to impersonal judgments over rights to things of market value. The invention of justice is therefore the invention of a new political perception of men: in the eyes of the public, men are viewed as bundles of reciprocal rights and duties related to objects and services of value. Competition between these bundles is both intense—leading to many conflicts—and impersonal. The satisfaction a "winner" receives in a civil suit is only his monetary due, the costs of the suit, and perhaps the amount obtained from a token fine on the other party. Needless to say, the state should get nothing.[36]

The logical coherence in the jurisprudence of Bentham and Austin is mirrored by a coherent psychological theory—the same theory which informed Hume's natural history of justice. Hume's formulation has the advantage of assuming that civil law was invented in isolation, or at least in a setting which did not contain competing theories of obligation and law. The coherence of utilitarian theories of civil law and psychology could only be achieved analogously by shielding that system from criminal law, physical punishments, and the entire panoply of values and resources which compose political power. To divorce civil law from questions of consciousness and personality is a necessary part of that enterprise.

Maine's analysis of Roman legal development in *Ancient Law* makes explicit the separation of law "properly so called" from politics, custom, and morality.[37] He posits a change "from status to contract" with the result that late Roman law and contemporary European law are the same: both are self-contained systems of individual economic relationships disconnected from all remnants of public power save that of interpretation and enforcement. Roman legal history provides the material from which Maine constructs his theory of law, and the logic of Roman legal development begins to repeat itself beginning in postmedieval Europe. Postulating that all primitive societies start with practices "best suited to promote [their] physical well-being," Maine goes on to show that in most societies expediential rules soon become mixed with irrational religious beliefs, rules, and rituals. When this happens, caprice reigns under the aegis of "patriarchal despotism."[38] In short, reasonable usage often evolves into unreasonable law, as paternal authority and priestly oligarchy corrupt usage and codify it into law. Roman law developed as an exception to this process because political revolution overthrew privileged groups while "usage was still wholesome." And because of this revolution, Rome began with uncorrupted written law.[39]

Having established these facts and postulates, Maine traces the means by which deliberate legal change from status to contract is effected. While the immediate cause of this legal change is "social needs" or utility, the motivational and cognitive means used by jurists and rulers changes over time. Legal fictions are first used to change law, then notions of equity or natural law, and finally direct legislation. In all cases, the direction of the law is away from political/legal actors defined by status and toward legal persons defined by contract. Maine views all of the change as "remedial," that is, as indirect responses to the social progress which uncorrupted extant law had encouraged. Except in ancient Rome and modern Europe, this "gradual amelioration" has not taken place.[40]

Legal fictions have the limited and preliminary purpose of extending the reach of Roman law. Later legislation tends to codify what equity has already wrought. Maine's focus, then, is on Roman equity jurisprudence, "the ancient counterpart of Benthamism."[41] Both equity and utilitarianism provide simple organizing principles for lawyers and jurists to adjust the law to the primary fact of moral progress.

The last stage of deliberate legal change is legislative will, both in Rome and perhaps in post-Bentham England. In Rome, legislation is coequal with the decline of the Republic and the increasing dominance of the emperors. In the Roman Republic jurists reformed the law gradually and in the courts. Only under the Empire did legislative will come to determine law. Curiously, Maine simply leaves Roman history at this point. Following a summary of analogous patterns of change in England, Maine states that, with the decline of natural law in Rome and the stagnation of equity in England, "we are brought close to the ideas of our own day."[42]

The second half of *Ancient Law* is simply a charting of progressive changes in Roman civil law: testamentary succession, wills and successions, property and contracts. The importance of this analysis is that *patria potestas* is viewed by Maine as the *nidus* or seed out of which the "law of persons" becomes defined in terms of the "law of things."[43] Civil law emerges as a coherent system of law divorced from political, social, and moral values. Legal equality is the result of this reduction. In brief, ancient "civil" law and ancient political authority were initially "patriarchal" and combined: both were centered in the "father" as private legal actor and in the "father-king" as citizen and family ruler. In terms which would apply more generally, status symbolizes not only "father" or "father-king" but lord, peasant, bishop, and, indeed, any imposition of personality apart from that derived from relationships to things of value. Thus, the progress of law is stated by Maine as a decomposition of the centrality of "status." "Jurisprudence fell gradually to pieces" within each of the various categories of the civil law. And, in pursuing this inquiry, Maine cautions that

> we need not suffer ourselves to be stopped by the imaginary barrier
> which separates the modern from the ancient world. For one effect of
> that mixture of refined Roman Law with primitive barbaric usage,
> which is known to us by the deceptive name of feudalism, was to
> revive many features of archaic jurisprudence which had died out of the
> Roman world, so that the decomposition which had seemed to be over
> commenced again, and . . . is still proceeding.[44]

The last chapter in *Ancient Law* is curiously out of place. Entitled "The Early History of Delict and Crime," it consists of a very short and inclusive query into why, even in the developed stages of Roman law at the end of the Republican period, such a scanty and poorly arranged body of criminal law existed. Maine first suggests that crimes were the province of ad hoc judgments made by legislative or popular assemblies. He then points to the fact that ad hoc courts were established for particular crimes because there were so few crimes committed. Moreover, many "crimes" that did take place were handled within family units, where fathers had quasi-political power. Only during the final stages of the *imperium* did "the list of crimes in the Roman State [become] as long as in any community of the modern world."[45] More ominously, in view of his parallels to the modern period, Maine ends by raising the question why the death penalty was rare and even, at times, nonexistent in republican Rome. Though he alludes to specific institutional causes, Maine concludes that the absence of this penalty "led distinctly and directly to those frightful Revolutionary intervals, during which all law was suspended simply because party violence could find no other avenue to the vengeance for which it was thirsting." This general "abeyance of the laws" was the ruin of Roman political liberty. In more general terms, he concludes, "the punishment of death is a necessity of society in certain stages of the civilizing process."[46] That stage is when status is superseded by contract.[47] Modern civil law loses

> the assistance of superstition, probably that of opinion, certainly that of spontaneous impulse. The force at the back of law comes therefore to be purely coercive force to a degree quite unknown to societies of the more primitive type.[48]

Leviathan seems to make his appearance not at the beginning of civil society but at the culmination of a natural history of justice. As Hume admitted in the *Treatise*, "without the separate sanction of government," contractual promises "would have little efficacy in large and civilized societies."[49] The other half of legal theory is criminal law and political sanctions. It is here that the other world of liberalism makes its appearance.[50]

Criminal Law and the Hobbesian Connection

Considerations of criminal law and punishments necessarily require a closer examination of political power than do discussions of civil law. Indeed, criminal law is the means by which these writers cross over into a world of motives and actions quite removed from the logic of legal obligation and economic interest. In so doing, Adam Ferguson's other actor—"he who first ranged himself under a leader"—reappears in many different guises, all of them fitted to the requirements of criminal law and executive power.

Hume's natural history of justice ends with the invention of private contracts. This ending is also the starting point for his discussion of the need for a political magistrate. Hume initially says that the creation of government is analogous to the invention of justice. Every individual finds it in his interest to appoint "indifferent persons" who "have no interest . . . in any act of injustice and . . . have an immediate interest in every execution of justice which is so necessary to the upholding of society." Through this artifice other men are relieved from the burdens of upholding law and "begin to taste at ease the sweets of society and mutual assistance." In this formulation, Hume is following one of Locke's paths in the *Second Treatise:* no mention is made of thieves, but attention is drawn to luxury and inequality. Society without government "is one of the most natural states of men." Only "an increase of riches and possessions could oblige men to quit it" and only after this increase is so great "as to disturb men in the enjoyment of peace and concord." Hume adds another explanation for the rise of government. Wars between societies without governments cause civil wars. In civil war, "the laws, which may be well enough observed while men were calm,"[51] are no longer observed. The father-general in war becomes, with victory, the civil magistrate. War, like sex, throws men into an environment which has advantages not previously recognized—conquest becomes utility. Hume does not even bother to suggest a legislature as agent in this transformation.

All three explanations, pure utility/self-interest, increasing inequality and crimes, and the accidents of war, are rather lamely tendered by Hume. What he appears to maintain is this: the legal bonds of civil society consist of ownership, transference, and networks of contractual promises. Adherence to these rules is first "learned" by perceiving the utility of obedience. Similarly, whether through deliberate action or the accidents of war, the utility of a separate executor of justice is perceived. Allegiance, like justice, is grounded in self-interest—what Hume calls natural or self-enforcing obligation. Only when Hume moves his discussion to the contemporary period and explores the relationsips between government and law do contracts tend to lose their earlier natural qualities of obligation. Once de facto governmental power is granted and he is discussing the workings of historically advanced societies, Hume can make a series of other qualifications to his earlier argument. For example, "reason tells us that there is no property in durable objects such as land or houses, when carefully examined in passing from hand to hand, but must in some period have been founded on force and injustice."[52] Once the system of justice is operative and, more important, once a system of public power that backs justice is in place, philosophical issues must take a back seat to experiential, historical, and psychological necessities. The origins and justifications of economic inequality and the origins and justifications of magisterial power cannot bear the strict scrutiny of reason.[53]

Rules protect inequality founded on fraud and injustice. Were governments also founded that way? Hume's answer, even in the *Treatise,* is a qualified yes. The importance of government, like justice, does not lie in its origins—rational or irrational—but in its utility. Natural (self-interested) obligation can attach itself to a government whose origin was in conquest as easily as it can to one founded on election or contract. And in either case, submission per se "produces a separate sentiment of morality,"[54] called allegiance, divorced from promises and the entire range of maximizing behavior which describes contracts. Except in cases of overwhelming oppression leading to revolution or civil war, maxims such as long possession, present possession (including conquest), and succession (inheritance) are perfectly valid sources for "right of magistracy." "Men are mightily addicted to general rules," Hume asserts, "and we often carry our maxims beyond those reasons which first induced us to establish them."[55]

Hume makes no serious attempt to give us definitive answers regarding justice and allegiance. One paragraph, sounding like a combination of Ascham and Hobbes, must be weighed against others sounding much closer to Locke. The rational core of natural history is the artifice of justice which makes possible the systematic satisfaction of desires. The major argument is not the origins of government but its necessity for present-day happiness. The central motif is not the origins of property but the necessity of property for present-day industry.

The one lesson which Hume's natural history does teach is that the origin of law is separate from the origin of political power and that the sentiments which support justice and allegiance are also separate.[56] Throughout his discussion, criminal law and physical punishments for crime are not mentioned. These concerns are implicit in his discussions of inequality and luxury, but even in these contexts the stress is on the light burdens which political allegiance imposes on contemporary men. With superfluous goods come superfluous labor, so even the sacrifices of war are now reduced to postponing the purchase of luxury goods while the producers of those goods are fighting the battles. Civil law is indeed a gift of the gods, linking "industry, knowledge and humanity . . . by an indissoluble chain."[57] No hint of a crisis of liberalism appeared on Hume's horizon. No matter what the history of liberal society, contemporary men—at least the "middling rank . . . who are the best and firmest basis of public liberty"[58]—do not see in it any deep conflicts between justice and allegiance and between self-interest and feelings of benevolence. Only with Bentham's analysis of crime and punishment do we see the true extent of the problem posed by natural history.[59]

Bentham's discussions of criminal and penal law span his entire intellectual life. Just as he had made it his task to create a felicific calculus to measure the civil law, so he attempted to calculate the costs and benefits of penal law. As a result, we are in Bentham's debt for discovering the darker side of the relationship between law and politics. In the realm of criminal law, all equations from civil law connecting individual to public interest are simply false. The marginal utilities of private contracts seem to prove that nature is benevolent and history is kind; the immeasurable pains of physical punishment and the incalculable loss of death reveal a different side of human nature, a side which cries for vengeance and even savors its higher pleasures. Were these aspects of human nature vestiges from a distant past, Bentham's discovery would be less important than it is, but the contrary is true: only with the liberation of the individual from past servitudes do these passions find direct expression in criminal law and political executives.

In Bentham's discussion of civil law, the purpose of government is to protect expectation and thus to guarantee aggregate benefits clearly greater than before. Without crime, civil law would be, in Adam Smith's phrase, like "the immense machine of the universe [producing] the greatest possible quantity of happiness."[60] But crime is a threat, a "penal code" must complement the civil code, and a physical punisher of criminals must stand behind the impersonal judge of civil suits. In shaping a penal code, the legislator must weigh two evils: "the evil of the offence, and the evil of the law; the malady, and the evil of the remedy."[61] Calculating the former set of evils is Bentham's first task. In the example of theft, the first quantum of pain would be that suffered by the victim of a crime and, indirectly, by members of his family, by his creditors, etc. This must be weighed against the happiness gained by the thief. The net results of these calculations were discussed earlier.

Beyond these "first-order" evils on the part of the victim, "second-order" pains—alarm and danger—are suffered by strangers to the victim.

> Alarm is a positive pain, a pain of apprehension, the apprehension of suffering the same evil which we see has already fallen upon another. Danger is the probability that a primitive [first-order] evil will produce other evils of the same kind.[62]

Bentham has some difficulty in showing that danger (based on real probability) is always related to, and precedes, alarm or feelings of insecurity. He concludes, however, that this evil-danger-alarm sequence does hold and shows that, after a certain point, alarm "extends to [man's] active faculties; it deadens them, it throws them into a state of torpor and decrepitude."[63] The justification for erecting certain acts into criminal offenses rests, therefore, on the *intangible alarm* created, not on the measurable values of "first-order evils." This reckoning adds immeasurably more than economic value to the calculation.

> I compare all the pleasure, or, in other words, all the profit, which results to the author of the act, with all the evil, or the loss, which results to the party injured. I see at once, that the evil of the first order surpasses the good of the first order. But I do not stop there. The action under consideration produces throughout society, danger and alarm. The evil which at first was only individual, spreads everywhere, under the form of fear. The pleasure resulting from the action belongs

solely to the actor; the pain reaches a thousand—ten thousand—all. This disproportion already prodigious, appears infinite, upon passing to the evil of the third order, and considering that if the act in question is not suppressed, there will result from it a universal and durable discouragement, a cessation of labor, and at last, the dissolution of society.[64]

It does not require much imagination to conclude that the punishments of torture and death are miniscule compared to the aggregate pains suffered by all men with the dissolution of society. Both sets of pains, however, are of an entirely different order than the "economic" pains and pleasures within the matrix of civil law.

The natural history of interest and utility is mocked by a parallel history of crime and punishment. Many of the tragic elements of Maine's Roman history are anticipated here. But Bentham seeks to defy the result: rather than conclude that thieves should be tortured beyond endurance and then killed, Bentham barely discusses physical punishment and death penalties at all—except to assert the exact opposite: with the proper reforms, almost all physical punishments and the penalty of death itself can be abolished. Bentham's task is not simple, for he is attempting a revolution in the basic structure of liberal political philosophy that had prevailed since Hobbes. Bentham's promise, symbolically put, is that the first half of *Leviathan* can vanquish the need for the second half. It is no wonder that the enterprise required the efforts of his entire adult life.

Bentham's "Principles of the Penal Code" is actually a wide-ranging discussion of alarm and of how to combat it in order to guarantee "security" which yields labor and utility.[65] If civil law alone seems to Bentham a good bargain, the criminal—whether a private thief or a public one—appears to be a vengeful god of false religion. His act against one man terrifies all and overwhelms the careful calculations of contractual men. When Bentham addresses himself to the problem of alarm and criminal law he deals with two quite different sets of equations. On the side of civil law and security alone, pleasures are always only slightly greater than pains. On the side of criminal offenses and penal remedies, with the exception of the insignificant happiness of the thief, Bentham confronts nothing but pain.

Bentham's first step in ridding civil society of the need for physical punishment is to show that many actions denominated "crimes" need not be punished criminally because they do not create sufficient alarm to warrant it. In all contexts where apprehension leads immediately to compensation of the victim, the state should view the conflict as if it were a civil suit in which the victim always wins the case. Alarm is not created by offenses "which none but such as are responsible can commit. Where compensation is certain, punishment is needless."[66] This construction of the act should prevail even if "criminal consciousness" is obvious and despite societal feelings of moral outrage or calls for vengeance. To put this order of crimes on the footing of civil law makes them nonmischievous acts until after trial, for in a civil suit, prior to the judgment, "there neither is nor can have been any offense whatever in the case."[67] Bentham's equation—no alarm equals no imputation of criminal consciousness equals no justification for punishment—rests on compensation.

All private contracts create mutual watchmen, so all violations of contracts are quickly detected and monetary retribution is expected. Analogously, responsible men who commit crimes are those who threaten only specific others and within established relationships. Bentham uses the example of guardian and ward. Society at large feels no alarm when it learns that a guardian has embezzled a ward's savings. Thus, almost all "crimes" committed in the context of legally established economic relationships can be transmuted into civil offenses. The injured party gets back everything he deserves and should be satisfied. To ask for more satisfaction "consecrated to the sole object of vengeance would be pure evil."[68]

If most criminal offenses were followed by detection and immediate compensation for loss, the creation of societal alarm would be reduced to an absolute minimum. The sequence of crime-danger-alarm would be broken. The law could be purged of what Bentham termed "the arbitrary principle . . . of sympathy and antipathy."[69] To rid criminal law of passion and moral judgment requires that alarm cease, for men who feel alarm demand satisfaction: they want to lay aside their labors to partake in the joys of vengeance. Lockean men in the state of nature presumably *wanted* to exercise "executive power" on thieves. Believers in a Hobbesian society presumably felt satisfaction in witnessing the viceregent of God do God's work on earth when he pronounced final judgment on a criminal. Bentham rejects the religious elements in this reasoning, and attempts to purge man and society of its secular forms.

The first proposal by Bentham is a system of public indemnity to serve as "satisfaction" for those injured by obviously criminal actions. "Everything that can be made up for by a pecuniary indemnity, may soon become as if it had never been . . . the alarm caused by the offence ceases altogether."[70] As he pursues this logic, Bentham's formal distinctions between civil and criminal law begin to evaporate. If "criminal consciousness" is only imputed from the alarm the action causes and is only a fictional hook on which to hang demands for physical punishment, to be rid of alarm is to make consideration of consciousness superfluous. The whole discussion of criminal offenses (i.e., *very* odious, *very* mischievous, etc.), he finally says, makes "the application of the word crime altogether uncertain." One cannot, he concludes, really use the word "criminal . . . to characterize any branch of law as subsisting in contradistinction to that which is called civil."[71] Men often bring penal actions against other men, rather than civil actions, only because of "natural partiality . . . in their own favor and . . . natural propensity to be angry." In fact,

> whatever right is capable of being determined upon in a penal action is equally capable of being determined upon in a civil action: but there are cases proper for a civil action, which cannot without a departure from truth be determined in a penal action.[72]

In truth, Bentham simply has no rational standards for punishment to match those for alarm. In the first place, alarm is invisible and immeasurable; in the second, the harm is potentially infinite; and in the third, it is to be abolished. To use alarm to measure culpability—what Bentham termed "criminal consciousness"—is an impossible task. In Bentham's discussion of the penal code, more than one-fourth of the total is devoted to various schemes of compensation; just short of one-half is devoted to "indirect means of preventing offences;" and less than one-eighth to punishments. Even in that section Bentham has little to say: he is against statutes of limitations, shows where punishments ought not to be applied, speaks of mistaken and misapplied punishments, shows that the pardoning power increases uncertainty, and praises a system of securities for good behavior.[73]

This failure to articulate a theory of punishment could be said to be inevitable, since at the end he states that the purpose of penal legislation is:

> 1st. To reduce all the evil of offences, as far as possible to that kind which can be cured by a pecuniary compensation.
> 2nd. To throw the expense of this cure upon the authors of the evil, or, in their default, upon the public.[74]

Bentham requires an end of alarm because no punishment could compensate its pains. He utilizes every device imaginable to rid the world of "criminal consciousness" and, therefore, of the existence of a passionate and vengeful public symbolized by the executioner. All men might be indelibly tatooed; each man might be required to have a unique name; vegetable gardening should be encouraged; tea and coffee should be popularized at the expense of liquors; music, drama, and card games should be encouraged. "Time is to be filled up," so even one acquitted on a charge of indigence must be made to give an account "of his means of subsistence for at least for the last preceding six months. If they were honest this inquiry can do no harm; if they were not honest, he ought to suffer the consequences." Marriages contracted for limited periods of time ought to be permitted to drain off sexual passions of men whose situations are such that they cannot maintain a family. Prostitution should be permitted to prevent private vengeance for adultery.[75] Bentham even attempts to substitute symbolic for real punishment.

The emblematic robes of the inquisition may be usefully applied to criminal justice. . . . [E]mblems appropriate as far as possible to each offence, would have an additional advantage. It would furnish allusions to poetry, to eloquence, to dramatic authors, to ordinary conversation. The ideas thence derived would be re-echoed . . . by a thousand objects, and would be scattered on all sides.[76]

By explicitly raising the issue of criminal punishment and its pains, Bentham casts a shadow on the measurable utilities of civil law. No one in that philosophic tradition, before or since, has explored it with such reckless courage without the aid of the gods or of necessity. Bentham's daring is understandable and his passionate dislike of criminal punishment is explicable when one adds the grandest reform proposal of all: his Panopticon prison. This life-long project protected his jurisprudence, integrating that jurisprudence to utility theory and making it a practical possibility.

Bentham's plans and projects underwent many changes over time, but James Mill captures their central features in an essay "Prisons and Prison Reform."[77] Prisons, Mill begins, could be said to serve three purposes: (a) the provision of safe custody for those who are to stand trial; (b) the punishment of convicted criminals; and (c) the reformation of criminals. There are three types of men in prisons: those who are to stand trial; persons already convicted who are awaiting the punishment stipulated by the judge; and debtors. Speedy trials would rid prisons of the first group and rational debtor legislation would rid them of the last. Since all three classes of men are in prison, however, debtors and those detained before trial should not be "punished" while in prison. Neither are they there, as yet, for "reformation." For these men, the prison should provide a subsistence level sufficient to prevent impairment of health. They should be permitted through voluntary paid labor or by use of savings to purchase "unexceptional indulgences" to supplant the subsistence standard. These men should be treated with "benevolence consistent with economy."[78]

"Prisons are not the best instruments of punishment," Mill continues, even for convicted criminals. Granting that confinement per se might be thought of as punishment, he dismisses that argument out of hand.[79] Criminal punishment is involuntary physical pain or bodily harm. Prisons should confine and perhaps reform men but not punish them. Mill especially attacks the practice of forced labor. "Most of the persons who come to prisons as criminals, are bad, because they have hated labour." Since "men seldom become in love with their punishments," compulsory labor as a punishment would make reformation impossible. "What sort of lesson do you teach [those outside the walls] whose lot is labour, whose lot is hard labour, harder than any which it is in your power to impose?"[80] Mill's plans to reform the prison inhabitants are surprisingly close to theories of learning in the state of nature. Like nature's god, the prison should guarantee a subsistence floor to the convicts. The artifice is capital equipment and supplies to provide work for the convicts if they choose to work at the wage level set by the jailer. Whatever the convicts get they can use to purchase additional items sold by the jailer. The jailer receives funds to pay for wages and subsistence expenses from the sale of the products of convict labor to the world at large.

According to James Mill, the central question of reformation is "what are the best means of producing the performance of those acts, the habit of performing which we desire to render so perfect, that it may be relied upon for effect, even in a state of freedom?" His answer is lawful labor for reward. The only way that labor can be a means of reformation is that it "be a source of pleasure, not of pain. The way in which labor becomes agreeable to men out of a prison, is the way in which it can be made agreeable to them in prison, and there is no other."[81] The jailer symbolizes the whole system of political economy outside the walls, but artificial means must be created to prevent his monopoly position as buyer of labor and seller of commodities from being misused. If the jailer maintains the subsistence floor, his profit will come only if he can motivate prisoners to labor. Mill would establish additional checks. The jailer gets his position by competitive bid. He is fined if the death rate within a prison population is greater than actuarial equivalents in the world outside. He is fined if convicts commit crimes when released proportionate to the amount of time these convicts were under his care. He must publish audited accounts of his enterprise and, without legal immunities, answer to inspecting magistrates. So thoroughly had Bentham's prison been integrated into the economic and motivational mechanism of civil society that Mill closes his essay by answering charges of "unfair competition" with the larger economy.[82]

The similarities between prison walls and a utilitarian state are striking. John Austin's jurisprudence codified both the logical and the psychological connections with meticulous clarity. Political power and prison walls, he says, are both general contexts of suffering within which we involuntarily find ourselves. We do not will or desire to be born in a particular political society any more than we would voluntarily walk through the gate of a prison. Both contexts, however, shape our character: "change in the mind may be wrought or prevented, whether we desire the change or whether we do not desire it."[83] Our way of life is bound by the strictest servitude, necessity itself; our unending desires are granted the widest liberty. Prisons and governments surround and protect a realm of civil law and—if rightly ordered—vouchsafe the liberty which civil law sustains. Unlike convicts, however, men outside the walls are capable of establishing and disestablishing governments and of deciding which men shall go to prison. This entire realm of action and decision is outside of Austin's legal theory.

Utilitarian theories of jurisprudence complement their reform proposals by purging law "properly so called" of all elements of "involuntary suffering." Absolute obligations are not a part of law but flow from necessity: "Suffering, therefore, is the ultimate sanction . . . [and] every obligation is ultimately sanctioned by suffering." Physical confinement and physical compulsion are ultimate sanctions. One cannot even speak of a separate category of criminal law except in the minimal sense of "the different tendencies of Civil or Criminal Procedures." In all cases of offense against a legal right, the injured party may pursue satisfaction at his discretion; in some cases, this is done for him by the sovereign or his subordinates.[84]

Criminal law and criminal punishments are really exercises of sovereign power, but sovereign power has nothing to do with legal obligations—except to guarantee their existence. Austin's jurisprudence banishes the mysteries of crime and death from law only to place them firmly in the lap of political sovereignty. The result is a theory of government merging a most authoritarian Hobbes and a most liberal Locke:

> Now since it is not restrained by positive law from dealing at its own pleasure with all things within its territory, we may say . . . that the state has a *right* to all things within its territory, or is absolutely or without restriction the proprietor . . . thereof. Strictly speaking, it has no legal right to any thing, or is not the legal owner or proprietor of any thing.[85]

To grant the state legal right to any "thing" would be to say that the sovereign power confers all the relative rights and duties created by civil law. If this were the case, all civil law would be sovereign command and all duties would be absolute. No man could be said to have any legal rights at all, no property and no liberty. If this were the case, the keystone of his legal logic, namely, civil law regulating rights and duties in relation to things of value, disappears. All property would legally belong to the sovereign.

To escape this logic, Austin simply reverses his reasoning. All "law" relating to the use and distribution of sovereign power could be integrated into civil law, as part of "the general law of procedure" or as "miscellaneous and supplemental" limbs of the law of persons. No distinct body of public "law" would remain, only public power. Since every legal relationship—from private contracts through the rights of the hangman—is "designed, among other purposes, for the prevention of crime,"[86] any logical demarcation between private and public rights is "too loose to justify." In positive terms, "every part of the law is in a certain sense public, and every part of it is in a certain sense private also."[87] On the one hand, Austin's sovereign is all-powerful because his power is the determinate context of involuntary suffering and is the ultimate sanction. On the other hand, Austin's sovereign and all of his material resources dissolve into the regular and predictable workings of civil law. As in Bentham's prison, the characters of men are not shaped by the will of the jailer but by the aggregate voluntary desires, will, and actions of each individual within the walls.

> [A]lthough, in logical rigour, much of the so-called law which relates to the Sovereign, ought to be banished from the *corpus juris,* it ought to be inserted in the *corpus juris* for reasons of convenience which are paramount to logical symmetry. For though, in strictness, it belongs to positive morality or to ethics, a knowledge of it is absolutely necessary in order to a knowledge of the positive law with which the *corpus juris* is properly concerned.[88]

In strictness, then, any obligations which the sovereign might have are either rules of morality dictated by "general opinion" or "ethical maxims which the Sovereign spontaneously observes."[89] The use of sovereign power rests on opinion. Opinion rests, in turn, on the character of the public and/ or the sovereign. The penal code, prisons, and police are external ultimate sanctions. Opinion and character are internal ultimate sanctions. A world of difference may separate the proven utilities of civil law and the commands of political power: "Herein lies the difference between governments of law and governments of men."[90] The natural history of law requires a natural history of opinion to insure the victory of justice and the logical coherence of jurisprudence.

To this point in the discussion of law, I have led the reader in a circular path. Bentham's inquiries into the costs and benefits of law began with his discovery of David Hume's *Treatise of Human Nature* but ended with Panopticon prisons. The major link between reading Hume and inventing prisons is a book compiled from Bentham's writings by Etienne Dumont, called *Traité de Législation.*[91] The centrality of this book to utilitarianism is insured by John Stuart Mill's *Autobiography:* "When I laid down the last volume of the *Traité,* I had become a different being. . . . It gave unity to my conceptions of things. I now had opinions; a creed, a doctrine, a philosophy; in one among the best senses of the word, a religion."[92] Mill's later "mental crisis" and rejection of much of Benthamism was not because it ended in prisons but because Mill saw the doctrine as self-enslaving. Mill's reexamination is doubly appropriate: first, because he went back to Hume's concern with moral opinion and, second, because Mill again brought to light how an indifference to the other world of liberalism results in an edifice of reason and power precariously resting on opinions which its science could neither integrate nor do without.

The separation of law from morality in the legal positivism of Austin and Bentham is another means of stating the fragility of utilitarian notions of politics. This fragility is not only true from the standpoint of political supports but also from the standpoint of freedom. Mill began his political life dedicated to liberating men by appeal to their interests; he ended it by asking whether an interest morality might be a subtle form of self-enslavement. The crucial determinate in this question is the quality of shared opinions in the society. To examine freedom in terms of opinion and belief is to reopen issues which Hobbes raised in the second half of *Leviathan* and Locke examined in his many writings on religion and morality. By separating law from morality, Bentham and Austin also separated "consciousness of freedom" from civil law. But if consciousness of freedom is essential for a government of laws, the location of freedom shifts to opinions and beliefs. This is not the only possibility. Contemporary men may live in prisons of their own designing: lacking all memory of freedom and all commitment to any ends of life at all, they might mindlessly act out their "desire for power after power until death." Within the logic of natural history, the result would surely signal the end of all history. Hobbes's promise of "civil eternity" in the first half of *Leviathan* would be kept.

12

Opinion

Nature will always maintain her rights, and prevail in the end over any abstract reasoning whatsoever.

DAVID HUME, *An Enquiry Concerning Human Understanding*

Hobbes and Locke see moral opinion and religion as intimately connected. Part of their task was to unravel this connection by showing how political and religious leaders manipulated ideas of good and evil for their own secular and institutional advantages. In the process of reconnection, Hobbes and Locke try to demonstrate how a purely biblical religion requires and supports true moral philosophy and is consonant with natural religion, that is, a religion derived solely from reason. And, finally, both men conclude that popular moral opinions supportive of a liberal polity are historically possible only insofar as true religious beliefs are victorious. Locke outlines a parallel possibility: practical moral opinions can be acquired indirectly through the economic, legal, and political relationships created by man's history of industry. In discussions of the relationship of moral opinion to politics in writings after Locke, this latter possibility is central. David Hume and Adam Smith begin with a natural history of "moral sentiments" but, like later utilitarians, are more concerned to explicate a theory of contemporary moral sentiments. Their concern is with the present state of opinion—its stability, its material basis, and its relationship to legality and virtue.

Contemporary moral sentiments are built upon the artifact of justice and on the natural feelings of benevolence. For all the stress on opinions within an ongoing liberal society, however, the problem of religion and history still intrudes. Are men in liberal societies fundamentally different from men in preliberal ones? If supernatural religious belief no longer dominates moral opinion, what takes its place? Is there a functional equivalent to popular religious belief or can religious feelings be displaced by practical concerns?

141

To say that preliberal moral and religious beliefs can be explained by a more comprehensive psychological and social theory is to suggest that social and psychological mechanisms might power contemporary opinion without the requirement of religious belief. The prominence which Hume and Smith give to natural "instincts" or spontaneous "feeling" implies that, for them, the important conflict is not between supernatural religion and liberal moral opinion but between one class of sentiments and another. For them, the conflict is psychological: spontaneity, personality, and instinct battle with calculation, impersonality, and utility. Paradoxically, however, the former class of beliefs has a public and recorded history while the latter are only postulates of empirical psychology and a hypothetical history. The focus on contemporary man disguises this fact in their writings and seems to transform the issue solely into a psychological one. In many respects, however, the category "supernatural religion" is simply imported into the discussion under the label "instinctual feelings." Whether feelings thus labeled are subversive or supportive of true moral opinion remains at issue.

Three problems dominate discussions of opinion in these post-Lockean writings. The first problem concerns the relationship of moral opinion to religious belief. The second problem concerns the tensions which exist between sentiments supportive of the strict demands of justice and sentiments surrounding the spontaneous and particularistic virtues of benevolence. A third problem concerns moral opinion and political power. This last problem is the most important. If public opinion determines each individual's view of himself as well as his views of others, which particular sentiments or sets of sentiments are most germane to political life? Does contemporary government require different kinds of supportive opinions and, therefore, different types of human character than past governments? Some provisional answers to this last question have already been given. Bentham discovered "alarm," the collective and spontaneous thirst for vengeance, as a source of shared belief, but he feared this discovery as much as he feared the morally distorting effects of supernatural religious belief: to act on the basis of either destroys both utility and happiness. Austin and Maine also raise the problem of vengeance and criminal law but are more concerned to show that justice requires the breaking of connections between spontaneous personal feelings and political life. Like religion, these constituent elements of personality must be relegated to the private and subjective realm.

The natural history of opinion, then, points in two directions. One direction is toward new, somewhat ominous forms of spontaneous connections among men; the other is toward a world in which the cultural creations most significant to individual purpose increasingly lose public and political relevance. John Stuart Mill mirrors this dual portrayal of opinion when he examines the interdependence of moral feelings, moral associations, and their justification. All moral associations "are wholly of artificial creation"—

they have a history. In the modern period, this artificiality becomes a source of fragility, for "as intellectual culture goes on" these associations "yield by degrees to the dissolving force of analysis." Are *feelings* of moral duty, Mill asks, equally fragile and equally dissolving in the modern period? His answer is ambivalent. Our moral faculty "if not a part of our nature, is a natural outgrowth from it" because it is grounded in a powerful natural sentiment, "the social feelings of mankind—the desire to be in unity with our fellow creatures."[1] Neither intellectual culture nor a liberal society can destroy the natural sentiment even though the particular growths cultivated in the past are dying and no new ones seem to be growing in their place. Mill's view seems to confirm the persistence of state-of-nature logic in the natural-history assumptions of the utilitarians. In utilitarian theory, natural history ends in a condition resembling a new state of nature—liberal society—wherein men and cultures are stripped of their unique attributes. For Mill, this condition was a personal crisis and a philosophical starting point; for his predecessors, this condition was a necessary and desired goal.

Religious Opinion

Locke's *Reasonableness of Christianity* is an attempt to reconcile the changing religious obligations in biblical history with the dictates of natural reason. Reason is an aid in understanding biblical revelation and the revealed duties are a motive to follow the dictates of reason. Hume's *Natural History of Religion* begins with two very different problems concerning religion: "That concerning its foundation in reason, and that concerning its origin in human nature."[2] The first question is easily answered: religion as a product of reason has never and will never prevail in the world and therefore cannot be the subject of a history. Even though rational religion and its duties can be resolved into duties of evident morality and justice, natural religion lacks features which make it psychologically compelling to most of mankind. Natural religion is powerless in the world of opinion and in history. Popular religion, on the other hand, is supernatural religion whose origins can be traced in human nature. Beneath the caprice, variety, and change so evident in popular religions over time and among different societies, a sequential logic can be discerned. Religious history can be understood not as the plan of God's providence but as the result of "ordinary affections of human life; the anxious concern for happiness, the dread of future misery, the terror of death, the thirst for revenge, the appetite for food and other necessities." Hume's reliance on Hobbes's "seed of religion" argument is obvious: "Agitated by hopes and fears . . . especially the latter, men scrutinize . . . the course of future causes. And in this disordered scene . . . they see the first obscure traces of divinity."[3] Hume, however, postulates a changing pattern of popular beliefs and a natural history to explain the change. Needless to add, this explanation owes nothing to Old Testament covenants or New Testament messiahs.

The earliest religions are polytheistic. In the primitive world of accident and caprice, the terrified mind of the "ignorant multitude . . . deifies every part of the universe and conceives all the conspicuous productions of nature, to be themselves so many real divinities."[4] Belief in these divinities is grounded in stories about real events and transmitted in narrative tradition. The power of polytheism is greater than speculation which derives a single god from logic not only because the former answers to psychological needs but also because adaptive oral history is more accessible to men than is complex logic.

An account of the defeat of popular polytheism and the victory of monotheism is the second stage of Hume's natural history. According to Hume, the cause is to be found in the psychological tensions occasioned by the very nature of polytheistic belief. Early polytheism becomes idolatry. Of the idols worshipped, one among them is usually considered a "peculiar patron, or as the general sovereign of heaven." In propitiating this god, increasingly exaggerated forms of address and worship are invented. As his power is thus increased, "men's fears or distresses become more urgent" so they "invent new strains of adulation." This process continues "till at last they arrive at infinity itself, beyond which there is no further progress."[5]

The coincidence between the rise of monotheism and "the principles of reason and true philosophy" is merely fortuitous. Indeed, such is the "vulgar comprehension" that middle-range deities (saints, angels, etc.) are reintroduced and idolatry again intercedes between coarse man and pure divinity. Thus, religious belief fluctuates between "deity as a pure spirit and perfect intelligence" to a "limited and corporeal one" requiring intermediaries. And, as these lesser deities are worshipped as idols, men's thoughts are again elevated to a conception of an "infinitely perfect deity, and creator and sovereign of the universe." Reason is never victorious. Nature dictates that "the same anxious concern for happiness which begets the idea of these invisible, intelligent powers, allows not mankind to remain long in the first simple conception of them."[6] In the sphere of religious belief, nature will always prevail over reason.

An analogous ambivalence occurs even within nonidolatrous forms of theism. The more men exalt the power and knowledge of God, the more they fear him. The fear which "no secrecy can conceal" is the fear of God's terrible vengeance. Men "must then be careful not to form expressly any sentiment of blame and disapprobation." "Popular monotheism" must remain forever "a species of daemonism":

> The heart secretly detests such measures of cruel and implacable
> vengeance; but the judgment dares not but pronounce them perfect and

adorable. And the additional misery of this inward struggle aggravates all the other terrors, by which these unhappy victims to supersitition are for ever haunted.[7]

The same sequential order of "sacred history" is outlined in Hobbes and Locke: first paganism, then one god of covenant with intermittent idolatry (Old Testament) or saints and angels (Catholicism), and, finally, one god plus unmediated anxiety concerning punishment after death. Moreover, Hume has preserved intact the motivational distinction between political/religious and moral/legal obligation. So clear is Hume on this latter result that he recounts his natural history of morality but concedes that "a superstitious man finds nothing [in those duties], which he has properly performed for the sake of his deity, or which can peculiarly recommend him to the divine favour and protection." Indeed, if a church were found whose only tenets were justice and benevolence, "so inveterate are the people's prejudices, that, for want of some other superstititon, they would make the very attendance on these sermons the essentials of religion, rather than place them in virtue and good morals."[8]

The pessimism which concludes Hume's essay is only partly qualified in his other writings on religion.[9] Reason teaches us that the true purpose of religion is to enforce "motives of morality and justice," but nature compels men to set religion up as a "separate principle" where it inevitably becomes "only a cover to faction and ambition."[10] In Hobbes's words, "worship amongst men is power" and the power of "humane politics" in Hume's analysis cannot be transcended by reason and it will not be redeemed by revelation.

Hume escapes the dilemma which Hobbes poses in the first half of *Leviathan* in two ways. If nature cannot be overruled, its pernicious effects on politics and morality can be checked and channeled. The passions in men can be manipulated by artifice so that irrational motivation might yield rational result. The first way out of the dilemma is provided by the recent history of Great Britain. Hume maintains that the seventeenth-century battles between the "enthusiasm" of independent sects and the "superstition" of the established church resulted largely in the victory of the former. The energy and combative spirit of those under the sway of principles of religious enthusiasm had the unintended effect of weakening the institutional power of religion and thus the power of religious motivation to effect everyday life. Popular religion and true morality are always opposed in principle but fortunately not always in history. Reformed Protestantism is a more effective agent against "priestly power . . . than sound reason and philosophy," while remaining a "friend . . . to civil liberty."[11] Great Britain was especially lucky in this respect.

The political and moral opinions of the "cooled" enthusiast are generally appropriate for a liberal society. To maintain that cooled state requires institutionally weak churches, preferably in competition with each other. Adam Smith's *Wealth of Nations* suggests that a free state should mandate at least two hundred independently organized sects. In this way, religious doctrines might be reduced "to that pure and rational religion . . . such as wise men in all ages of the world wished to see established." Without this precaution—and a few others which come perilously close to cynicism—Smith warns that a free society would be forced to rely more directly on standing armies, fear of coercion, and religious persecution to maintain freedom.[12]

Hume's reliance on British history and Smith's suggested artifice to consolidate that good fortune suggest that the irrational impulses of religion might be contained within the psyche of liberal man. But the contemporary cooled enthusiast still has faith which might heat up again under the proper circumstances. A second path away from the dilemma leads to a consideration of moral sentiments whose origins and expression are not religious at all. These sentiments are more directly the product of natural passions and they too have a natural history. This history, like religious history, consists of opinions and connections among men which do not depend directly upon calculations of utility or flow from material self-interest. Like belief in prophecy, the power of these sentiments is both natural and beyond the power of reason to compel. Moral sentiments, like our belief in causality, "are a species of natural instincts, which no reasoning or process of the thought and understanding is able, either to produce or to prevent."[13]

Moral Opinions: Justice and Benevolence

Public opinion is shaped by more than religion. Hume's psychological explanation of religion owes much to Hobbes; his more novel theory, however, is that public opinion separated from religious belief increasingly holds sway in modern society. This suggestion also rests on a psychological explanation, one which asserts that contemporary man is, in some important respects, more "natural" than before: his sentiments and opinions are more directly the product of instincts, desires, and ordinary activity. This makes it possible to construct (in Smith's phrase) a "theory of moral sentiments" in the modern age without the need to examine the rather varied constructs of theology and popular religious belief. The more universal features of civil society can now be studied in combination with our knowledge of human nature to produce psychic maps of men's sentiments and coherent explanations for their opinions and conduct.

Moral sentiments have different psychological origins from religious beliefs. Religious principles are indirect results of passion and instinct; moral sentiments are direct passions. Because religious beliefs are secondary results, they are less stable and "easily perverted by various accidents and causes." Moral sentiments flow directly from instincts "absolutely universal in all ages and nations." Religious feelings are stimulated reflexively; they appear most strongly when the mind is turned back upon itself. Moral sentiments are most strongly felt in active engagement in the social and material world when we have "little leisure or inclination to think of unknown invisible regions."[14] If uncorrupted by the more distorting elements of religious belief, public opinion will largely reflect the aggregate of moral sentiments.

For Smith and Hume, the scientific understanding of moral sentiments—their cause, content, and power—rests on a knowledge of psychology on one hand and the prevailing material environment on the other. This science is a possibility in the contemporary period because of the weakening power of supernatural religious beliefs over public opinion and because the social and economic world is relatively stable.[15] For these and other reasons, moral sentiments and public opinion appear as increasingly autonomous phenomena in the contemporary world.[16] In this sense, natural history points to a science of morality: in the words of the subtitle to Hume's *Treatise,* it is "an attempt to introduce the experimental method of reasoning into moral subjects." Viewed this way, dominating opinion anchored in the bedrock of civil society and powered by natural instincts is a new phenomenon in history. Weak in the past, submerged and dependent upon religion, public opinion is now on the edge of triumph. The reason for the victory is not to be found in the power of men's reason but rather in the by-products of his passions—in this case, the passions which produced the mechanisms of civil society. In Smith's terms, our survival and happiness have not been "entrusted to the slow and uncertain determinations of our reason" but to "original and immediate instincts." In the contemporary period we can simultaneously construct a natural history and a science of moral sentiments. The knowledge gained can in turn teach us our moral and legal duties. This knowledge of obligation is now placed on a firm empirical footing, for the inquiry "is not concerning a matter of right, if I may say so, but concerning a matter of fact."[17]

The shift in perspective occasioned by this new theory of opinion is remarkable: the primary distinction is between opinions which cluster around the value of justice (men are born to freedom) and feelings which are associated with benevolence (men are born to servitude). The virtues of justice and of benevolence are quite separate in origin, in social effects, and in the views of self which result. To explore their distinct logics is my immediate purpose. My larger purpose is to examine how each can constitute a separate theory of moral duty, political loyalty, and personal identity. It then remains to ask in what respect these separate theories are compatible.

According to both Smith and Hume, justice (Smith terms it "utility") is an artificial virtue. Rules of justice and the belief in their rightness develop over time. Rules of justice come to constitute an immensely complex system of relationships; each rule is connected to all others. Sentiments supportive of justice must be supportive of its systematic nature and relatively indifferent to any particular results. Feelings of obligation to rules of justice require an impersonal view of self and others. And because these feelings are both impersonal and universal, they do not require complex judgments. Indeed, says Smith, the single passion behind our feeling for justice is resentment, "given us by nature for defense, and defense only."[18] Sentiments of justice are purely negative ones, aroused only at the sight of injustice.

Innocence is the highest virtue in the realm of law and we can remain innocent "by sitting still and doing nothing." Opinion which is constructed from sentiments of justice only seeks to punish injustice; innocence is its own reward in a properly constructed society. "In order to enforce the observation of justice," says Smith, "nature has implanted in the human breast that consciousness of ill desert, those terrors of merited punishment which attend upon its violation, as the great safeguards of the association of mankind."[19] Collective resentment itself is a punishment and constitutes the support for governmental punishment. Because resentment flows from our own passionate self-interest, contemporary men are naturally able to discriminate among degrees of injustice and degrees of merited punishment. Victim, spectator, and agent alike recognize that murder and physical suffering are greater evils than forceable loss of goods and view the violation of contractual expectation as a lesser injustice than theft. But in all instances and within each category the standard for measuring actions applies equally to all and can be understood by all. Those standards are laws. The magistrate as the agent of vengeance and punishment represents the real feelings of the community. If all men felt the same way, resentment would connect men to each other and the community to its governors.[20]

Both Smith and Hume assert that a society could subsist powered by the sentiments of justice alone. Security, industry, and happiness can be achieved "without any mutual love or affection; and though no man in it should owe any obligation or be bound in gratitude to any other, it may still be upheld by a mercenary exchange of good offices according to an agreed valuation." The edifice of happiness "raised by the social virtue of justice" is likened by Hume "to the building of a vault where each individual stone would . . . fall to the ground [without] the mutual assistance and combination of its corresponding parts."[21] The passions of resentment and fear of punishment insure this correspondence.

Smith, to a greater degree than Hume, explores the ways in which the sentiment of justice could substitute for religious belief and sanctions. For Smith, public opinion becomes the modern equivalent of an avenging God.

When the lawbreaker confronts this hostile opinion, Smith portrays him as plagued by "demons" and "avenging furies" who allow him "neither quiet nor repose" and drive him "to despair and distraction." He can neither live outside of society and its collective judgment of him nor live happily in it. Remorse or death are the only escapes. Such is the power of resentment that, to those who confess to great crimes, "the horror of blameworthiness seems . . . to conquer dread of blame." By confessing and submitting themselves to the block, they hope "by their death to reconcile themselves at least in their imagination, to the natural sentiments of mankind."[22]

To construct a society solely on the virtue of justice is to construct powerful supports for political power. Bentham's discussion of "alarm" is a direct extension of this theory of sentiments and points to the feeling of unity which vengeance provides. The abyss that Bentham confronts, however, is his calculation that the pains of vengeance would clearly outweigh the utilities of justice. For Bentham, a society based on the happiness of justice alone would require the extirpation of crime, resentment, and punishment. But to do this might sever the only remaining spontaneous bonds among men. In an ironic reversal of Smith's logic, Bentham seems to suggest that society can neither do with nor do without the criminal and the binding moral sentiments he arouses among the innocent. These sentiments arise among men as gradually as the invention of justice and inequality. To contend that justice is the sole end of politics is to suggest that resentment is the only political connection among men that is available as an unambiguous support.

The moral sentiments of justice are clearly tied to self-interest and individual reason. These sentiments explain why men might support a powerful political executive but fail to explain why men, given a choice, might want to create such a society and whether they would sacrifice themselves in its defense against challengers. In light of this problem, Smith and Hume point to an entirely separate category of benevolent moral sentiments which seem to redeem men and society from this grim logic. Sentiments of benevolence are as natural to man as sentiments of justice. The sentiments of benevolence can also order society and politics. If resentment voices the judgment of an avenging god, the sentiment of benevolence echoes the blessings of a merciful one.

In contrast to the impersonal and legal quality of justice, sentiments of benevolence always have in view a particular object or action. Each individual has separate motives for the exercise of benevolence and sees his own motives and actions as good in themselves. The individual happiness resulting from benevolent actions is immediately "complete and entire." The collective happiness resulting from these acts is not a tight-fitting vault of justice but a "wall built by many hands, which still rises by each stone that is heaped upon it, and receives increase proportional to the diligence and care of each workman."[23] The virtue of justice is negative and impersonal; benevolence is positive and personal. Judgments founded in benevolence require great powers of discrimination in judging our own actions and the actions of others. Unlike justice, which rests on coercion and duty, beneficence "is always free; it cannot be extorted by force, and the mere want of it exposes to no punishment."[24] Feelings and actions of benevolence are outside the legal order. No injustice can be caused by private benevolence or its lack, and no "civil interests" are directly threatened. Actor and recipient receive unpurchased pleasures as if grace itself were being showered on the earth. The sympathetic bonds created among men are spontaneous, particular, complex, and architectonic. Each man is centered in a series of concentric circles of recipients and providers of affection. Family, friends, colleagues, and, through the powers of imagination, humanity itself encircles, reflects, and shares the joy of each benevolent act.

Obvious questions intrude at this point: while one can evince many material causes for the rise of sentiments of justice, it would appear that sentiments of benevolence have neither a progressive nor a logical history. Altruism and affection take a bewildering variety of secular and sacred forms and always seem mediated through layers of cultural artifacts which shape their expression; moreover, their specific contents reflect more closely the inherited traditions, tastes, cultures, and ideals of any given society or its subdivisions. While common standards of approbation and disapprobation may be contained in these sentiments, their sources and forms of expression are exceedingly complex. Smith and Hume, however, point to general features of the history of benevolence which in part overcome these difficulties. First, with increasing civilization, benevolent feelings—whatever their content—become more refined in the dual sense of more exact and more exacting. In comparison to men in less civilized societies, contemporary men can more easily enter into the feelings of others and share more complex kinds of feelings. Feelings of unity increase as civilization advances. Second, in a civilized society, sentiments of benevolence are more broadly shared. Contemporary men can enter into the feelings of more men and even extend those feelings to embrace all of mankind.[25]

Political Opinion

Although these explanations do not completely obviate the difficulties, they at least point to ways in which modern sentiments of benevolence might be related to political supports for a liberal regime. The first important relationship is indirect and arises from contrast with standards of justice. Both Smith and Hume start by pointing to and reconciling potential conflicts between the two. Inequalities which result from the enforcement of justice tend to rank-order men into subcommunities. Thus, the more powerful feelings of goodwill and affection flow among those of similar status and condition. The happiness generated in these settings tends to buttress the prevailing system of rank and reputation. Because men's fears of a fall in status are greater than their hopes for a rise, their "love of reputation" prevents them from risking a reshuffling or leveling of social distinctions in the name of a larger benevolent motive.[26] The same system of justice which yields inequality generates the setting within which benevolence is nurtured, a generosity, in Hume's phrase, "required by . . . situation and fortune."[27]

This form of reconciliation is not held applicable in the same degree to all men. Those of "middling rank" most easily see that "the road to virtue and that to fortune . . . are, happily, in most cases very nearly the same." At its extreme limit, these men can see in the strict system of justice a larger system of benevolence. And because their "stations in life . . . can never be great enough to be above the law," the farthest reach of benevolence would not exceed the grasp of justice. These men can usually integrate the conflicting virtues of benevolence and justice so long as their world is bounded by such as themselves.[28]

Hume and Smith suggest here that, among some men at particular times, sentiments of justice and of benevolence almost become one. In this situation, common feelings, shared commitments, and a willingness to risk one's own happiness for others conspire to further the virtues of justice. Middling men who gather in cities multiply opportunities for communication and concerted action. John Millar, a Scottish contemporary, gave direct political expression to this idea when he pointed to the fact that "a great proportion of [such] people are easily roused by every popular discontent, and can unite with no less facility in demanding a redress of grievances." Merchants, artisans, and independent professionals, unlike farmers and landed gentlemen, evidence a concern for private advantage with a sure instinct for group benefit through collective action.[29]

Far above and far below such men, however, are those whose position and reputation in life are not achieved by assiduously practicing the virtues of "prudent, just, firm and temperate conduct."[30] Further problems now intrude. If benevolence is such a powerful sentiment, would not the pity engendered at the sight of the wretchedly poor overcome the sentiments of justice which permit and even enforce that condition? Conversely, when middling men view the very rich and powerful, might not their feelings of envy be augmented by the standards of benevolence to condemn a legal order which protects those whose high stature is unearned? Or, if such men enter into the transutilitarian feelings and values of those far above them, might not the standards of that happiness turn back to condemn the moderate way of life which justice rewards? To extend Hume's metaphor, what prevents the feelings of middling men from taking their "rocks" of benevolence and hurling them at the vault of justice? Less drastically put, under what conditions might men trade the joys which benevolence gives for the happiness which justice produces?

The class problem is discussed on two different levels. Smith forthrightly confronts the tension between resentment and compassion in the example of a criminal about to receive "that just retaliation which the natural indignation of mankind tells them is due to his crimes." The criminal, now "broken and humbled," is transformed by our feelings from "an object of fear" to "an object of pity." Our benevolent sentiments "are disposed to pardon and forgive him." Only the reflection "that mercy to the guilty is cruelty to the innocent" can withstand the compassionate emotions. This reflection is not the rational one that justice is a "necessity to the support of society" but rather that justice is "a more enlarged compassion which [we] feel for mankind."[31] Resentment becomes a higher form of benevolence.

A more general discussion of the class problem concerns the sentiments called forth in the presence of great poverty. Smith and Hume say that pity is the immediate response but that this feeling gives way to contempt rather than to compassion. "The fortunate and proud wonder at the insolence of human wretchedness, that it should dare to present itself before them . . . to disturb the serenity of their happiness." An aesthetic principle operates to prevent a sympathetic response to poverty: "the loathesome aspect of its misery" repels and deflects those sentiments which would condemn the enforcers of the law.[32] The same aesthetic principle also operates to shape men's views of the very rich. The average spectator might be thought incapable of entering into the feelings of the very rich. Like the thief, the rich could be viewed as possessing undeserved objects of value. Does this mean that the rich become objects of envy, resentment, hatred, and, finally, expropriation? Not at all. According to Smith, the spectator does not see the person so much as "the beautiful clothes, equipage, garden [and] house." This beauty gives pleasure. And added to the pleasures derived simply from the hope of sharing in "the generosity and liberality" of the rich, "an agreeable sympathy" is produced by the vicarious pleasures of seeing or imagining the enjoyments which the rich themselves derive from their possessions. Hume says that this factor is the source of that "esteem and approbation" which attaches to men of fortune more powerfully than it does to age, wisdom, or even distinguished family lineage.[33] The benevolent bonds of sympathy are often engendered by aesthetic and imaginative responses. Such is the power of imagination confronting harmony and beauty that the spectator's reason is of small consequence. Reason says that the beautifully arranged accoutrements of the rich cannot protect them from "fear . . . sorrow . . . disease . . . danger . . . and death," but nature's sentiments banish such thoughts.

When we consider the condition of the great in those delusive colours in which the imagination is apt to paint it, it seems to be almost the abstract idea of a perfect and happy state. It is the very state which, in all our waking *dreams* and *idle reveries,* we had sketched out to ourselves as the final *object* of all our desires. We feel, therefore, a peculiar sympathy with the satisfaction of those who are in it. We favour all their inclinations and forward all their wishes. What a pity, we think, that anything should spoil and corrupt so agreeable a situation! *We could even wish them immortal;* and it seems hard to us that death should at last put an end to such perfect enjoyment.[34]

Through imagination and illusion, benevolence is tied directly to political authority. Whether this foundation is more stable and more rationally defensible than supernatural religion is less important than the fact that this kind of foundation is deemed necessary at all in a society ostensibly justified by utility. Although middling men "covet equal laws," they are also swept up into a system of higher pleasures which directly answer to major requirements of political life. These sentiments and pleasures are concretely expressed in literary and aesthetic culture, in institutional tradition, and in custom. However expressed, such sentiments provide for Smith and Hume a naturalistic means of accounting for political allegiance which neither reason nor resentment can supply. Smith's example of the power of resentment to propel a criminal to a voluntary death is not very convincing. His examples of military courage and patriotism are more compelling because they are more common and because the actions rest clearly on transpersonal ends. The young soldier whose own life "is of infinitely more value than the conquest of a kingdom . . . feels that he cannot be too prodigal of his blood, if, by shedding it, he can promote so valuable a purpose." Admiration for heroic action and the capacity to follow historical example have something of the quality of prophetic times. "Our admiration is not so much founded upon the utility, as upon the unexpected . . . the noble, and exalted propriety of such actions."[35]

The much-remarked gap between the penetrating and destructive rationalism in Hume's history of justice and his complacent, confusing, or even "Tory" discussion of the sources of contemporary political obligation have foundation in the contrasting sentiments of justice and benevolence.[36] Less remarked and less obvious are the psychological and political parallels between sympathy and benevolence on the one hand and supernatural religious belief on the other. The theory of benevolent sentiments provides ample room for non-self-interested actions and broad scope for their exercise in society. The capacity for "sympathy"—which makes it possible for "all the affections readily [to] pass from one person to another"—is utilized more to communicate benevolence than resentment. In either case, however, this capacity is the primary reason that men are both able and willing to subscribe to purposes and even ways of life which are quite removed from individual utility and the truths of psychological individualism.

The history and the theory of "benevolent" moral opinions raise as many questions as they answer, especially when viewed against the backdrop of earlier formulations in Hobbes and Locke. Feelings of unity and the capacity for collective action always have a real history as well as a hypothetical or natural one. Like popular religion, sentiments of benevolence seem to rest as much on remembered stories, myths, and unique traditions as they do upon direct and ad hoc psychological mechanisms. For all the stress on universal causes, whether psychological, economic, or demographic, the reliance on benevolence and not vengeance as guarantor of individual liberty raises still more questions. Sympathetic connection and feelings of unity are formal postulates with no guarantee that the ideas actually shared are appropriate to or supportive of a liberal society and politics. The spontaneity and freedom of this class of sentiments constitute both its hallmark and its danger. And like its analogue (one might say precursor) in popular religion, benevolence can invent new stories, establish new traditions, and value new ways of life. Adam Ferguson's other actor—"he who first ranged himself under a leader"—seems to make his reappearance, even though the leader may be a shaper of ideas and intellectual culture rather than a prophet or a commander of hangmen and soldiers.

13

Authority

In the writings of Hobbes and Locke, supernatural religious belief constitutes a higher form of self-interest which yields opinions sustaining political loyalty and social altruism. Psychological truths are not directly denied but are transformed when placed within a context of supernatural revelation and sacred history. Analogously, in their writings on the power of moral sentiments, Smith and Hume alter the meanings of "self" and self-interest. If we receive our identities by "viewing ourselves . . . with the eyes of other people or as other people are likely to view [us],"[1] then the ideas and opinions shared by the spectators must be specified in order to understand the meaning of both personal identity and self-interest. When each person's self-conception is located in public opinion, the content of that opinion becomes a central issue of politics. Even more, public opinion which serves this function operates like religion in that it provides for each individual a plan of life and a set of sanctions to hold him to that plan. Public opinion in the modern period attains an authoritative stature approaching earlier religious belief in providing a final judgment on each man's life story. Two implications follow from this view. First, the ideational content of sympathetic bonds are of critical importance to political loyalty. Whether or not there must be an identity between moral sentiments and the values required to sustain political power is something of an open question. With the exception of positing a loose fit between standards of justice and middle-class virtue, Smith and Hume would say no, for political loyalty rests as well on illusion, deference, and habit. A second implication is that liberal regimes upholding impersonal standards of justice require increasing levels of popular support even as they undermine the political resources of religion, custom, and aristocracy. The natural history of justice points to both conclusions, so that personality becomes more distant from politics while political power becomes more dependent than ever before on moral sentiments and popular opinion. Smith and

Hume emphasized the latter view. The facts of sympathy and benevolence do not contradict the truths of utility and justice, but they do make problematic the obligation and support which justice receives. The assurance that contemporary men are less irrational because they are less superstitious does not and cannot constitute a claim that reason and opinion have become one.

Neither Smith nor Hume thought that man had so changed his nature that opinion, belief, imagination, and even illusion were not crucial for contemporary political authority. Only with Bentham and the utilitarians is a sustained effort made to construct an entire public world on the logic of justice and reason alone. This result requires not only the destruction of the power of supernatural religion but of all sources of public opinion which may bind men on any other basis than contractual exchange. For the Benthamites, sympathy and benevolence are the last outposts to be conquered on the way to a just and rational society. The greatest happiness of the greatest number, says Austin, is only an "index" and should never be a conscious human end. The principle of general utility "imperiously demands that [a man] commonly shall attend to his own rather than to the interests of others; that he shall not habitually neglect that which he knows accurately in order that he may habitually pursue that which he knows imperfectly."[2]

Moral sentiments, as invisible patterns, lie outside the direct control of law, coercion, and calculation. Even the resentment which compels strict justice is a threat to the maximization of happiness. How much more indeterminate and dangerous to public life are those "unseemly parts of the human mind" which harbor both benevolence and self-consciousness. Smith and Hume could show the independence of modern political life from supernatural religion, but many of the indeterminacies and dangers of religion were brought back into politics in the guise of benevolence. Thus, preliberal standards of intellectual culture, of unearned social "place," and of personal and family connection all conspire to buttress a system of political authority which departs widely from the psychological postulates of civil law.[3] Each of these standards has a particular location in time and space—in short, a real history—in which each generation of men participates and from which each generation of men receives part of its identity.

Utilitarian moral theory and utilitarian reform proposals can be viewed as complementary attempts to subordinate benevolence to the demands of justice. Bentham stresses the relationship of benevolence to reputation and strongly suggests that the latter is the motive force of the former. Justice, rank, and reputation must envelop and dominate benevolence. The purpose of the legislator is "to regulate [the] application [of benevolence] according to the principle of utility."[4] The sustained attack on aristocracy and "corruption" is an attempt to rid political life of publicly coerced benevolence. As sternly as Hobbes in *Leviathan*, the reformers admonish the sovereign to give no unmerited rewards and seek to rid parliament, church, and king

of the connecting webs of sinecure, favoritism, patronage, and profit.[5] Benevolence as a political principle is merely another name for corruption; as
such, it constitutes a mild but continuous form of public theft. In Bentham's
words, "the province of reward is the last asylum of arbitrary power."[6] The
justification for unpurchased reward is benevolence. Were corruption banished, the state would become a mirror image of the impersonal god of
nature; all-powerful but, withal, "a creature of reason with which I have
no quarrel."[7]

Sentiments of justice and benevolence—public opinion—must never determine the legislative and executive actions of the utilitarian state. Utility
and reason have nothing to do with vengeance or grace. Carried further—
as John Austin surely carried it—political authority cannot rest firmly on
any form of consent informed merely by "preference." Collective sentiments
and public opinion must be severed finally from the idea of political obligation. In its place must be "the best of moral securities . . . a wide diffusion,
through the mass of the subjects, of the soundest political science." Only
if this form of objective truth becomes opinion can we assume that dislike
of an established government has any relationship to real faults or imperfections.[8] Under these conditions, the "gods" of liberalism would finally
be driven out of politial life and all connection between culture, self-understanding, personality, and political obligation would be broken.

It is not to be wondered that John Austin prefaced this theory of obligation
with a long discussion of Hobbes's *Leviathan*. Austin defends Hobbes's
enterprise against charges of atheism and despotic political principles but
does charge him with two "capitol errors":

1. He inculcates too absolutely the religious obligation to
obedience. . . . 2. He ascribes the origin of sovereignty, and of
independent political society, to a fictitious agreement or covenant.

Despite these faults, *Leviathan*—at least its first half—contains one principle
lesson: "that good and stable government is simply or nearly impossible,
unless the fundamentals of political science be known by the bulk of the
people."[9]

There is irony in this use of *Leviathan* as authority in the nineteenth
century—an irony which Austin's pupil, John Stuart Mill, was to confront
on many levels in the course of his personal and intellectual life. Hobbes
ends the first half of *Leviathan* pretending indifference to whether or not
his true principles of civil philosophy would come to be accepted in the
world. At some time in the future, he says, a good prince might come upon
his book and apply its principles. Only in the second half of *Leviathan* does
Hobbes's vain hope become a real expectation, but the book which creates
that possibility is not *Leviathan* but the Bible. *Leviathan* interprets the
meaning of historic prophecies whose truth and power rest on revelation,

not reason. Such was the confidence afforded by the substitution of natural for sacred history, that John Austin can point to *Leviathan* itself as an authoritative text to legitimize political power exercised in the name of the scientific truths it contains.

Sir Henry Maine unintentionally caught one dimension of this irony in a lecture on why both imperial and national governments must rest on pure power and not on the opinions of either colonial subjects or European citizens.

> But if the Analytical Jurists failed to see a great deal which can only be explained by the help of history, they saw a great deal which even in our day is imperfectly seen by those who, so to speak, let themselves drift with history. Sovereignty and Law, regarded as facts, had only gradually assumed a shape in which they answered to the conception of them formed by Hobbes, Bentham, and Austin but the correspondence really did exist by their time and was tending constantly to become more perfect.[10]

Two centuries separate Hobbes and Austin. The inescapable conclusion is that Hobbes is more prophet than philosopher, while Bentham and Austin drift with history using their reason only to codify more exactly the results foretold in *Leviathan*. Without the writing of *Leviathan* and its transformative effects on later philosophy, those results might not have prevailed. Thus, *Leviathan* has an authoritative status for two entirely separate reasons: as a collection of truths and as a cultural vision of such power that it helps to create the very historical conditions it seeks to prove are universal.

But the *Leviathan* which Austin and Maine saw was only the first half, so its use as authority and as reason by the utilitarians had obvious weaknesses. To suggest that political science could replace opinion and belief as a ground of political obligation and then to assert that only a handful in any society could understand political science is to admit failure before starting. The utilitarian moral sciences not only exclude all trace of sacred history but reject aesthetic, cultural, and benevolent elements as well. As such, these sciences become weapons to attack the lingering effects of popular opinions in politics and law. As Maine and Austin warned, political democracy, with its reliance on popular opinion, is in direct conflict with a rational theory of liberalism.[11]

To put it differently, utilitarian moral science shares with the first half of *Leviathan* the assumption that man is born free. Reason and obligation are restricted to what the mind can reconstruct and consenting individuals can create. Supernatural religion and moral values can only remain sentiments. But man is also born to servitude: the objects and language of religion and benevolence are not the autonomous products of individual will but are historical "givens" flowing in a stream of real time which transcends the life span of individuals and generations. Common opinion and, therefore, individual consciousness are irrevocably connected to this history, yielding values and purposes which necessarily outweigh those of material interest and contractual justice. The reason of man did not write biblical history; prophets only recorded messages received. So, too, in the case of secular culture: the ideas and standards which constitute moral sentiments and sympathetic bonds among men have a real as well as a natural history. This real history is often marked and transmitted by particular books. Their authors are not gods, but their ideas are equally distant from those flowing from personal desires and aversions. Speculative ideas—the province of philosophy—are as integral a part of real history as religious ideas and play as central a role in the shaping and transmission of moral sentiments. Utilitarian reformers did battle against the literary and institutional marks of this autonomous historical world wherever they appeared. In Bentham's words, "It is from the folly not from the wisdom of our ancestors, that we have so much to learn."[12] For the utilitarians, *Leviathan* can only be authority because it contains (despite occasional lapses) some truth which timeless reason can reconstruct, not because it contains prophecies come true in history.

In contrast to the utilitarians, Hume and Smith write more within the larger framework of *Leviathan*. The problems they raise regarding the relationship of opinion to political authority echo those from the second half of *Leviathan* and raise the larger issue of the relationship of personality—and personal history—to political obligation. And like the second half of *Leviathan*, their writings point to a realm of personal and political freedom quite foreign to utilitarianism. This realm of freedom requires a prior servitude, if only in the form of an acknowledgment that our most important personal and political purposes are never of our own making.

John Stuart Mill clearly recognizes these same lacunae in utilitarianism. In his essay "Bentham," he says that every action has three dimensions: "its moral aspect, or that of its right and wrong; its aesthetic aspect, or that of its beauty; its sympathetic aspect, or that of its loveableness." Bentham, he says, only concerns himself with the first, which "addresses itself to our reason and conscience." Left out of his social theory are those aspects of life which address both our imagination and "our human fellow feeling."[13] Correspondingly, Bentham narrows the problem of government to means of checking abuses of political authority. Left unanswered, says Mill, are two prior questions, namely, "to what authority is it *for the good of the people* that they should be subject?" and "how are they to be induced to obey that authority?"[14] Anwers to both must be found elsewhere. In any case, to admit the legitimacy of the two questions is already to reject fundamental tenets of utilitarianism.

It does not occur to Mill to recommend *Leviathan* for either its aesthetic or its sympathetic values. What does occur to Mill is that *Leviathan*, like all works of genius, consists of speculative ideas that have no direct connection to the author's self-interest or to prevailing material conditions but that do have antecedents and sequels—in short, a history. Hobbes is not a religious prophet, but the product of his mind—the first half of *Leviathan*— is itself a form of prophecy because it helps to shape the leading ideas of the present age. The history and destiny of man cannot be embraced entirely by natural history or by the charting of psychological response to material conditions. "The state of the speculative faculties, the character of the propositions assented to by the intellect, essentially determines the moral and political state of the community." Changes in the state of opinion derive "not from the practical life of the period but from the previous state of belief and thought."[15] Ideas are connected to ideas to create the chain of man's history and development. *Leviathan* is an important link. Political authority rests on opinion. Some opinions are created by speculative philosophy which, allied to politics and consciousness, becomes true prophecy.

The image of public power in the last half of *Leviathan* contains this same insight. At the end of the first half, power is simply de facto and rests on the fear of death. The God behind this Leviathan is the god of nature, a product of our reason, so the right to rule rests on the de facto power of the ruler to kill. The God behind the Leviathan in the second half of the book is prophetic and historical: his power rests on covenant. Correspondingly, the right to political rule lies not in the power of our material natures but in our willingness to transcend necessity by means of collective belief and agreement: the power of this ruler is de jure. This same dual logic obtains in Hobbes's notion of liberty: the liberty of the natural man rests on freedom from physical impediments to act out his desires. Power to act is freedom, but the use of that power is thoroughly bounded by material and psychological necessity. The liberty of the faithful in the second half of *Leviathan* is clearly more extensive. They can topple and create kingdoms, withstand the fear of death, and, finally, decide whether or not to construct a regime resting on interest and reason. The source of this power and this freedom is the capacity for collective action and personal risk—the same source which Hume and Smith categorize as benevolent moral sentiments.

Mill's criticism of the utilitarians is also a criticism of the first half of *Leviathan*, but his answer to the utilitarians recalls more directly the writings of Locke, Hume, and Smith, rather than the other half of *Leviathan*. Mill would agree with Hobbes when he says that the sword of justice is powerless without the sanction of the Word, but the Word which rules kingdoms is found in many books and speaks in many voices. The history of ideas is as central and even "sacred" to the political philosophy of John Stuart Mill as is biblical history to Hobbes and Locke.

Through this history of ideas—especially British political ideas from the Puritan Revolution to his own time—Mill seeks to escape from the de facto world constructed by Austin, Bentham, and his own father. His attempted liberation is wide-ranging: religion, culture, economics, law, and politics are all realms in which a higher freedom is possible than that honored by his immediate predecessors. To Mill, their history of nature is the celebration of timeless necessity, while his own history of ideas is proof of man's progress and freedom. Both histories are simultaneously true, but only one can be authoritative if man is to remain free. And insofar as Mill sees his personal history as part of the history of ideas, his life's work resembles Locke's in taking on the character of a calling in which his own freedom and that of mankind are equally at stake.

Part Four

John Stuart Mill

The change which is thus in progress, and to a great extent consummated, is the greatest ever recorded in human affairs. . . . Whoever can meditate upon it, and not see that so great a revolution vitiates all existing rules of government and policy, and renders all practice and all predictions grounded only upon prior experience worthless, is wanting in the very first and most elementary principle of statesmanship in these times.

JOHN STUART MILL, "Civilization"

In the examination . . . of Rights and of the causes of how they are forfeited, the familiar canvasing of the supreme Rights appears to be the dangerousest. For it unloosens the very pins of Government, and so lets all the Frame fall into confusion. . . . [M]y hands tremble to write further of this.

ANTHONY ASCHAM, *Confusions and Revolutions*

Utilitarian moral theory is the philosophical inheritance of John Stuart Mill. Utilitarian social reform is his political inheritance. In one view, both sets of ideas are the refined product of almost two centuries of liberal political theory. Mill's intellectual inheritance is twice blessed: grounded in a rigorously empirical view of human psychology, its central truths had withstood generations of criticism and amendment. In another view, however, Mill's philosophical inheritance is impoverished. The systematic attempts to banish uncertainty and subjectivity in social and political theory had left the liberal tradition of thought radically reduced. Mill's intellectual inheritance is twice cursed. Beginning with a flawed masterpiece, a rich and complex body of thought came to be created. But by Mill's own time, those parts of tradition which always answered to the last half of *Leviathan* were discarded, leaving a diminished and incomplete theory of man, society, and politics.

Both of these views are defensible. The point of raising them is not to preface a choice but rather to indicate in broad terms John Stuart Mill's own attitudes toward his intellectual inheritance and (since the two are blurred) toward himself and his vocation. Mill himself encourages us to view liberalism from both of these perspectives: in his *Autobiography* his intellectual training is portrayed as both rich and impoverished. In *Utilitarianism* the received doctrines of utility are vigorously defended in the realm of law but revised almost beyond recognition for political and moral life. In the *Logic of the Moral Sciences,* the history of ideas is portrayed as driven by the cumulative progress of empirical science in some areas of social inquiry and in other areas as propelled by the inspired visions of prophets. And, if further evidence is required, the essays "Bentham" and "Coleridge" stand as proof that Mill saw his Benthamite inheritance as one-sided and in need of ideas, impulses, and feelings drawn from traditions of thought quite foreign to "the prevailing schools of Liberalism."[1]

The secondary literature on Mill confirms this judgment regarding Mill's inheritance. Whether put in terms of logical contradiction, psychological strains, or intellectual tensions, Mill's thought has often been portrayed as "two-sided."[2] But even when Mill's particular methods, principles, or values are defended as coherent, scholars disagree on the nature of that coherence. Thus, Mill has been portrayed as a spokesman for and against scientific method, as a firm supporter of individual utility and as its subverter, as a democrat and as an elitist.[3] Some of these differing interpretations reflect explicit changes in Mill's positions. But even if one could detect "traces of every wind that blew in the early 19th-century"[4] incorporated somewhere in his writings, significant disagreements persist regarding his position at every stage of his intellectual career.

The most challenging and sophisticated study of Mill in recent times places this variety of tensions in a more comprehensive framework. Mill's thought is said to reflect long-standing tensions between a "behavioral" and a "reflexive" view of man. His immediate inheritance is decidedly behavioral: its "sociology" and its "history" are grounded in material interests and the human responses predicated on those interests. The revisions which Mill made and the intellectual vocation he accepted consist not in rejecting this entire mode of thought but in placing it "in second place," subservient to a view of man who is capable, at his best, of creating himself from his own thoughts. This study concludes that the antagonisms between these two views are built into Mill's methods and teachings, giving to us, in turn, our characteristic views of liberalism in the twentieth century.[5] One of the many strengths of this study consists in tracing the ways Mill's own account of the stages in his "mental history" are directly related to his view of the history of ideas in the modern world—as if the intellectual stages in Mill's own life represent periods in the spiritual history of modern man. The task of reconciling the antagonisms in his own life—to create a completed story—then becomes part of the larger task of integrating this self-understanding with the meanings contained in the larger story of the progress of ideas.

While no such comprehensive treatment of Mill and modern liberalism can be attempted here, the analysis which follows is based on Mill's concern with time and history. The focus is on the valuations Mill places on liberal thought when viewed from the separate perspectives of past, present, and future. While this approach cannot claim to resolve the differences within Mill's own writings and the disputes within the secondary literature, it can place them within two clarifying contexts: Mill's own understanding of history and the history of liberal ideas as outlined in this study.

As preliminary and warrant for this way of understanding Mill's political thought, a brief comparison of his defense of utilitarian morality in *Utilitarianism* and the designation of his own intellectual life in his *Autobiography* is useful. What is remarkable about these works which address such diverse concerns is the similarity of language. In *Utilitarianism*, the central chapter is titled "Of the Ultimate Sanction of the Principle of Utility." In that discussion Mill shows first that utility is logically defensible as a moral principle and next that this principle can become the object of man's highest duty. The "ultimate sanction," however, cannot be found in self-interest, in external coercion, or in truths implanted by education. All of these sources of obligation are artificial, depending upon the interaction of internal desires and the artifice of the external world. Because these moral feelings are "not a part of our nature," they are "susceptible, by a sufficient use of the external sanctions and of the force of early impressions of being cultivated in almost any direction."[6] Stated differently, an obligatory grounding for utilitarianism cannot be discovered within the categories of associational or behavioral psychology—a set of understandings as old as Hobbes and as recent as Bentham.

In Mill's *Autobiography,* a middle section is titled "Mental Crisis." In tracing the cause of his crisis, Mill points to the incompleteness of his early education. The doctrine of utility "appeared inexpungable" (irrefutable) to him, but his teachers had not been able to ally his life and feelings to that doctrine. Trusting to the "old familiar instruments, praise and blame, reward and punishment," they could only produce in him an "artificial and casual" allegiance to utilitarian truths. His mental crisis and the ensuing transformation of his intellectual life had its origins in the failure by his teachers to discover and cultivate a "natural tie . . . essential to the durability" of association of mind and feelings. His training and reason commanded a life dedicated to Benthamite reform, but "an irrepressible self-consciousness distinctly answered, 'No!' "[7]

Mill's personal crisis and his philosophical need to discover a new source of obligation for utility have the same origin: the inherent weakness of both associationist psychology and "geometric" methods of inquiry. The language used to convey the weakness of his education and the weakness of prevailing utilitarian theories of obligation is almost identical. In *Utilitarianism,* Mill speaks of all moral associations in the modern age yielding by degrees "to the dissolving force of analysis," thereby weakening any felt obligation even to those associations based on utility.[8] In his *Autobiography,* Mill recounts the failure of his education "to create . . . feelings in sufficient strength to resist the dissolving influence of analysis." Resolution of his personal crisis lay in the rediscovery of "the permanent sequences in nature; the real connections between Things, not dependent upon our will and feelings; natural laws . . . which . . . in proportion as they are clearly perceived and imaginatively realized, cause our ideas of things which are always joined together in Nature, to cohere more and more closely in our thoughts."[9] Resolution of the crises of obligation lay in a parallel rediscovery of "a natural basis of sentiment for utilitarian morality."

> This firm foundation is that of the social feelings of mankind; the desire to be in unity with our fellow creatures, which is already a powerful principle in human nature, and happily one of those which tend to become stronger, even without express inculcation, from the influences of advancing civilization.[10]

In both of these projected resolutions, Mill suggests that there are direct historical relationships among the "dissolving influence of analysis," the increasing importance of material interests, and the weakening of altruistic feelings and commitments to higher forms of happiness. Recalling his early days as a Benthamite reformer, for example, Mill says that "we did not expect the regeneration of mankind from any direct action on [feelings of] . . . unselfish benevolence and love of justice . . . but from the effect of educated intellect, enlightening the selfish feelings." Now, however, only "those who are themselves impelled by nobler principles of action" should be entrusted with doctrines of self-interest. "I do not believe that any one of the survivors of the Benthamites of that day, now relies mainly upon [educating the selfish feelings] for the general amendment of human conduct."[11]

Mill's *Autobiography* consists of "stages" or distinct periods in his mental life. Mill's understanding of human history is also based on stages consisting of changing relationships between leading ideas, opinions, authoritative institutions, and actions. Mill maintains that some stages of individual lives as well as collective life are marked by a seemingly natural fit or complementarity of religious, moral, and institutional beliefs and authorities. These are "organic" periods. Between these periods are "transitional" ones, caused by deep divisions between those who wield "worldly power" and the ideas and ideals held by groups in the community more fitted for leadership. In these periods, the leading and dynamic ideas are in conflict with the earlier, institutionalized ideas. When a society has "found itself out in a grievous error, and has not yet satisfied itself of the truth,"[12] a transitional state in politics, culture, and intellect begins. In individual lives, the equivalent period is a mental crisis.

This parallel understanding is important to underline because Mill's analysis and revisions of liberal political ideas are shaped within the contours of a transitional period of history. The crisis Mill recounts in his own life merges into his critique of liberalism. The path which Mill takes to resolve his crisis also leads to the revisions he makes in utilitarian doctrine. The ends of both projects are the same: to create an organic life and to insure a new organic age under the auspices of revised liberal values.

One difficulty confronting our understanding of Mill's relationships to the tradition of liberal philosophy is in deciding where Mill locates the intellectual sources of weakness in contemporary utilitarianism. Liberal philosophy and reform movements have their origins in the critique of a prevailing intellectual, moral, and political world. These critical ideas achieve intellectual dominance and major influence on political opinion; but in the process of cultivation, says Mill, these same ideas dissolve away elements in the intellectual culture which had sustained political unity and the capacity for altruistic action. Are the "dissolving effects of analysis" directly attributable to the theories of Bentham, Austin, and James Mill, or are these effects to be found in earlier writings? Is the connection between philosophical truth and natural feeling stronger in the time of Hume or even of Locke than in the contemporary period? How far back does Mill go in tracing the intellectual causes of the present "stagnant" and incomplete state of utilitarian moral sciences? To enter into Mill's understanding of the past is to gain a clearer perspective on Mill's critique of the present. If Mill sought to recapture features of an earlier "organic" state in order to usher in a new one, we must know what "pasts" he had in mind. In this way we are enabled more fully to understand our own intellectual inheritance for, like Mill's, our understanding of the meaning of liberty is critically affected by how we understand and write the history of liberal ideas.

The strategy I follow in the analysis of Mill's philosophy is to examine his interpretation of morality, religion, economics, and politics within the separate contexts of past, present, and future; that is, I follow the pattern of Mill's *Autobiography*. In all of the contexts I examine, a single feature of his thought is foremost: that beliefs, opinions, and ideas—and not material interests—are sovereign in the world, and therefore consciousness rules both motives and actions. His self-understanding, his understanding of history, and, most important, his understanding and critique of liberalism rests on this central assumption. Without actions ruled by consciously shaped ideas, man would have neither a history nor freedom. The story of liberal ideas is contemporary proof of man's freedom, but the truths the story teaches must be grounded in this view of man and history. Both the first half of *Leviathan* and Mill's early education in utilitarianism deny this grounding. Mill's vocation was to supply it, and thereby unwittingly to supply an alternative second half to the *Leviathan*.

14

Liberalism Past

Religion and morals . . . bear, even when they are at their calmest, the traces of having been established by word of command. . . . A religion is first preached by a single person or a small body of persons. A certain number of disciples adopt it enthusiastically and proceed to force their views upon the world by preaching, by persuasion, by the force of sympathy.

JAMES FITZJAMES STEPHEN, *Liberty, Equality, Fraternity* (1873)

Every considerable advance in material civilization has been preceded by an advance in knowledge, and when any great social change has come to pass . . . it has had for its precursor a great change in the opinions and modes of thinking of society. Polytheism, Judaism, Christianity, Protestantism, the critical philosophy of modern Europe, and its positive science—each has been a primary agent in making society what it was at each successive period.

JOHN STUART MILL, *On the Logic of the Moral Sciences* (1843)

Opinions move men and history; ideas must precede opinions; ideas make history. "And thus, the state of the speculative faculties, the character of the propositions assented to by the intellect, essentially determines the moral and political state of the community." Both in his study of Auguste Comte and in his *Logic of the Moral Sciences*, Mill places the "history of opinions, and of the speculative faculty" as the "leading element in the history of mankind."[1] The practical life of men in history, men's interests and passions do not have a primary existence, for passions divide and neutralize both individual men and society; "it is only by a common belief that passions are brought to work together and become a collective force,"[2] sufficient to produce a coherent individual life and to rule society. Moreover, ideas are

169

linked to ideas; each historically powerful mode of thinking is "an emanation not from the practical life of the period, but from the previous state of belief and thought."[3] In an older vocabulary, history is a record of faith—not of works.

Mill need not have relied on Comte to support his theory of "the order of progression in the intellectual convictions of mankind." (Indeed, in revised editions of the *Logic of the Moral Sciences,* he systematically deletes references to Comte.)[4] Mill's periodization of history, at least up to "critical philosophy," is the same one that was used by Hobbes in the beginning and end of *Leviathan,* by Locke in *Reasonableness of Christianity,* and by Hume in *Natural History of Religion.*[5] In his study of Comte, Mill goes to some lengths to defend Protestantism against Comte and in a manner hardly distinguishable from Hume's begrudging praise of seventeenth-century "enthusiasm." In England and Scotland, Calvinist beliefs paved the way for the development of critical philosophy. Protestantism "makes a demand on the intelligence; the mind is expected to be active . . . in the reception of it." The notion of individual responsibility for an active intelligence "is almost wholly a creation of Protestantism."[6]

The whole corpus of Mill's later writings abounds with references to the decisive role played by Calvinist religion in giving efficacy to the truths of utilitarian reform proposals and in raising the levels of morality and justice. But Mill did not think in terms of a static complementarity between Protestantism and critical philosophy. The former is in a single series and must be supplanted by critical philosophy—at least among speculative men and in the realm of ideas, if not among most men and in the realm of opinion. In the past, however, Protestantism was the midwife of critical philosophy, both for the few creators of ideas and for the many recipients of them.

When Mill, later in his life, explores more exactly the relationship between religion and moral philosophy the movement from religion to philosophy appears more problematic. In "Utility of Religion" the movement is seen more as a potentially dangerous break in man's history than as a continual ascent. The break, in turn, creates exactly the problems he outlined earlier in the *Autobiography* and *Utilitarianism,* the problems of whether philosophical ideas that are liberating can ever constitute a way of life and whether those values can become of highest obligation. A central problem of *On Liberty* is also raised here: what might motivate the average man to accept and internalize higher ideas and more refined moral standards in the modern age? A counterpossibility might seem more probable—an "age of disbelief" combining with a complacent, mediocre, and omnipotent mass culture.

Mill's view of the past assumes that religion was the framework within which all important ideas were shaped, criticized, and transformed. Intellectual and moral progress depends on priests and prophets, sacred texts and remembered stories. The distinguishing break between past and present is that Protestantism alone among religions utilized a secular and critical philosophy. Indeed, the postulate for Mill's "Utility of Religion" is exactly this: for the thinking portion of mankind today, critical philosophy has already supplanted even the most intellectually refined forms of Protestantism. More pointedly, Mill assumes that religion, the vehicle or "form" for speculative ideas and opinions in the past, might now serve to keep ideas stagnant. His examination of the "utility" of religion, then, is in two parts—the use of religion in the individual creation of new ideas and its use as a vehicle for common moral opinions.

> The inquiry divided itself into two parts, corresponding to the double aspect of the subject: its social and individual aspect. What does religion do for society, and what for the individual? What amount of benefit to social interests, in the ordinary sense of the phrase, arises from religious belief? And what influence has it in improving and ennobling individual human nature? The first question is interesting to everybody, the latter only to the best.[7]

Mill first considers "social interests." Authority and early education are the reasons for the particular content of the religious belief of any large body of people. Mill calls this influence "involuntary—[the] effect on men's conviction, on their persuasion, on their involuntary sentiments." Among the mass of men, the "general concurrence of mankind, in any matter of opinion, is all powerful." Even though in the past most men might have disobeyed the moral teachings of their particular religions, "they did not doubt" what they were taught. For children, commands of parents are like commands of God; beliefs simply begin and end with acceptance. Even later, when the opinions taught are rejected by the mind, the "hold of these first impressions [is retained] over the feelings." So powerful is this education that "there is *not one natural inclination* which it is not strong enough to coerce and, if needful, to destroy by disuse."[8]

The most crucial feature of religious belief as it affects social interests, however, is its hold on public opinion. This "third power . . . operates directly on . . . actions, whether [men's] involuntary sentiments are carried with it or not." Coercive public opinion consists of specific sanctions for specific actions. When allied to conscience, "it is then of all motives which operate on the bulk of mankind, the most overpowering."[9] For the bulk of men, conscience and public opinion are usually identical. For most men, Mill's lament that moral associations can be "dissolved away" does not appear warranted: authority, education, and opinion are sufficient to sustain men's highest obligations.

In Locke's writings, material interests and speculative beliefs are mediated and merged in a third category called "practical moral opinion." In "Utility of Religion" Mill extends Locke's theory. He takes pains to remind the reader that supernatural beliefs need not be considered uniquely essential for these benign social effects, even though they are the historical form through which secular moral opinion was articulated and communicated. Most men are not saints: the real power of religion and therefore the proof of its utility for the average man is derived primarily from the sanctions of public opinion. Almost as if the ghost of Locke were guiding his pen, Mill states that the moral progress of man has depended on the progress of moral opinion, but that shifts in that opinion have required prior shifts in the "truths" of religion. Religious belief is the weapon to destroy religious belief: new and purer forms of belief destroy the corrupt and historical forms. Changes in supernatural belief undermine older forms of public opinion and usher in new ones. In this process, the role of prophetic individuals is critical. These individuals seek new speculative religious truths, not new moral rules and not new methods of reasoning. But critical philosophy appeared in history as a by-product and tool of this religious quest and the result was progress in moral standards. In contrast to Locke, who buttressed a similar theory with a more prosaic history of private property, contractual exchange, and money, Mill sees a more freely created moral past. This is especially evident when Mill turns from the conformist and reactive many to the creative few. Religion dominates morality, but religion in turn is the product of the few. Mill seems to praise what Hobbes condemned in the opening chapters of *Leviathan:* "all formed religion, is founded at first upon the faith which a multitude hath in some one person, whom they believe not only to be a wise man . . . but also to be a holy man."[10]

Mill shifts ground to consider the utility of religion for select individuals—martyrs, great religious teachers, and philosophers. Here Mill turns from moral ideas to speculative beliefs, from the mass of men who are directed by opinions to a few men who literally transform themselves by transforming the state of ideas, thereby making history.

> Their impulse was a divine enthusiasm—a self-forgetting devotion to an idea; a state of exalted feeling by no means peculiar to religion, which it is the privilege of every great cause to inspire, a phenomenon belonging to the *critical moments of existence*, not to the ordinary play of human motives, and from which *nothing can be inferred* as to the efficacy of the ideas which it sprung from, whether religious or any other, in overcoming *ordinary temptations* and regulating the course of daily life.[11]

Moral opinions are explicable from ordinary understandings of human desire and responses; religious ideas and their sources are not. Religion is not morality. Indeed, morality in the past depended upon religious authority and supernatural sanctions.

When viewed historically, all will admit that "religion may [have been] morally useful without being intellectually sustainable." So too Mill grants that, "considered as a matter of history," religious teachers and teachings made some few men "disinterestedly desire to conform their conduct to the presumed preferences" of supernatural gods "independently . . . of personal hopes and fears." Historically, the very mystery which religion attempts to penetrate "at once awes our feelings and stimulates our imagination." Religion is a "craving to know" whether ideal conceptions "have realities answering to them in some other world than ours." Those with higher sensitivities and intellects and with a "craving for higher things" will always seek and find "obvious satisfaction in religion," as long as they cannot obtain it through "the cultivation of a high conception of what [the world] may be made."[12] Political revolutions "originate in moral revolutions," Mill writes in 1833. "The subversion of established institutions is only one consequence of the previous subversion of established opinions."[13] In the past, religious teachers and their followers have been both the subverters and the sustainers of established opinions. In either case, however, these certain few were "born to servitude" and were thereby freed both from the chains of hopes and fears and the prevailing system of sanctions which preserved their dominance.

Given the audience Mill addresses, he often carries this logic to conclusions about the past which seem almost too tolerant of religion. Thus, in "The Spirit of the Age," he praises the Catholic priesthood for calling on "the moral sentiments of mankind in all their energy, against the inducements of mere physical hopes and fears." Evidently religion could do then what philosophy could not: "Reflecting on these things, I cannot persuade myself to doubt that the ascendency of the Catholic clergy was to be desired, for that day, even by the philosopher."[14] Most men's altruism often is a higher form of selfishness, to be sure, but they believe in the value of morality even as they follow dominant moral opinion only because of its coercive power. The few, however, operate on different principles. In the words of a contemporary of Mill's, the true votary is "a loving, trusting, believing spirit [who] wants neither reward nor punishment. He falls in love with his creed as a man might fall in love with a woman."[15] Mill would hardly disagree. This kind of association cannot be dissolved away by even the most powerful intellectual analysis.

The model of Mill's "Utility of Religion" was Bentham's *An Analysis of the Influence of Natural Religion on the Temporal Happiness of Mankind* (1822). On some levels, the essays are in agreement. Inducements of heaven and hell, says Bentham, provide "no rule of guidance whatever" and produce a vast catalogue of unnecessary pains: "unprofitable suffering, useless privations, undefined terrors, preliminary scruples and subsequent remorse." Mill would not disagree. Bentham's second argument in his brief against all religion is that the institutional by-products of belief are kings and priests with power "sufficient to enslave and lay prostrate the whole community." Mill would give a qualified agreement to this criticism. The last major argument in Bentham's critique is that "the substratum on which all [pernicious] influence is built" is "extra-experiential belief" causing some men to give to other men "a general power of attorney . . . of predicting future events."[16] Mill would agree with the truth of the relationship (collective power and extra-experiential belief), but insist on its necessity and value. Moral rules based on experience alone are insufficient historically, psychologically, and philosophically. In Mill's view of the past, all of the praiseworthy elements in man's history—indeed, the very preconditions for moral progress—rest precisely on what Bentham condemned. Two other factors divide the essays: Mill's praise of religious beliefs for the "gifted few" as the historical agents of progress, and Mill's application of this historical argument even for utilitarian morality.

The utility of religion for morality is closely related to Mill's perception of the history of liberal ideas and the problem of obligation in modern utilitarianism. In "Utility of Religion" Mill concludes that the speculative ideas of the best men have now surpassed the inherent moral limits of supernatural religion. To put it plainly, philosophy must now replace religion as the source and vehicle of the leading ideas of mankind. A major difficulty suggested but not resolved in the essay is projecting the effects of the destruction of religious motives on the moral sentiments of the many. All Mill forcefully stresses is that contemporary moral opinion sanctioned by supernatural belief is now a bar to progress in ideas and moral opinions. Because of this central fact, the question of utility must now be raised, because "arguments for its truth . . . in a great measure [have] ceased to convince." Recent acquisitions of knowledge have been double-edged: positive knowledge has been wholly beneficial but negative knowledge, the knowledge that in certain areas of life "nothing can be known," does not yield "any new fact by which to guide ourselves." Although we have to admit the historical interdependence of religion and progress because men in the past "would not have received either moral or scientific truths unless they had supposed them to be supernaturally imparted," today "we are disabused of our trust."[17] Mill does not necessarily assume that the common man is disabused, only that truth-seekers and the cultivated are (or should be) disabused. In either case, supernatural religious belief can no longer serve as a stimulus for further intellectual and moral progress.

With this image of stagnation in the background, Mill asserts that contemporary intellectual energy is being wasted in trying to "prop up" traditional religion. In the name of progress, truth-seekers in the immediate past—he seems to have Locke in mind here—have suffered "the hardest burden, . . . that of improving religion itself." But this improvement must "be assumed to be complete."[18] A purified Christian belief leaves nothing remaining except natural religion and supernatural reward and punishment. Mill fails to reflect on the incredible coincidence between religion stagnating in this way and the intellectual victory of Benthamite utilitarianism. Although the process of the purification of religion *was* the victory of critical philosophy and moral reform and although the purifiers [Locke?] were also the innovating moral philosophers, these creative links are now a binding chain. No matter how purified, supernatural beliefs tempt a man

> to regard the performance of his duties to others mainly as a means to his own personal salvation; and are one of the most serious obstacles to the great purpose of moral culture, the strengthening of the unselfish and the weakening of the selfish element in our nature.[19]

Even the best men who have stressed the rewards and not the punishment of religion have ended, because of their belief in personal rewards and punishments after death, by corrupting both the minds of the vulgar who fear punishments and the idea of virtue in all men. Mill assumes that the final improvement of religion—the motive of reward in heaven and true moral philosophy on earth—is a condition to be transcended.

This confident judgment expressed at the close of "Utility of Religion" belies the difficulties it raises. Progressive moral opinion must be severed from supernatural religion, says Mill, so that a philosophically respectable "religion of humanity" will become inspiration for man's speculative faculties and moral sympathies. In other writings, however, Mill's analysis remains the same but the judgment is reversed: contemporary life is stagnant because it is now severed from religious belief. Without a powerful "internal ultimate sanction," modern morality teaches only narrow justice and prudential self-interest. As if the historical legacy of higher sentiments were suddenly stripped away, nothing but the passions of nature and the reason of natural religion seems to remain. In these writings Mill speaks, in the language of crisis, of a "transitional period" in which both motives and reasons for preferring right to wrong conduct seem lacking. This is both an intellectual and a political problem. If taken seriously, it ironically twists the history of moral progress sketched in *The Logic of the Moral Sciences* and "Utility of Religion."

As a young Benthamite, Mill could confidently foresee a future in which reason and science would supplant the need for any form of extra-experiential beliefs. Mill soon began to doubt that assumption, but his later writings display a deep ambivalence concerning the status of "critical philosophy." On the one hand, it is a system of ideas which seems to have supplanted religion and thus, part of a series indicating man's moral and intellectual progress. On the other hand, this new system of ideas does not and cannot fulfill the moral, political, and philosophical functions of its religious predecessors. This latter view is surely suggested in Mill's writings, but is found most clearly articulated by James Fitzjames Stephen, a contemporary and sometimes a critic of Mill.[20] Stephen's history of the rise of liberalism is unambiguous: both its leading ideas and historical power can be traced to religious elements. The result for the contemporary period is two distinctly different forms of utilitarianism: one which assumes a future state of punishment and reward and one which does not. The former can justify the use of criminal punishments and provide motives for all citizens to defend the regime of utility. The latter form of utilitarianism is fraught with intellectual and moral contradiction and lacks all possibility of strong political support. The reason for the appearance of this latter theory can be traced to historical circumstances. Because early liberals "were a weak and unpopular party making its way towards power," they introduced notions of toleration as an edge for their religious and political beliefs. Not realizing how closely connected religious liberty is to a simple destructive skepticism, these men undercut the religious power of their moral beliefs, ultimately producing the present crisis. Locke is singled out by Stephen as the crucial figure in this unfortunate transition and Bentham as the product.[21] For Stephen, Hobbes still furnishes the model of a powerful and defensible liberalism.

Mill's historical judgment is much more ambivalent and parallels ambiguous features in his diagnosis of the contemporary crisis. In Mill's essay "Bentham," David Hume is singled out for searing criticism: although Hume is England's "profoundest negative thinker on record," even the shallowest man can become "a first-rate negative philosopher." Further, this "absolute scepticism in speculation . . . agreed very well with the comfortable classes." The rich could be content without a faith, but the poor could not. The practical effect of Hume's ideas was that "religion and morality came into fashion again as the cheap defense of rents and tithes [i.e., church establishments]."[22] In contrast, Bentham's ideas were constructive though narrow, and encouraged selfless political activity among his followers. Mill's judgment of Hume suggests one interpretation of the relationship of liberal philosophy and religion in the past: critical philosophy without reformed Protestantism or without an alternative secular faith yields either political conservatism or the possibility of class conflict and anarchy.

This interpretation receives some corroboration in two related contexts, one in which Mill discusses how intellectual activity is necessary for continued moral improvement and the other in which he discusses the natural allies for a reorganized reform party. The intellectual context is raised in an essay, "Professor Sedgwick's Discourse" (1835). There Mill bewails the decline of English speculative philosophy which "once stood at the head of European philosophy." Now, however, except for mathematics and physical science, not a vestige of a reading and thinking public [is] engaged in the investigation of truth *as* truth, in the prosecution of thought for the sake of thought. Among few except sectarian religionists—*and what they are we all know*—is there any interest in the great problem of man's nature and life: among still fewer is there any curiosity respecting the nature and principles of human society, the history or philosophy of civilization; nor any belief that, from such inquires, a single important practical consequence can follow.[23]

In the past religion and intellectual curiosity were broadly joined, producing progressive practical consequences. To destroy that connection is to destroy a major source of intellectual stimulation and the possibility of the diffusion of ideas among broad sections of the population.

The political context is in an 1839 essay, "Reorganization of the Reform Party." Mill fluctuates between a logic of reason and interest and one of belief and altruism: half the section on "natural radicals" is addressed to those "disqualified" by class bias, legal privilege, and superstition from reaping the merited rewards for their talents. With the help of the cutting edge of philosophy, men's interests must out. However, this part ends on the sober note of fears of conflict between middle-class and laboring-class interests, both groups naturally radical and presumably allied in reform. After discussing this conflict in terms of the troublesome question of suffrage, Mill abruptly turns to religion as another source of "natural radicals," showing that all groups opposed to the present Church of England are also natural allies for reform. In this discussion, he takes pains to demonstrate that "infidels and indifferents" tend to prefer church establishments to the more demanding world of nonconformity, voluntarism, or moderate church reform. In a veiled reference to Hume, Mill says that those "who are not much in earnest about religion, would prefer for the sake of their own ease and quiet, an endowed to an unendowed clergy"[24] and ally with those on the side of privilege and reaction. He makes no overt attempt to relate economic and class interest to religious belief but only suggests that, without religious connections and motives, pure interest-demands by the working class might drive the middle class into the arms of the political and religious conservatives.[25]

A decade later, in his discussion of the English working class in *Principles of Political Economy*, he attributes to dissenting preachers one of the main causes for the immunity of the working class to corrupting "paternalistic" theories for the amelioration of their condition.[26] Indeed, he goes on to suggest that the dissenting tradition of religious instruction tended to immunize the working class against *all* religious appeals for docility and deference while making it "quite consistent with this, that they should feel respect for intellect and knowledge, and defer much to the opinions, on any subject, of those whom they think well acquainted with it."[27]

Reform Protestantism taught the working classes to respect intellectual authority—distinctly a product of the middle classes. The question which increasingly seems to trouble Mill as he reflects on the present is what might happen to men and society instructed only by his immediate and antireligious intellectual ancestors. Would they listen? What is there to teach? In a culture permeated with the logic of self-interest, could the average man be motivated to act in a non-self-interested way? This constitutes the starting point for Mill's analysis of the present-day political and moral crisis. The problem of loyalty to reason alone was also the beginning of Mill's personal crisis.

In his essay *On Liberty* Mill speaks of the contemporary period as one of "intellectual pacification" wherein a small island of dissidents exist in a sea of complacency. Peace reigns on the island and the sea never threatens to swamp it because men of intellect speak frankly only among themselves. When "active and inquiring intellects" now address the public, they "fit as much as they can of their own conclusions to premises which they have internally renounced." Contemporary intellects lack "moral courage," becoming thereby "mere conformers to commonplace." Perhaps Mill assumes that the speakers no longer believe in religious obligation but that their audiences do. This would explain why he calls modern intellectuals "time-servers for truth, whose arguments on all great subjects are meant for their hearers and not those which have convinced themselves."[28] Two other explanations suggest themselves: intellectuals do not really fear the wrath of a conformist public outraged that moral doctrine is severed from religion. Rather, modern intellectuals might fear the political consequences of preaching a doctrine of self-interest annexed to a theory of obligation which only men of ideas could understand and love.

A second explanation, and one which will be examined below, is that the failure of contemporary intellectual courage is a necessary accompaniment to secular ideas. Blame is not to be placed exclusively on the conformist masses, with their capacity for moral coercion, but shared with the inherent weakness of liberal philosophy divorced from religion. Only in these circumstances is toleration of ideas a crucial requirement for their efficacy, for modern ideas—at least those urging higher morality—do not have enough power to reign in the face of significant opposition.

However the problem of modern men of ideas is explained, Mill seeks ways to deepen their resources for courage and efficacy by recourse to the past. An antidote to Bentham is Coleridge, who can teach contemporary men of ideas "truths which Tories have forgotten, and which the prevailing schools of Liberalism never knew." Mill's use of Coleridge—"his greatest object was to bring into harmony Religion and Philosophy"—corroborates an interpretation of the past which assumes that "there is little prospect at present that philosophy will take the place of religion, or that any philosophy will be generally received in this country, unless supposed . . . to be consistent with . . . Christianity."[29]

Mill's critique of utilitarianism is double-edged and seemingly inconsistent. One part is based on an attempt to recapture the past, reintegrating religious and philosophical elements into a theory of politics broad enough to encompass felt loyalty. Another part rests on an attempt to transcend this interdependence by discovering in history—the history of ideas—sources for a new kind of religion for the future. To see only one or the other source of his critique is to miss what Mill plainly saw, namely, a present state of moral philosophy which is intellectually and politically fragile.

15

Liberalism Present

The progress of inquiry has brought to light the insufficiency of the ancient doctrines; but those who have made the investigation of social truths their occupation, have not yet sanctioned any new body of doctrine with their unanimous, or nearly unanimous consent. . . . [R]eason . . . will teach most men that they must in the last resort, fall back upon the authority of still more cultivated minds, as the ultimate sanction of the convictions of their reason itself.

JOHN STUART MILL, "The Spirit of the Age"

To Mill, the most cultivated minds of the immediate past were his own teachers: primarily his father, Bentham, and John Austin. One understanding of their teachings is historical. Mill sees utilitarianism as a product of earlier Protestantism and critical philosophy. Another understanding of their teachings is philosophical; Mill sees utilitarianism as a series of sciences which can be examined analytically. In Mill's analysis of the present state of moral philosophy, historical understanding tends always to inform the philosophical. Without this location in the history of ideas, much of his critique of utilitarianism and the suggested amendments to its foundations is inexplicable. Mill's sense of the present is defined by the present state of speculative ideas—utilitarianism without religion.[1] Symbolic of his analysis of the present weakness and even the danger of liberal ideas is Mill's posthumously published essay, *Nature*. Mill's analysis of the past had concluded that heavens and hells were useful in the past but not in the present and future. His analysis of the present, however, condemns the attempt to substitute a purely empirical world view based on nature, natural sentiments, and associational psychology. Nature cannot have a primary moral significance for man because nature does not have a history which can provide meaning for men. Were we to create a world hewn to the contours of nature, both within us and without, boundless cruelty would result.

> Nature impales men, breaks them as if on the wheel, casts them to be devoured by wild beasts, burns them to death, crushes them with stones like the first Christian martyr, starves them with hunger, freezes them with cold . . . has hundreds of other hideous deaths in reserve.[2]

Without the creation of a distinctly human history, "the ways of Providence as manifested in Nature" exhibit neither justice nor benevolence. Indeed, Mill concludes that the awe men exhibit toward nature has nothing whatsoever to do with moral feelings. To follow nature is to replicate the terrors of nature. Such is its power, cruelty, and caprice that it operates outside the measure of human pains and pleasures from which men derive moral good and evil. More pointedly, natural sentiments can blot out the very reasons for establishing justice. Nature's most vivid expression of power is in "inflicting evil," and our response is often "a feeling which though in its higher degrees closely [borders] on pain" we often seem to prefer to ordinary pleasures.[3]

Nature can be read as an extension of Bentham's *Theory of Legislation* informed by Hume and Smith. Sentiments of justice call for vengeance. Nature can speak to man as well as through man. Unless checked by ideas and beliefs, men often prefer vengeance to utility and reason. In the past, sentiments of justice were mediated through custom, religion, habit, and natural feelings of benevolence. As the regime of utility grows increasingly to dominate the ends of political life, however, previous controls are weakened, leaving nature and natural feelings to dominate. The prominence of natural sentiments in the present day are the result of the loss of past artifices and beliefs which blunted or at least channeled the expression of vengeance. Past cultures bound men together as persons with shared commitments and not as bundles of rights and duties with similar natural desires and aversions. In political terms a religion of nature is only a religion of necessity, vengeance, punishment, and death. In this respect, Mill's judgment exactly parallels Hobbes's conclusion regarding "the Kingdom of God by Nature."

For Mill the problem of nature is a contemporary one, peculiar to a moral philosophy built on the rejection of supernatural beliefs. Our duty now is not to follow nature but to "amend it . . . in respect to [our] own nature as in respect to the nature of all other things . . . not so much [by] subduing the original nature as merging it into . . . the most elevated sentiments of which humanity is capable, [to become] a second nature." When this is done, the awesome and painful terrors which men prefer to pleasures born of contracts, calculation, and intellect "may some day be compelled to an unconditional surrender."[4]

Mill's call for a victory over nature might be viewed as superfluous in light of the achievements of his own teachers. Bentham's proposals in *Theory of Legislation* to cut down on alarm, to make the state "a creature of reason," and to make all punishment external to the body would seem victory enough. And surely Austin's complex system of jurisprudence as a codified system of interests symbolizes a victory of sorts over natural man. Mill's essay, in contrast, suggests an incredible irony in these achievements. The utilitarian victory over nature is also the victory *of* nature: the prior victory destroyed or threatened to destroy the political foundations of civil society—the beliefs, opinions, and feelings binding men to each other. The single artifact of justice remains to conceal the spontaneous power of feeling which Bentham called alarm. Now that religion has lost its power, a "second nature" for man must be created, for without it only mass imprisonment or fear of the hangman might remain.

The truths which constituted Mill's intellectual inheritance are not denied by Mill but put "in second place," subordinate to authoritative ideas which are not derivable from experience and interests. As a critic of the older utilitarianism, then, Mill consistently attests to its truths and denigrates their importance. Mill's writings on Austin's jurisprudence and Bentham's *Theory of Legislation* and his discussion of justice in *Utilitarianism* all point to this understanding of older utilitarianism: it was an empirical theory of law and morality based on the limited truths of an empirical psychology. In his review of Austin's *Lectures on Jurisprudence*, he casually observes that the considerable talents Austin displays there "would have fitted him as well for the problem of inductive psychology." His criticism of the *Lectures* follows from this observation. Mill unerringly singles out the fallacy of attempts to define all legal duties as counterparts of individual rights. Austin would call every legal duty the expression of someone else's right; Mill counters with the spectre of absolute duties and public power: "It is [the jailer's] duty to keep [prisoners] in confinement, perhaps in bodily fetters." Is this a prisoner's *right*? "Again, it is the duty of the hangman to inflict capital punishment upon all persons lawfully delivered to him for that purpose; but would the culprit himself be spoken of as having a right to be hanged?"[5] Empirical psychology as the basis of a positive science of law cannot reach to embrace the most important questions of jurisprudence and legal philosophy.

To one who finished Bentham's *Theory of Legislation* as "a different being," one who "wound up with what was . . . a most impressive picture of human life as it would be made by such opinions and such laws as were recommended in the treatise,"[6] Mill's later criticism of Austin demonstrates the distance he had traveled. Jailers and hangmen are not simply the clever counterexamples of a book reviewer. Behind the jailer and hangman stand the political power and collective beliefs of society, whether "animal" sentiments or specific ideals. Mill quickly grasps, therefore, the intimate connections between analytic jurisprudence, physical punishment, and *Leviathan*. Taking note of Austin's praise of Hobbes, Mill remarks that Austin "devotes to Hobbes perhaps the noblest vindication which that great but unpopular thinker has ever received."[7]

Jailers, hangmen, Hobbes: what have these to do with speculative faculties and opinions which supposedly rule the world and make history? What ideas or opinions have "made" the world pictured by Austin? If purified religion is nothing but natural religion plus heaven and hell, does it necessarily result in the harsh world of Austin's jurisprudence, an illegitimate hangman, a Leviathan in a world without grace? When Mill addresses the philosophical present, purified religion, nature as pure power, and politics as hangman tend to become one. Mill's ambivalence is not in his analysis but in how he views the results. This double effect is most evident in Mill's discussion of justice in his essay *Utilitarianism*.

In *Utilitarianism* Mill begins his discussion of justice by raising the problem of nature: the "feeling of justice might be a peculiar instinct," an "animal desire to repel or retaliate a hurt or damage to oneself or to those with whom one sympathizes." As if this combination of Bentham and Hume were insufficient, he adds the language of Smith: the feeling of justice is a "secret hankering" for retribution, a "natural feeling of retaliation or vengeance." Having said all this, he subtly damns such feelings even as he praises their efficacy. As men progress morally, the resulting social equality makes these feelings become more inclusive and thus more powerful "by the human capacity of enlarged sympathy and the human conception of intelligent self-interest."[8]

No less than Bentham, Mill holds that for contemporary men security of expectation is "the very groundwork of our existence."

> All other earthly benefits are needed by one person [but] not needed
> by another; and many of them can, if necessary, be cheerfully
> foregone . . .; but [on security] we depend for all our immunity from
> evil, and for the whole value of all and every good, beyond the passing
> moment; since nothing but the gratification of the instant could be of
> any worth to us, if we could be deprived of everything the next instant
> by whoever was momentarily stronger than ourselves.[9]

Law and the natural sentiments for justice do in fact hold the "present" together. Life would soon become nasty, brutish, and short without these feelings which back the hangman who backs the law. The interest of security is, "to everyone's feelings, the most vital of all interests."[10]

As if writing a gloss on the first half of *Leviathan*, Mill holds that law serves the deepest and most important of our self-interests. Natural sentiments attest to the importance of these interests and point to reasons why Mill can speak of "fellow-feeling" as the natural basis of the principle of utility, the "internal ultimate sanction." But this conclusion is not the last word. Natural sentiments, for Mill, can never be expressed directly but must be mediated and shaped by consciousness—a consciousness consisting of specific political, moral, and religious ideals. As a young Benthamite reformer, Mill thought that "enlightening the selfish feelings" was an adequate form of consciousness. After his mental crisis, Mill concludes that articulating natural passions is not a worthy form of consciousness and perhaps not even an authentic form of historical consciousness at all. To view utilitarianism from this historical perspective, then, results in a series of revisions which lift the utilitarian notion of justice from its empirical and scientific groundings and place it on the rising spiral of the history of man's spirit.

Logical analysis can trace utilitarian theories of justice to natural feelings, but history records the variety of ways in which law is justified and supported. Recent history has been dominated by the ideas of Mill's utilitarian teachers, but their writings are part of a larger history of ideas which have progressively refined the idea of justice.[11] The culmination in utilitarianism, however, is both novel and dangerous. Mill recognizes that these theories now rest on vengeance and selfishness—the victory of "animal instincts" over higher obligations. The nature in us "impales men . . . burns them to death, crushes them with stones"—a rather high price to pay for "enlarged sympathy" and the growth of "intelligent self-interest." Having peered over that precipice, Mill turns around and assures us that this natural sentiment for justice, "in itself, has nothing moral in it; what is moral is the exclusive subordination of it to the social sympathies, so as to wait on and obey their call." Our "animal instincts" only supply this "enlarged sympathy" with "its peculiar impressiveness and energy of self-assertion."[12] The central elements in moral progress are the shared ideals to which our instincts are subordinate. The novelty and danger in the present period is that the increased collective power of these instincts does not yet manifest agreement over "any new body of doctrine" which might direct and control them.[13]

Mill's discussion of the problem of natural instincts lying below the surface of justice seems to belie his larger theory of history which rests on the assertion that contemporary human feelings are far removed from nature. He states in his study of Comte, for example: "as society proceeds in its development, its phenomena are determined, more and more, not by the simple tendencies of universal human nature, but by the accumulated influence of past generations over the present." Human beings are not "abstract or universal but historical human beings, already shaped, and made what they are, by human society."[14] This same notion of artificiality and historicity is replicated in Mill's discussion of individual character which begins his *Logic of the Moral Sciences*: "It is only when our purposes have become independent of the [natural] feelings of pain or pleasure from which they originally took their rise that we are said to have a confirmed character."[15]

Mill's picture of the present, in contrast, suggests a state of nature just beneath the veneer of contemporary culture. Unlike previous eras of history in which new religious doctrines superseded old religious doctrines in the world of speculative ideas and dominant opinions, the present period is one of "intellectual anarchy" in which no contending ideas seem to represent a new and vital faith. Critical philosophy represents timelessness and nature against history and spirit; the logic of analysis threatens to dissolve the culture of history. In short, Mill's recounting of the victory of "critical philosophy" is pitched in negative terms, placing the positive or scientific accomplishments of utilitarian reform on a most precarious footing.

The Other World of Mill's Liberalism

In recounting the history of his own ideas, Mill tells us his mature views were grounded in history and not in analysis. He became less dogmatic concerning choices of political institutions and less democratic regarding issues of suffrage and majority rule. These changes resulted, he says, because he increasingly saw questions of politics in the context of historical culture and moral progress, rather than in the analytical mode of passion and material interests.[16] This altered view of politics parallels an altered view of his own role as reformer and intellectual: he and other "survivors" of an earlier Benthamism no longer seek to enlighten the self-interest of their contemporaries. Reform in the present and future must be achieved by altering directly contemporary political and moral consciousness. This is a task which can only be attempted from within the tradition of ideas and therefore in servitude to the past. Mill's critique of utilitarianism propels him to the other world of liberalism, a world for which his early training had not prepared him but which was a barely suppressed part of his inheritance.

Higher forms of consciousness can only be created by exceptional men and require the help of a dedicated few in order to insure their transformation into public opinion. But this program is fraught with difficulty. Unlike in the past, the power of supernatural religion is an obstacle, not an ally. The help of political coercion is forsworn from the start. Universities, while a potential aid, are hopelessly tied to regressive values and conservative interests. The burden of moral progress rests on the individual men who choose to take it up. The forum is public opinion. Modern intellectuals and reformers are uniquely equipped for the task, if they can be convinced to undertake it.

Mill sees himself as the one who must point the way. His personal history teaches him, however, that this new political/moral vocation is confronted by two contemporary dangers: stagnation and fragility. His search for an "internal ultimate sanction" is in answer to both dangers. Mill's vocation—and one which he urges others to follow—serves both personal and world-historical ends. Older utilitarianism set the stage for Mill's own crisis and transformation and symbolizes the crisis of authority in the contemporary age. The dimensions of his personal crisis and "transitional period" cannot be explored here, but the language he uses to convey this stage in his own life is dominated by the two images of stagnation and fragility. Mill's autobiography records how he escaped entrapment in a way of life he was so carefully trained to lead; the process of transition, however, was most dangerous, for he ran the risk of renouncing all past certainties and ushering in personal chaos. Endless stagnation or sudden and unpredictable revolution are also equal possibilities for European civilization.

In larger perspective, these two images—stagnation and fragility—have always been an integral part of the structure of liberal political philosophy. Mill's characterization of the present as on the edge of endless stagnation or of anarchy reflects this dual structure of liberalism in utilitarianism. The assumption that men are born to freedom yields the hope and the promise of eternal order in the first half of *Leviathan*. The assumption that men are born to servitude raises the ever-present prospect of apocalyptic change in the second half. Hobbes first promises "civil eternity," an endless collective life of desire after desire within a structure of impersonal order, a life achievable only if the logic of his civil philosophy were instituted. True civil philosophy, however, is only a moment in prophetic history, its truths existing only on the sufferance of a prophetic history.

Civil eternity—"as long as men are men," says Hobbes—is only the more extreme expression of changelessness in images of civil society throughout the history of liberalism. As the product of learning in a state of nature, civil society stands timelessly above the commitments and chaos of historical culture. As an ever-expanding set of predictable behaviors in "natural history," civil society is an engine destroying both prophetic gods and the external uncertainty giving rise to them. As expressed in a system of civil law, the image appears as a certain standard which destroys arbitrary political authority by insuring the emergence of impersonal political power, a power straddling a legal system bound together by passion, logic, and science. As a system of morals and law, civil society expresses the limits within which men's imagination can safely rise to encompass feelings of benevolence and sympathy. The power of this image is such that in Bentham it seems finally to encompass and define law, power, science, religion, and even self-consciousness. Yet civil society, like Bentham's security of expectations, is "assailed on every side—ever threatened, never tranquil, it exists in the midst of alarms."[17] From the earliest discussion of the "seed of religion," which could always sprout new loyalties through the latest recognition of the seething power of popular vengeance and alarm, the elements preserving and protecting civil society contain the very features which might devalue or destroy it. The "gods" of liberalism—the mysteries of body, crime and punishment, personal identity, political obligation, and, finally, sacred history and political power—are all marshalled outside the gates of civil society.

The composition and presumed need for armies outside the gates constitute the reason for most of the "history" within English liberal philosophy. The attempts to work out relationships between these armies and civil society within the gates seem to give the appearance of continuous change even while the central tenets of the philosophy hardly change at all. And further, no matter which armies are posted at the gates, there is always the fear that one or more of them might turn around and destroy the society within. Hobbes's concern that religion and religious imagination would derail rational trains of thought; Bentham's concern about alarm and consequent demands for physical punishment; Austin's concern that a simple mistake in the arrangement of law would logically make every voluntary act a coerced one—all these indicate that political allegiance and legal obligation are two distinct but mutually dependent levels of life, as different from each other as the changing drama of sacred history from a timeless state of nature. As John Stuart Mill puts it in *Utilitarianism,* without the aid of natural feelings and nonrational sentiments, "moral associations which are wholly of artificial creation . . . [would] yield by degrees to the dissolving force of analysis; and . . . the feeling of duty . . . would appear equally arbitrary."[18] A contemporary utilitarian, James Fitzjames Stephen, expresses an analogous but more Hobbesian doubt framed in terms of sacred history, which culminates in the end of the world: until that time, "knowledge, science, and power are, after all, little more than shadows in a troubled dream—a dream which will soon pass away from each of us, if it does not pass away at once from all." Only then would "the world, whether more comfortable or not, . . . at least see and know itself as it is, and . . . the real gist and bearing of all the work, good and evil . . . at least be made plain."[19]

Psychological counterparts to these potentially mutinous guardians are also to be found throughout the writings in this tradition. The counterparts, too, are both necessary and dangerous: necessary to sustain coherent historical personalities, but capable of devaluing the unceasing ends of desire and aversion. A personality constructed from the knowledge supplied by an empiricist psychology is not strong enough to sustain a coherent way of life or a just political order. Religious faith, moral sentiments, instinctual fellow feeling, illusion, or simply habit are required to give reality and power to such fictional and feckless men. Mill only stated forthrightly an assumption shared at some point by all of the writers in the liberal tradition when confronting men in history: "The distinction between will and desire . . . is an authentic and highly important psychological fact." However much the will can be determined by natural desires, belief, habit, and authority make the will independent of desire, "so much so that in the case of a habitual purpose, instead of willing the thing because we desire it, we often desire it only because we will it."[20] Epistemological truth is contingent truth: natural desire is ultimately dependent upon historical will. Without the cultivation of higher ideas to inform the will, contemporary men will lapse into endless mediocrity and conformity. But with the cultivation of false ideas, the legal and moral order will be destroyed and chaos will follow.

Those elements in the tradition located in timelessness and original freedom constitute the core of Mill's intellectual inheritance. It finally appears to Mill that civil society faces, rather than armies at the gate, simply a blank wall. It is as if the entire tradition of liberal moral philosophy has been cramped within the confines of Hobbes's *Leviathan*, Parts I and II. The wall is both awesomely strong and laughably weak; it is impregnable so long as no one touches it. The corresponding wall within each man is equally vulnerable. A simple act of imagination or, in Mill's case, "an irrepressible self-consciousness" suffices to destroy it. James Fitzjames Stephen concludes that systems of morality and law are simply coercive "dams and floodgates which regulate the stream of life" but provide no knowledge of the content and character of the stream. Analogously, moral and legal systems and their appropriate sciences are quite inappropriate as standards for serious judgments of persons, cultures, or nations. "If it were put to a vote, no one would sacrifice the history of his country for the sake of a history of unbroken inoffensiveness." Thus, "both greatness and crime are each in some way traceable to causes which lie deeper than the distinction between right and wrong." To be manipulated into innocence by dams, floodgates, and everyday self-interest might mean innocence, but "innocent men and nations are not the greatest, and therefore not the best or most admirable."[21] As Mill puts it in *On Liberty*, "One whose desires and impulses are not his own, has no character."[22] When Mill considers the causes of revolutions in politics, morality, philosophy, and religion, he points directly to impulses outside of, and inherently subversive of, "the ordinary play of human motives." These impulses are a "divine enthusiasm" from which "nothing can be inferred concerning moral standards of good and evil."[23]

The crisis which Mill sees in the state of the English moral sciences of his day is closely related to his recognition of the radical split within the psychological, legal, and political theories of English liberalism. The victory of the analytic and epistemological half of that theory—the necessities of civil society, jurisprudence, and political economy—might be a hollow one. One result is to produce both moral and intellectual "stagnation"; men and civilization are frozen into an endless repetition of predictably mediocre responses. A second and more distant result is the destruction or weakening of the beliefs and opinions necessary to maintain even that system. Men and institutions become vulnerable to destructive alternatives in the form of more compelling systems of belief directly opposed to utilitarian moral and legal standards.

John Stuart Mill has dominated the images and vocabulary of contemporary liberalism and has provided much of the grist for the mills of liberal philosophy in academia. In these circumstances, an analysis of his writings on future liberalism that views them as the last gasps of tradition rather than as a breath of fresh air might appear churlish. If one believes, however, that every revolutionary is, in the words of Professor Quentin Skinner, "obliged to march backward into battle,"[24] Mill at his most untraditional can be seen as drawing on earlier tradition. But the conclusion to be reached here is intended to be stronger than that. In seeking to transcend his immediate utilitarian inheritance, Mill has nowhere to go but back to Hume and moral sentiments and finally even back to Locke: not to the Locke of the *Essay on Human Understanding* so much as to the Locke of the *Reasonableness of Christianity.* The truths of utilitarianism, to quote Locke, did not constitute a morality "whereof the world could be convinced." For Mill, as for Locke, contemporary moral philosophy "seemed to have spent its strength." Locke's philosophical task was to destroy utterly the false religious doctrine which caused "the slow progress and little advance" of morality. Lest this destruction undermine all authority, Locke also took upon himself the task of urging new obligations by showing why "it was not without need that [Christ] was sent into the world."[25] Locke's appeal to men's highest obligations is both revolutionary and restorative. The ideas which constitute Locke's appeal are not the constructs of timeless reason but of historically revealed authority: man is born to servitude. As Mill put it in *Spirit of the Age,* reason only teaches "most men that they must in the last resort, fall back upon the authority of still more cultivated minds, as the ultimate sanction of the convictions of their reason itself."

It falls to the lot of some few men to preserve, reinterpret, and perhaps transmit new authoritative ideas in history. Lest this analogy seem unfairly weighted to stress a Calvinist Locke rather than a liberal Mill, it is worth noting the image Mill uses to describe the prophetic role of these men: "Eminent men do not merely see the coming light from the hilltop; they mount the hill-top and evoke it; and if no one had ever ascended thither, the light, in many cases, might never have risen upon the plain at all."[26] Liberal philosophy as articulated by Hobbes and Locke and the liberating philosophy which Mill called for in the future are more intimately related to each other than to the utilitarian moral sciences of Mill's own day.

The examination of Mill's intellectual and political program for the future both reveals this connection and places a dual burden upon those today who would draw upon his teachings. Like Mill, we are the heirs, refiners, and transmitters of truths which each generation can criticize and re-create by its own "timeless" reason. More important, if we would be true to Mill's entire range of political and moral concerns, we must also see ourselves as keepers of a historic tradition of authoritative ends which, if ever lost to memory, could never be recalled by reason. This latter task requires different disciplines and training than the former—as different, in fact, as those required by Locke's *Essay Concerning Human Understanding* on the one hand and his *Reasonableness of Christianity* on the other.

Mill held that authoritative ends shaped by particular men of inspiration and genius can best be understood and remembered by an integrative history of ideas and through the symbols and rituals by which culture in general is maintained and transmitted. He and his most creative contemporaries and followers were quite aware of this fact. It is not an accident that much of their "philosophy" consists of commentary on the work of their predecessors.[27] This task differs markedly from the enterprise of analytic philosophy and the specialized social sciences. Political life requires authoritative ends and science; an appropriate political education must include both forms of understanding as well. Mill saw his own intellectual vocation as an integration of these two sides of the liberal tradition, but that self-perception did not ease the difficulty which he confronted. To begin with the assumption that reason and interest—the foundations of analytic philosophy and the social sciences, respectively—are the product of a history of authoritative ideas, places both intellectual enterprises together in second place, both in time and in value. The primary fact is that man is by nature a "progressive being" able to create and re-create himself through time.

Another way of putting this difference is to say that the intellectual as "priest," with his stories and rituals, has always held more effective sway over moral and political opinion than has the intellectual as philosopher-scientist, with his postulates and proofs. Does this fact mean that future truth will also depend upon the standards and judgments of men who preserve and tell stories? If supernatural religion finally becomes exhausted, might the role of "priest" and "philosopher" become one? That possibility was surely not lost on Mill. He saved his most searing criticisms for those negative and narrow intellects who insisted upon staying within the bounds of certainty while individual action and collective progress called for ideas outside those bounds.

Mill knew that to step outside the clearing created by the liberal moral sciences, without the help of the traditional gods and stories of liberalism, is a most dangerous venture. For Locke, the biblical messages and promises constituted an unreliable map but one which at least pictured the end of the journey. The stories which Mill might use include many of Locke's but also many new ones whose warrant rests entirely on men and not on gods. And if we are required to choose among them, which ones shall they be? A related problem arises. Locke held that the biblical story "suit[s] the lowest capacities of reasonable creatures," even as it "reaches and satisfies, nay, enlightens the highest." Mill's stories must include the story of philosophy itself, so many of the chapters are inaccessible to the mass of men. Those who follow Mill's guideposts cannot have the confidence that they are leading a collective journey at all. Locke's map, faint and ambiguous as it is, contains guideposts familiar to all and comes with "the credit and authority [of Christ] and his apostles . . . by the miracles they did." Moreover, because the stories had this origin, those who follow their teachings can be assured that their guides are free of "any conceits or self-interest" and that the paths bear no "foot-steps of pride or vanity, no touch of ostentation or ambition."[28] Those who claim to be the authoritative readers of Mill's map into the realms of uncertainty may have a greater difficulty convincing themselves of their own pure motives and will most assuredly have a greater difficulty convincing the many who are asked "to fall back upon the authority of [their] more cultivated minds." Despite these differences, both Locke and Mill venture outside the clearing with maps presuming man is born to obligations and duties. They start, in fact, where Hobbes does in the second half of *Leviathan* when he says, "But the question is not of obedience to God [read "authoritative ends"], but of *when,* and *what* God hath said."[29]

Mill and Tradition in Modern Liberalism

Let it be remembered that if individual life is short, the life of the human species is not short; its indefinite duration is practically equivalent to endlessness; and, being combined with the indefinite capability of improvement, it offers to the imagination and sympathies a large enough object to satisfy any reasonable demand for grandeur of aspiration.

JOHN STUART MILL, "The Utility of Religion"

I will conclude this study of liberalism with an examination of Mill's philosophy for the future. Mill directly appropriates many elements of liberal tradition and raises problems reflecting concerns of long standing in his own thought and in that of his predecessors. No writer since Mill has addressed the entire range of issues which earlier proponents of liberalism thought relevant to political thought and life. After Mill (and, to some extent, because of Mill) liberal political philosophy is parceled into various provinces of academic scholarship. Theories of obligation, morality, religion, justice, and economics each become separate concerns; the distinctly political elements in each can become lost. Admittedly, Mill's attempt to be both embracive and synthetic too often meets with disappointing results, so we frequently turn instead to his more specialized contemporaries. But again we are disappointed. To be sure, Mill's own enterprise consciously rests on other minds—Bentham, Comte, Coleridge, are examples—but Mill's own use of them should hold our attention if we are to understand the larger tradition of liberalism and Mill's part in it. Unlike his contemporaries, but rather in the spirit of those who earlier shaped the main contours of liberal thought, Mill knew that political life demands authoritative answers to questions which are neither posed nor addressed by unaided reason or specialized knowledge. Mill's stress on "intellectual culture" as a locus of political power and as a source of political authority attests to his comprehensive view of political life and reminds us of the centrality of religious culture in the political writings of Hobbes and Locke. In the writings of all three men, the status of law and morality changes when viewed in light of intellectual culture or religious belief in history.

In his *Autobiography* Mill describes the passage of his ideas away from Benthamism and toward his own mature theory as being marked by "rediscovering things known to all the world, which I had previously disbelieved, or disregarded."[1] By these rediscoveries Mill is able to define his position with respect to utilitarianism and, with further additions, to shape his own theory of politics and society. In this process of reformulation, Mill alters utilitarian psychology by reintroducing the idea of consciousness and will; he becomes less committed to democratic majoritarianism as a political principle; his economic values change toward collective principles; and he places the burden of political and moral reform increasingly in the sphere of culture and opinion as opposed to legislation and state coercion. Although these changes and others are important and should be explored separately, all of them together can be examined as part of Mill's anticipation of the future—as a legacy and program for future generations.

This task confronts two difficulties. Because his program encompasses everything from realistic expectation of the immediate future to dreams of the distant future, the interpretive possibilities are extremely broad. A second pitfall is that any reconstruction of Mill's hopes for the future inevitably shades into our own valuations of the present state of liberal philosophy. One way in which to avoid—at least temporarily—such pitfalls is to measure Mill's contributions in terms of his understanding of earlier liberalism and his critique of utilitarianism and the intellectual culture of his day. Thus, one can isolate central problems which Mill sought to solve and exclude solutions which Mill had already considered in these other contexts. Having done this, we still have the task of entering into Mill's understanding of how his new teachings ought to stand in relation to earlier liberalism.

In what areas and to what extent do older utilitarian doctrines still hold true? In what areas of life should primary reliance still be placed on fear of punishment or, more generally, on motives of self-interest? What ideas and practices of an earlier liberalism must be discarded as barriers to both collective progress and individual freedom? Answers to these questions must begin by taking into account both context and audience. The essays "Bentham" and "Coleridge" suggest two different contexts and audiences. Bentham the man and "Bentham" the essay are the scourge of aristocracy, privilege, and custom—all barriers to the achievement of democracy, justice, and utility. The audience of "Bentham" is the middle and lower classes and the message is self-interest. As we have seen, however, Mill does not believe that purging society of past corruptions will necessarily create a future worthy of men of virtue and intellect. Indeed, the very weapons used and allies attracted in battles against a lingering past may constitute so many future barricades and enemies to the achievement of future ends.

As the companion essay, "Coleridge," proves, Mill does intellectual battle on two fronts with quite different weapons. Here he turns to fight political and cultural egalitarianism and even does battle with the remains of reformed Protestantism. In "Coleridge" Mill seeks to convince us that the leading ideas of Coleridge and Bentham are potentially complementary and that any future reform must combine both sets of ideas. Mill sees his own ideas—indeed, his own life—as the first such attempt. The treasures of past civilization must somehow be integrated with the timeless principles of utility. Benthamite reform tends to destroy the past; Coleridgean sensibility seeks "to preserve the stores and to guard the treasures . . . and thus to bind the present with the past; to perfect and add to the same, and thus to connect the present with the future."[2] This cultural-intellectual enterprise is as relevant to politics as the effort to make political and legal institutions conform to tests of utility. Such simultaneous tasks might, however, be radically at odds with each other.[3] In the examination of Mill's view of future law, morality, and, finally, religion itself, we can see the outlines of Mill's resolutions. At the same time we can witness the structure and the imagery of an earlier liberalism being reproduced and transformed.

Law and Progress

"The succession of states of the human mind and of human society cannot have an independent law of its own; it must depend upon the psychological and ethological laws which govern the action of circumstances on men and of men on circumstances."[4]

In both Hobbes and Locke, psychological and natural laws constitute the grounding for legality and legitimacy in their respective regimes. In Hobbes, these laws have a timeless and static quality; in Locke, they have a "natural" history but culminate, in time and truth, in the modern day. Mill carries forward this same desire to discover the laws behind the laws. In his case, however, the task is somewhat altered. Intellectual progress and material advance now make possible the creation of a science of society. The foundation of this science is "the progressiveness of the human race." A view of man and society from this dynamic perspective facilitates the discovery of laws of development. These laws appear to replace Hobbes's true moral philosophy and Locke's call for a demonstrable morality. These laws distinguish past states in man's history and may make it possible in the future consciously to shape more virtuous societies and persons of higher character.[5] In earlier liberal theory civil law and human nature are intimately connected. Whether the context be the state of nature, natural history, or formal jurisprudence, human needs, material scarcity, and calculation combine to knit together psychology and civil law. Natural law—whether defended directly by Hobbes and Locke or indirectly by Hume and Bentham—expresses the interdependence of man's nature and the rules which guarantee peace and happiness. The political power to enforce these rules in society might require irrational, historical, or religious supports, but the basis of civil law and morality is knowable and certain.

Mill's promise of a new science of society is also an attempt to integrate natural law and human nature, yielding enforceable rules of conduct. The initial result of Mill's developmental perspective, however, is to devalue the centrality of law, property, and economic life in contemporary liberal political philosophy. As Mill outlines a new science of society, the impression grows that man's moral progress, like Locke's view of heaven, "will cast a slight upon the short pleasures and pains of this present state"[6] which civil law and ordinary morality so carefully apportion out and protect. Man's future progress, like his past history, will evidence higher laws than those which protect the civil interests of "houses, money, lands, furniture and the like."[7]

"The universal laws of human nature" are the foundation of an authoritative science of society. Man's progressiveness is the central assumption of this law. Progressiveness, in turn, is in the first instance spiritual (mental) and moral, not material. The creation of a science of society, therefore, requires the creators to subordinate empirical truth to higher law: "If a sociological theory, collected from historical evidence, contracts the established general laws of human nature . . . we may know that history has been misinterpreted, and that the theory is false."[8]

Note what this does to the status of empirical evidence and generalization built on that evidence. Not the palpable data of desires and actions and laws and institutions but the laws of human nature constitute the ground of Mill's social science. These laws of human nature are not at all bound even by the external necessities of civil society, its positive laws and its externalized psychology. By implication, then, Austin's jurisprudence, the necessities of economics, and even the endless series of pains and pleasures cannot constitute sources of obligation; those regularities "amount only to the lowest kind of empirical laws" and are only true under conditions determined by higher law. From the data of history and from experience, we can derive only "the approximate truths [of] practical knowledge." When and if these truths can be "exhibited as corollaries from the universal laws of human nature on which they rest," they can become a science authoritative in the world.[9] Only then can truth become law and empirical generalization become duty.

Human nature is not static, not a series of faculties. Human nature is defined by the state of man's consciousness. Thus, laws of human nature are "discovered" in history by truth-seekers and articulated first as "speculative ideas." Because man's nature is morally progressive, so too are the laws which chart moral progress. The implications for a liberal theory of law of Mill's projected science can be profoundly damaging. Both in *Utilitarianism* and in *Logic*, Mill strongly suggests that civil law and the justice which it guarantees are now of secondary importance. In the past, "one custom or institution after another" has been placed before the bar of justice and become transformed from "a supposed primary necessity of social existence" into "a universally stigmatized injustice and tyranny."[10] Justifications of artificial distinctions among men have therefore crumbled in the wake of liberal theories of justice. And what of the future? Legal equality is on the threshold of final achievement. Although *Utilitarianism* raises some legal issues which still remain after formal equality, Mill concludes that problems such as economic distribution and justifications for and amounts of punishment simply cannot be resolved within a theory of law. Appeal must always be had to social utility, and social utility, in turn, can only be understood within a theory of man's progressiveness in history.

Given his theory of progress and the possibility of a science to insure its achievement, Mill's treatment of the role of law and issues of legal justice seems almost cavalier. He suggests, for example, that law and physical coercion—like economic interest itself—have reached their inherent moral limits and must therefore pass from center stage in political thought and practical concern. The destiny of human freedom in the past was tied to law and the interests which law protects. In the future, the interests of security will remain important, but those interests can never again serve as authoritative ends. To continue to focus on the internal logic of law and the economic life which law commands as the location of social utility would be to confine men's ideas of human freedom to an extreme degree of pettiness and stagnation.

In the future the ends of law will remain important only insofar as they are subservient to other and higher ends. Private property, contractual obligations, and criminal punishments will not cease to exist, but their justifications must now be found in the willing subordination of instinct, interest, and individual rights to authoritative collective ends. Even as we demand our legal rights and the benefits which those rights entail, our motive should be found in a willing commitment to an idea of the general happiness. Political order as well as moral progress are involved here. The motives by which men act are also the bonds of opinions and values which bind them together. To bring an increasingly just legal order into being did require self-sacrifice and demanded generous visions of human capacity. Claims of merit and interest against privilege were initially made in the name of a better way of life for all. Once instituted and perfected, however, such an order rewards equally the motives of fear and selfishness and those of hope and virtue.

Hobbes and Locke share an understanding with seventeenth-century Calvinists regarding adherence to the "law of works": saint or sinner can both obey the law and that is enough in the eyes of the sovereign. The reward for those who adhere additionally to the "law of faith" is, God willing, in heaven. Saints do act in history but only in the most extraordinary of times and not at all within the bounds of justice. Mill's view of the future would seem to insist on the continuous necessity of higher motives for obedience, even though the law cannot command, recognize, or specifically reward them. The limits of law in liberal theory were always seen in the fact that laws, properly so-called, must be confined to external behavior. Mill now adds that laws, as the limit of measuring a man's political duties, may constitute a barrier to moral progress.

By placing motives for obedience to law at the center of his view of law, Mill tends to make a stable and coherent theory of justice impossible. Those who shape and cultivate higher ideals as motives undermine the extant system of rules as much as they support it. General utility or benevolence as *motive* not only denigrates the ends of civil law, which are irreducibly self-centered, but also casts doubt on those parts of the legal system currently deemed least progressive. It is an open question whether Mill foresees a distant future in which there is very little need for law and punishment at all. If a man's motives increasingly rest on "an indissoluble association between his own happiness and the good of the whole," the selfish motives which the laws always presume might wither away.[11]

Three related topics support this reading of law. In his writings on religion, Mill holds that men in the future can be so socialized that the rewards and punishments of supernatural religion can be dispensed with "as a supplement to human laws, a more cunning sort of police, an auxiliary to the thief-catcher and the hangman."[12] Future religion can draw its strength exclusively from non-self-interested motives. If this is the case, religion merges with enlightened public opinion to become the repository of morally progressive altruism and the highest standards of human motives. The lowly motives on which the law now relies are supplanted. A second topic of central importance to this new view of law is economics, specifically Mill's theory of stagnation, wage-fund theory, and Malthusian population doctrines. Mill seems to welcome a future of little or no economic growth because it makes possible a less self-interested system of morality. The vista of continuous economic progress has only encouraged the selfish concerns of "getting on" at the expense of higher ends.[13] As individual competitive ends recede in importance, the conditions requiring law and coercion also recede. Those who think seriously about political and social life in the future must look less to law and legal institutions and more to mechanisms of communication and public opinion.

A third topic of relevance to Mill's discussion of law is political institutions. In the opening chapters of *Representative Government*, Mill clearly distinguishes his views from earlier utilitarianism by insisting that the choice of political institutions be subordinate to questions of individual and collective moral character—the real repositories of human progress.[14] No autonomous science of government is possible because each society requires a unique mix of appropriate institutions. Geometric modes of reasoning about politics must give way to internal and cultural methods. Even more than in the case of law, political institutions must be subordinate to the higher laws of moral progress and human nature. Even less than the legal relationships of civil society, political relationships cannot be established on timeless truths, for no single set of governing institutions can serve to protect either the civil or the moral integrity of the governed. Indeed, Mill ends his introductory remarks in *Representative Government* by referring to the prophetic tradition in Judaism to underline the primacy of personality and belief over political institutions.

> Their religion, which enabled persons of genius and a high religious
> tone to be regarded and to regard themselves as inspired from heaven,
> gave existence to an inestimably precious unorganized institution—the
> Order (if it may be so termed) of Prophets. Under the protection . . .
> of their sacred character, the Prophets were a power in the nation,
> often more than a match for kings and priests, and kept up . . . the
> antagonism of influences which is the only real security for continued
> progress.[15]

Mill's projection of the future locations of moral progress reintroduces into modern liberalism elements from seventeenth-century prophetic history. What Locke termed the "law of faith" always constitutes a dynamic source of duty in contrast to a static "law of works." In Hobbes, the just man is always a more praiseworthy achievement than "justice of actions," even though the law cannot measure the man. Judging from the second half of *Leviathan*, no commonwealth can stand which rests only on material interest and fear of death. In all three formulations, actions motivated by higher obligations are crucial in making man's history. And in all three writings, motives encapsuled in law, fear, and coercion achieve their moral value from a subordination to these higher obligations. Seventeenth-century empirical psychology, built on the assumption of man's systematic depravity, was not intended to honor the result of that depravity.

From a Calvinist perspective, the danger to true Christianity and righteousness is blasphemy and idolatry, not natural depravity. Indeed, the motives of depravity, such as fear, self-interest, and calculation, are utilized as subordinate weapons in a grander struggle. In the seventeenth century these attributes and the regime of legality itself achieve their importance more for the historical enemies they help destroy than for the timeless natural ends they proclaim. In Hobbes's terminology, to destroy the prevailing institutions of "vainglory" is not to elevate self-interest and timidity in their place but to make possible receptivity to true righteousness. Even Benthamite appeals to competition, individual merit, and material benefit had the flavor of an antiaristocratic crusade. But to destroy aristocracy—or saints and prophets—in politics, church, and society leaves the victors somewhat empty-handed. John Stuart Mill shares with Locke the belief that the weapons used to achieve victory should not be confused with the reasons for which the battles were fought. The limits of critical philosophy for Mill are the same as the limits of reason for Locke: like motives of self-interest, they are not capable of shaping man's future. Man is destined—perhaps whether he likes it or not—for higher pleasures than the law allows and reason understands. The universal laws of human nature can no longer be fulfilled through the mechanisms of positive law and political coercion.

Opinion and Progress

"In politics it is almost a triviality to say that public opinion now rules the world. . . . This is as true in the moral and social relations of private life as in public transactions."[16]

Authoritative truths in the future will be increasingly independent of the depraved instruments of coercion, interest, and law. Past moral and material progress has now prepared men to be guided by public opinion. This is the case for a number of reasons. As men have become legally and morally equal, their inner lives increasingly share identical feelings: "influences are constantly on the increase which tend to generate in each individual a feeling of unity with all the rest." For modern man, public opinion is at once his individual conscience, his source of moral standards, his behavioral motives, and his religion. Public opinion can create in each person a habitual "will to do right" which "ought to be cultivated into . . . independence" from simple desires.[17] The particular ends which dominate shared moral beliefs will determine the direction of man's future moral progress.

In eighteenth-century natural-history explanation, discussion of moral sentiments is framed with an eye to their functions in support of political authority and civil society. Sentiments have a history of mutual interdependence with economic life and law, but the presumption is that the primary cause of these relationships is man's desire for material well-being. Mill shares this theory of interdependence but insists that the causal element is intellectual or spiritual, not material. Speculative ideas determine opinions and opinions determine most men's inner state, their "character." Material conditions in the past have been limiting conditions for motives of general happiness. Most generally, politically coerced inequalities prevented the inclusion of most men in any particular man's conception of the common good. The resulting differences in status, position, and power among men prevented a single and "public" opinion from forming or dominating. All conceptions of the common good were skewed by politically and socially enforced distinctions among men. Whatever the particular ideas and actions that powered the destruction of these enforced inequalities, material conditions now obtain which make it possible for public opinion to form and for common moral ideas to embrace equally all members of society.

If material conditions (including the existence of political coercion) are viewed as a limiting factor in moral progress, the purpose of public opinion changes. Rather than a system of supports for prevailing institutions and practices, public opinion in the future must constitute the dynamic force for change. Indeed, without the aid of opinion, future change is impossible. Exactly how this change manifests itself, however, is not always clear in Mill's writings. Evident in the background of Mill's entire discussion is a tension between altering only the state of men's beliefs (motives) regarding their actions and actually altering their actions. In the past a progress of internal "states"—the quality of feelings and motives of a few dedicated men—always foreshadowed progress in laws, governments, and material well-being. Even more important, political revolutions brought about in the past by creative minorities reflected and furthered changes in opinions. These political changes caused sudden forward movement in man's progress. Mill however does not suggest the use of these overt political and coercive means in the future.

As public opinion becomes more important and laws, political institutions, and economic conditions less so, the source of danger to moral progress shifts as well. Because of democratization and the power of public opinion, cultural egalitarianism—in today's term, "mass culture"—is now the greatest threat. Public opinion in a regime of social equality can prevent even the formation of higher ideals of life, the motor of past changes. The victory of nonvainglorious standards of behavior threatens to prevent the creation of more noble ideals of happiness. In *On Liberty,* Mill portrays the egalitarian concerns with welfare, security, and propriety as a form of complacent idolatry demanding no exercise of intellect or courage. Under these new conditions, the control of common moral opinion is no longer lodged in institutional elites, priestly castes, or hereditary orders. Today and in the future, says Mill, the average man must be persuaded that his own happiness is inextricably bound to the improvement of all men in future times.

Mill's discussion of future moral opinion is further shaped by his assumption that the sciences of law, economics, and psychology are now known and essentially complete. This means that further moral progress cannot rely on the manipulative methods implicitly taught by these sciences. Like supernatural religion, ahistorical behavioral sciences have reached the limits of their improvement and the limits of their capacity to improve men.[18] In *Utilitarianism*, Mill tries to recreate some notion of "consciousness" as a starting point for the discovery and articulation of a nonreligious theory of an inner self independent of successions of desire-will-action responses. More specifically, this new psychological perspective is said by Mill to be true *only now,* after laws and behaviors have reached a certain stage of development and men have achieved a substantial equality. As if Locke's divine coincidence between natural history and Christ's appearance were to be repeated in a secular form, Mill says that only now have feelings of unity among men developed sufficient strength to make possible the direct trans- formation of human character through the power of public opinion.

Such feelings make it possible for the mass of men to internalize motives of general happiness. Contemporary man is capable of such an "internal ultimate sanction," making both him and utilitarian philosophy truly moral—that is, independent of appeals to self-interest. What was only a benevolent result in the past—what Austin called an "index"—can now become a shared belief and the measure of a good man's duty. As if reaching back to the very beginnings of liberal moral philosophy, Mill's discussion of this psychological dimension employs the same metaphor used by Hobbes in his discussion of "manners" in *Leviathan*: a seed in all men which requires the proper nurture. In Mill's formulation it is the victory of true moral philosophy and the victory of a purer religion which ushered in these new psychological relationships and moral possibilities. Non-self-interested mo- tives are now possible for the mass of men without the auxiliary aids of legal coercion and supernatural religion. This was not the case in the past. Then most relationships among men were among unequals, so most relationships were colored by self-interest and even exploitation. However, "in every age some advance is made towards a state in which it will be impossible to live permanently on other terms [than equality] with anybody." The resulting "seed" or "feeling of unity" can now be shaped into a feeling of duty toward the general good. This feeling "is not naturally and originally part of the end [of men's desires and actions], but it is capable of becoming so; and in those who live it disinterestedly it has become so, and is desired and cher- ished, not as a means to happiness, but as a part of their happiness."[19] For Mill, this constitutes the new "law of human nature" which in turn will constitute both the binding source of authority for man and the basis for a new science of society. It is at this point that the tension intrudes between altering beliefs or intentions only or altering major patterns of behavior as well.

In *Utilitarianism*, Mill maintains that disinterested motives cannot and should not demand much change in our conduct, let alone require new and even revolutionary legal and political systems. He does suggest that in the future many men will be motivated—even in their objectively self-interested actions—by motives of general good. In "ninety-nine hundredths" of cases, no observable difference can be detected between selfish and unselfish behaviors. In the few remaining cases where actions dictated by self-interest would conflict with the general good, most men will be able to follow their duty spontaneously, because the general good has in fact become a "part ·of their [own] happiness [and] desired for its own sake."[20]

Whether one wants to act in a self-interested manner because it is in one's self-interest or because it is believed to be a moral duty can easily become blurred to anyone who is not omniscient. The least generous reading can view Mill's "internal ultimate sanction" in the way Locke's *Reasonableness of Christianity* is so often viewed in contemporary scholarship: as a kind of idealistic opiate in the face of great distributive injustice—and a rather ineffective opiate at that. If Mill's theory of moral progress is to be taken seriously, however, one must assume that Mill suggests new ideas and new actions outside the limits of liberal moral and legal canons. In short, Mill does seem to want to tell us how to make bad men good. This transformation in turn requires the altering of man's deepest beliefs in order to guarantee that the "universal laws of human nature" are true in thought and that they will become true in history.[21]

Supernatural religion can no longer be improved; critical philosophy and "geometrical" modes of reasoning have all but played themselves out. As a positive science of society supplants critical philosophy and as a "religion of humanity" becomes the source of ideal and transcending images of the future, new and truly "selfless" instruments must be found with which to mold men's characters. In the *Logic of the Moral Sciences*, a central part of a future science of society is said to be a science of "character formation," or ethology. This science is predicated upon and verified by "universal laws of human nature." It will provide the knowledge required for the proper nurture of "feelings of unity" and thus for the cultivation of the "internal ultimate sanctions" constituting moral character. This science will not dictate ends but it will make it possible

> for a competent thinker to deduce from those laws [of character formation] with a considerable approach to certainty, the particular type of character which would be formed in mankind generally by any assumed set of circumstances.[22]

Ethology does not discover the ends of human nature and does not provide us with character models, new ways of life, or visions of the future. Mill terms the content which is to inform the new social science an art, the "Art of Life," which, like sociology itself, "is, unfortunately, still to be created." It is this art "which enunciates the object arrived at, and affirms it to be a desirable object, whether in the realm of morality, prudence, or aesthetics.[23] No mundane processes of desire-will-action shall sully creation of this art and no ordinary processes of desire-will-action shall transpose this creation from speculative idea into common moral opinion. The art which powers science should be as spontaneous, free, and personal as the gift of grace itself. By this means, the definitions of general happiness which constitute the content of men's highest obligations can become the universal laws of human nature. In this sense, ethology is to speculative ideas (articulating the "art of life") what theology is to revelation.

The shaping of higher and nobler characters cannot be compromised, as in the past, by reliance on physical coercion and material interest. Definitions of good and evil which are to shape the very ground of our being must be freely given and freely received. Mere laws service the depraved world of works; as Locke reminds us, they are created only to protect external goods and physical bodies. In contrast, practical moral opinion penetrates to our motives and character, not only affecting our self-interested happiness on earth but also our final destiny after death. Mill's discussion of the process of future "character formation" for the many occurs within the Lockean framework of practical moral opinion. The moral coercion of the many can legitimately enter where the law must stop. At the very heart of Mill's defense of individual liberty, he reserves for moral coercion the most important role of "forcing men to be free": moral sanctions alone can punish "that portion of [a man's] conduct and character *which concerns his own good,* but which does not affect the interests of others in their relations with him."[24] If enlightened public opinion were the vehicle for "elevated sentiments" and higher ideals of life, progress would begin again; the stagnation and mediocrity informed by selfish interest would be transcended. Coercive opinion never violates legal rights; its "pains" cannot constitute a civil injury. No determinate person can be held accountable for any adverse effects moral coercion has on another individual. Legally innocent, self-regarding conduct deserves legal protection, but it does not constitute a standard of sufficient worth to be immune from moral coercion.

The power of public opinion over the average individual is coercive—it is painful to resist—but the process by which particular ideas come to dominate that opinion is not. In a regime of toleration, victorious ideas will be those which small groups of dedicated men persuade others to accept. The motives of the persuaders cannot be those of self-interest, because they are men of ideas, not men with public power or economic position to protect. Their "experiments in living" and their intellectual speculations are caused by a passionate desire to know. When new ideals of life are proclaimed by those of the highest intellectual culture, whose only ulterior motive is an earnest desire for the improvement of mankind, who could ever charge them with intending injury to others or exclusively benefiting themselves? Their motives can only be compared to the best of religious motives in past history.

The essence of religion is the strong and earnest direction of the emotions and desires toward an ideal object, recognized as the highest excellence, and as rightfully paramount over all selfish objects of desire.[25]

In Mill's writings, the creation of higher ideals of happiness is a kind of religious quest and the story of that quest is a sacred history. The willingness to translate higher ideals into powerful opinions is an act of faith in future man and future society. As Mill points out in his discussion of the power of a "morality grounded on large and wise views of the good of the whole," it is "claiming too little" to term the resulting sentiments simply morality.

They are a real religion of which, as of other religions, outward good works (the utmost meaning usually suggested by the word morality) are only a part, and are indeed rather the fruits of the religion than the religion itself.[26]

Without fully realizing it, Mill recreates the image of the elect seeking to establish a divine politics in a world steeped in depravity, idolatry, and self-interest. Toleration of opinion, like toleration of the sects, is a demand of freedom for the elect to serve a prophetic role in the teeth of complacency, self-interest, and moral cowardice. The translation of new ideals into ruling opinion meets with obstacles which require power to overcome. As in the past, idols born of false teaching and selfish passion stand in the way. Not all men receive full grace, but most men can follow in the footsteps of the faithful. For "superior natures" the internal ultimate sanction "would derive its power . . . from sympathy and benevolence and the passion for ideal excellence; in the inferior, from the same feelings cultivated up to the measure of their capacity, with the super-added force of shame."[27] Both kinds of men are thereby liberated from the shackles of interest and necessity. At the same time, liberal philosophy itself is liberated from its timeless necessities and its reason-derived certainties.

Mill's idealist theory of history contains a causal hierarchy extending from speculative ideas through public opinion to moral and legal rules and government policy. In a morally progressive society, somewhat less clearly articulated hierarchies of men correspond to this hierarchy of ideas. The eminent men who mount the hilltop to receive new light inform others who help to spread that light to the plains. The role of governing officials and ordinary citizenship would seem minimal in this model.

The main feature in this relationship of ideas and opinions, however, is the call for a new beginning for man. Not rational science but ideals in the mode of religious feeling are foremost in importance. The image which Mill evokes, then, is not that of Hobbes's take-it-or-perish logic but of Locke's poignant hope for a new start.

The rational and thinking part of mankind, it is true, when they sought after him, they found the one supreme invisible God, but if they acknowledged and worshipped him, it was only in their own minds. They kept this truth locked up in their own breasts as a secret, nor ever dared venture it amongst the people, much less amongst the priests. . . . Hence we see, that reason, speaking ever so clearly to the wise and virtuous, had never authority enough to prevail on the multitude.[28]

"Human reason unassisted" failed men in its great and proper business of morality. Like Locke, who pictured the weakness of philosophy in a contest with pagan forms of religion before Christ's appearance, Mill, too, seems to believe "that religion [is] everywhere distinguished from and preferred to virtue."[29] Locke, in the *Reasonableness of Christianity*, gives us a millennialist theology to power the truth of virtue. Mill gives us a religion of humanity—or perhaps only a history of ideas—to power a science of society. But will the bearers of this news be brave enough to "venture . . . among the people" and challenge the priestly defenders of complacency, mediocrity, and conformity?

The call for toleration in *On Liberty* is as much a condemnation of the cowardice of contemporary intellectuals as it is a testament to the power and mediocrity of mass culture. In comparison to past prophets and their disciples, contemporary agents of progress require much more favorable circumstances. In part this follows necessarily because these new agents have no institutional power—no church, no academy, no army, no hangman. But their alleged lack of courage may equally be caused by the secular ideals they teach. Related problems intrude. How one might recognize true from false prophets in the contemporary period is in doubt. Exactly what Mill would have them say is not always clear. His confidence that they will all bring the same news tends to waver. His faith often fails him that the mass of men will spontaneously accept the right message in preference to less demanding ones. That the future of freedom rides on the outcome is the truth that Mill never doubts. Both the problems and the urgency of their solution rest on a history of ideas—on stories understood and remembered and then recreated and extended into the future.

Religion as the History of Prophetic Ideas

"To see the futurity of the species has always been the privilege of the intellectual elite or of those who have learnt from them; to have the feeling of that futurity has been the distinction, and usually the martyrdom, of a still rarer elite."[30]

When John Stuart Mill seeks to articulate a new principle of authority behind the truths of the utilitarian moral sciences, he unabashedly combines the following terms into a single question:

> What is its sanction?, what are the motives to obey it? . . . what is the source of its obligation?, whence does it derive its binding force? It is a necessary part of moral philosophy to provide the answer to this [sic] question.[31]

As soon as history becomes important, sanctions, motives, and obligation become a single question asked of liberal political philosophy. The point at which historical change is raised is the point at which formal discussion of political and legal obligation run into questions of opinion, power, and loyalty. The requirements of political life—and especially the realm of political freedom—mandate this interconnection of sanctions, motives, and obligation. The tradition of liberal political philosophy up to Mill is proof of this mandate. The last half of Hobbes's *Leviathan* and Locke's *Reasonableness of Christianity* are positive proofs. The difficulties encountered by Hume and Smith in explaining political allegiance except in de facto terms are negative ones. John Stuart Mill explicitly located his theory of politics and morality in history. And by eschewing reliance on supernatural religion, his attempted merger is even more complete than the same merger is in Hobbes or Locke. His theory of political obligation begins and ends by combining questions of sanctions, motives, and loyalty without even the pretense of seeking independent foundations in legal or moral rationalism.[32] Mill's theory of history and progress assumes the subservience of legal and moral life to political life—that is, to the beliefs and loyalties which bind individuals and societies into coherent unities. The chain binding history together is the chain of those speculative ideas which become dominant opinions, that is, ideas which foretell the future. The understanding of history is found in stories independent of men's material circumstances as surely as Locke's biblical history is independent of the march from land held in common through the invention of money to the triumph of civil society.

In Mill's discussion of the future, prophetic ideas become the single locus of political obligation, political authority, and historical change. In contrast, Hobbes and Locke left conscientious men with two guides—a behaviorist epistemology and a biblical theology; Mill seems to have left only general intimations of a new social science powered by a yet to be created religion of humanity. Lockean political actors have two distinct sources of motive and obligation: biblical tradition informed and interpreted by reason and a natural history of legal and economic artifacts created and understood by reason. Locke's citizen as saint is firmly located in sacred history and his citizen as liberal is thoroughly grounded in the logic of the material world.

It is up to God to create a moment in history when the two become one and decisively change man's destiny.

Mill's distinction between organic and transitional periods accepts something of this logic insofar as revolutionary moments combine belief and interest to signal the passage from one period to another. The active agent in the combination, however, is always belief. Mill's "proof" of the utility principle rests on this assumption and on his belief in the efficacy of the new ideas to dominate change. In *Utilitarianism*, the fact that men's desires are subordinate to "habitual will" is used by Mill to show that a belief in general happiness both can and ought to attain the status previously occupied by religious motives. In *On Liberty*, Mill distinguishes between a creed "still fighting for its existence"—one able to "penetrate the feelings, and acquire a real mastery over the conduct"—and one suffering a "decline in the living power of the doctrine," which is increasingly unable to affect desires and actions. The idea of utility as of the highest obligation requires, like all past religious creeds, "a lively apprehension."[33]

When Mill attempts to specify the requirements of a creed appropriate for modern men living in a society dominated by equality and public opinion, he also confronts us with the dimensions and dilemmas of future liberalism. In one group of his writings, Mill presupposes a dangerous transitional age requiring men of ideas to construct positive consensual doctrines on which authority, stability, and morality can be reconstructed. Mill's quotation from Comte prefacing the first edition of *Logic of the Moral Sciences* best expresses this perspective:

> As long as individual intellects have not adhered by unanimous consent to a certain number of general ideas capable of forming a common social doctrine . . . the state of nations will remain, of necessity, essentially revolutionary.[34]

In another group of his writings, Mill presupposes an equally dangerous organic age not marked, as in past organic ages, by powerful beliefs, but by collective mediocrity of ideals, as if ordinary morality has finally conquered religion. Not disbelief and anarchy, but tepid remnants of belief and invariably timid behavior are the new dangers to liberty and progress. Here the appropriate role for men of ideas is not that of house ideologue but of skeptic and nonconformist. In this perspective, the future of liberty requires a permanent transitional period—an endless future of evolutionary change powered by incessant and varied challenges to prevailing practice and opinion. Modern egalitarian society naturally tends toward a deadening equilibrium. Because the thinking of most men today "is done for them by men much like themselves" and not, as in the past, by "dignitaries in Church or State" or through recognized books and intellectual leaders, the future problem is exactly the reverse of the past one.[35] On this reading, the task of the "more highly gifted and instructed One or Few" is to challenge prevailing popular authorities rather than to form "a common social doctrine." Ruling elites in the past were challenged by counterelites. In previous periods of transition and confusion, the alternatives posed to dominant values were worthy alternatives.[36] Mediocrity could never reign in the past because the many were led by the few, whether in defending or challenging prevailing values. Now, when the many rule, all true elites must in some respects be counterelites dedicated to a future of continuous reform.

The first supposition, that of a dangerous transitional period, calls for a common social doctrine dominated by science, expertise, and the proximate goals of material welfare. The ideas which constitute authoritative ends will be tied to the modest reach of rational analysis and social statistics and modified by a healthy respect for prevailing sources of order. Academic intellectuals could be the natural guardians and spokesmen of political and social theory; expert civil servants would translate ideas into reality. Mill suggests these conserving functions for a new social science while underlining its bureaucratic and managerial utility:

> to understand by what causes [society] had . . . been made what it was; where it was tending to any, and to what changes; what effects each feature of its existing state was likely to produce in the future; and by what means any of those effects might be prevented, modified or accelerated.[37]

Incremental decisions and evolutionary morals will be guided by an appropriate history of ideas honoring the march of rationality, social integration, and benevolence. Under the assumption of a dangerous transitional age, a history of liberalism would begin with Locke's warning that reason is a small clearing in a jungle and would end, perhaps, with expert commissions and Fabian socialism.[38] The limits of interpreting and extending the major texts of liberal philosophy will be set by the canons of critical philosophy and modified by the cumulative knowledge of social science. Any "art of life" inspired by this history of ideas will not challenge the necessities of logic, science, and law. The men of genius who are the engines of future historical progress should be men of strict intellectual discipline. Their teachings would celebrate those ideas in the past, present, and future which gradually extend Locke's clearing and reject as folly those ideas which try to discern what lies far deeper in the jungle. It is perhaps no accident that Mill begins the first substantive chapter of *Logic of the Moral Sciences* with a harsh critique of "free-will metaphysicians."[39] A properly taught history of ideas could end with a lesson on the dangers of ideological politics.

Under the assumption of a dangerous transitional age, moreover, the future will not consist of prophetic breaks in ideas and revolutions in political authority. Responsible intellectuals who are the guardians of the story of past ideas might celebrate past prophets and revolutionaries—as Mill did—even though they will have no intention of emulating them. Indeed, a central assumption of this history of ideas is that supernatural religion and violent political change have outlived their moral utilities. In this model of the ideas which constitute future authoritative ends, there is room neither for prophetic martyrs nor creative magistrates. Miracles have ceased. Without the visible signs which made clear to men in the past that major changes in fact were occurring, men in the future can only "fall back upon the authority of still more cultivated minds," taking it on faith that ever higher ideals guide the destiny of their species. This faith is the central tenet of a religion of humanity. The only remaining mystery is whether ideas in fact still rule the world or whether it is now ruled by sheer material and psychological necessity. Social science can chart the regularity of change, and the history of ideas will term that change moral progress. Finally, under this assumption of the future, liberal political philosophy will be the sum of its academic parts. A history of ideas which has purged each part of its irrational, ideological, or simply unsettling elements will assure a rough coherence. The writings of Leslie Stephen are a proof of this possibility in Mill's own time. His books, especially *Hobbes, English Thought in the Eighteenth Century* and, finally, *The English Utilitarians*, all point to the centrality of a history of ideas as the source of intellectual, political, and moral coherence. Fittingly, the last book of *The English Utilitarians* is entitled "J. S. Mill."[40]

The second supposition, that of a deadening age of conformity rather than one of destabilizing transition, gives us a rather different perspective on Mill's view of future authoritative ends and the appropriate history of ideas to inform those ends. In this more openly political and religious model, future men of ideas are closer to past prophets and rulers. Inspired by visions of new human possibilities, men of genius create more worthy images of human natures; other men internalize these visions, translating them into new standards of moral beliefs which come to dominate opinions and history. Ideas of this type, which are created by challenging or extending past ideas and "from which nothing can be inferred" of a directly moral nature, are always dangerous. Miracles have not ceased. Mystery remains, but some men now consciously assume the roles previously occupied by the gods and their spokesmen. The history of ideas is not initially to bind together or rationalize the prevailing moral sciences but to rule and transform them.

On this reading of Mill and of his impact on future liberalism, Locke's *Essay Concerning Human Understanding* occupies a secondary role in the history of ideas similar, perhaps, to that occupied by all of Hume's writings. Locke's small clearing takes on some of the characteristics of Bentham's prison and Hume's celebration of moderation as "a mediocrity, and a kind of insensibility, in every thing."[41] An appropriate history of ideas would make Bentham, the radical reformer of his time, an apostle of conformity and stagnation; Coleridge, the conservator of the past, becomes an apostle of change, transformation, and progress. On this reading, the simple act of preserving a history of authoritative ends is a radical enterprise. The history of ideas, including religious ideas, preserves dangerous memories and possibilities in an age that necessarily fears them. The best men who repair to that tradition are also the ones who will transform men in the present and shape the man of the future. The signs of this change, however, are not to be found in political institutions and laws. Revolution in the future will be in culture and consciousness because political authority in the future will increasingly be exercised directly by public opinion.[42]

Perhaps our understanding of Mill does not require us to make a choice between the assumption of a dangerous age of transition or one of deadening mediocrity. Both assumptions point to the need for particular men to uphold and articulate authoritative ends and, thus, to the need for a history of ideas. And whether Mill assumes that conformity or intellectual anarchy is the chief danger to moral progress in the future, the need for a religion of humanity is essential to provide motive, sanction, and obligation for the many and inspiration for the few. At issue is not the need for beliefs which have the status of faith but rather the content of the theology and the meaning of the chosen texts. Mill's religion of humanity is both a story of ideas and a prophecy of man's future. The real issue for liberal political philosophy is first whether this set of beliefs is tailored for the many or for the few and, second, whether it increases or diminishes freedom.

Mill inescapably confronts an order of problems which dominate the writings of John Locke. Locke's image of magistrate-captain assisted by citizen-crew sailing the ship of state on the tumultuous seas of the subject-multitudes has a counterpart in Mill's *Utility of Religion* and *On Liberty.* Because most men are neither saints nor intellectuals, they accept the authority of dominant opinions. Insofar as the threat of external sanctions by law, opinion, or supernatural rewards and punishments dominate their motives and actions, most men are condemned to live their lives within the realm of "works." Without sanctions and good men to shape and uphold them, most men would at best be enslaved by self-interest and natural passion or, at worst, by false prophets and grossly immoral purposes. One result which Locke claims for toleration of religion is that increasingly large numbers of men would be forced by circumstances to confront alternative religious opinions forcefully urged by a dissenting clergy. Undisciplined depravity yields superstition and illegitimate authority. Toleration would discipline depravity by forcing the depraved to confront and perhaps even to choose among differing sets of beliefs. Idolatry or righteousness is the only real choice. Locke seems not to doubt the outcome.

The main chapter in Mill's *On Liberty,* "Of the Liberty of Thought and Discussion," is true to this Lockean formula. Not only is the chapter preoccupied with religious ideas, models, and examples, but the chief social benefit claimed for toleration is that it encourages an "intellectually active people." Although "there have been and may be again, great individual thinkers in an atmosphere of mental slavery . . . we cannot hope to find that generally high scale of mental activity which has made some periods of history so remarkable."[43] To recapture the spirit and movement of these periods now requires a strong belief in toleration. The end, then, is to create a greater popular concern for authoritative beliefs by recreating earlier conditions in new circumstances. The object is not to destroy common moral opinion but to make it purer, more spontaneous, and more persuasive. As if Locke were speaking from his grave, Mill laments in *On Liberty* that now, "not one Christian in a thousand guides or tests his individual conduct by reference to . . . the maxims and precepts contained in the New Testament."[44] Mill's response, of course, is not to attempt a resuscitation of the New Testament (or of the Enlightenment, for that matter); these impulses "are well nigh spent." His intent is to make a "fresh start" by establishing conditions conducive to the reassertion of "our mental freedom."[45]

The interplay between toleration and a religion of humanity echoes some of the ambiguities found in Locke's *Letter on Toleration*. Locke provides a bald outline of the contents of practical moral opinion which will result from religious toleration: if true faith reigns, the political and legal future is known in advance. Toleration is to further the power of true moral opinion even as it seems to condemn the many lax and corrupt Christians in the established church and to strengthen the religious cause of the saints. Toleration is not to test the truths of civil society but to establish an ultimate sanction for them. This fit between belief and knowledge presumes but cannot guarantee a body of the faithful willing to sacrifice all to make the hope a reality in history.

Mill's ultimate sanction requires a slightly altered set of religious ideas and body of saints. Unlike Locke's saints, Mill's intellectuals do not teach a doctrine of grace. Mill's claim for the moral superiority of a religion of humanity is that it specifically lacks a promise of personal reward and therefore can teach pure selflessness. For Mill, even the most purified Protestant doctrines have one insoluble moral contradiction: salvation and eternity for *some*.

> It is that so precious a gift, bestowed on a few, should have been
> withheld from the many, that countless millions of human beings
> should have been allowed to live and die, to sin and suffer, without the
> one thing needful, the divine remedy.[46]

To repudiate finally this grace-giving god would indeed appear to signal an entirely new beginning for the liberal moral philosophy, a beginning that is scientific, secular, and autonomous.[47] Mill rejects such a beginning in the strongest terms. The determinate social relationship is still that of the few men of ideas to the many who accept or reject their teachings. The multitudes in both Mill and Locke are condemned to live, for the most part, in a realm of freedom firmly circumscribed by the complex of sanctions into which they are born. Mill's religion of humanity makes this distinction undeniably clear. No illusions should intrude to convince the many that moral mediocrity is virtue or that mere obedience to law is good citizenship. Important issues of politics and freedom are neither framed nor decided in the realm of works and within the confines of civil society.

At the end of *The Natural History of Religion*, David Hume says that popular religion is always in opposition to and more powerful than moral philosophy. The reason for this dominance of prophet and priest over philosopher is that religion rests on stories easily grasped and remembered while morality rests on complex processes of reason. The combination of "traditional stories and superstitious practices" often encourages actions necessarily removed from motives framed by interest, common sense, or logic.[48] Locke thinks of the Bible as a story easily accessible to the mass of men and, if properly understood, as an effective surrogate for moral and political duties derived from reason. In both Locke and Hume, history as story is perceived as powerful while pure philosophy as compulsive and timeless logic is thought weak and confined to the few. The very structure of Hobbes's *Leviathan* attests to the centrality of this dictinction.

John Stuart Mill, standing at the end of this tradition, almost reverses its significance. Insofar as the modern age is dominated by interest, sanctions, and science, most men are now condemned to act out the timeless logic of interest and philosophy. Their behaviors are in lieu of their understanding, but any intelligent observer can predict their actions—almost as if some awesomely powerful Leviathan were directing each of them. Mill saw this clearly. "Though the course of affairs never ceases to be susceptible of alteration" by "ordinary accidents [or] the character of individuals," such alterations are becoming increasingly rare. Because of "the increasing preponderance of the collective agency of the species," historical change now "deviates less from a certain and preappointed track." A predictive science of society is a growing possibility "not solely because [society] is better studied but because, in every generation, it becomes better adapted for study."[49] In this future, the past models of a transitional *or* an organic age no longer hold. The danger is neither anarchy nor hierarchic domination but rather a "negative organic age" typified by an absence of any authoritative ends combined with the most regular and docile social behaviors. The threats to freedom under these conditions are neither the breakdown of law and order nor the use of the state by a few to rule the rest. The primary threat to freedom is the culture itself: no stories, no examples, and no commitments are strong enough to withstand the routinization of desire after desire until death. The first half of *Leviathan* triumphs.

On Liberty charts the one means left to Mill of avoiding this possibility. A popular belief in toleration will create an audience which may be persuaded to transcend necessity and endless stagnation. Ironically, however, the few speakers must come bearing stories, not logic. The history of speculative ideas is the preserve of the few; a new religion of humanity reintroduces "traditional stories" and new prophecies to redeem men from spiritual enslavement to a world created in the image of Benthamism. Higher pleasures and higher freedoms are found in this history which is also a religion. The proof of freedom lies in the capacity of virtuous men to continue the stories, not in the capacity of most men to behave in ways which prove the truths of philosophy.

The future of freedom and morality depends upon how the story is told and upon the quality of future ideas which the story encourages. A religion of humanity can stress the timeless necessities of earlier natural religion or the apocalyptic and transcending actions of earlier supernatural religion. In the former case, a religion of humanity becomes a wall to keep out earlier Christianity and later ideologies construed now as dangerous forms of political religion. In the latter case, a religion of humanity is always potentially revolutionary, containing dangerous memories in the form of standing rebukes to the idolatrous worship of our interests, passions, and calculations. All would seem to hinge upon the particular stories remembered, told, and believed.

In Mill's conception, a history of ideas informing a religion of humanity is ambiguous—a kind of endlessness and a kind of eternity. It denotes an endlessness because the history of the species man is, according to Mill, a history of his leading ideas. This same history of ideas, however, is a kind of eternity because ideas, like the mystery of consciousness, imply "that something which has ceased, or is not yet in existence, can still be, in a manner, present."[50] Those who live within this story combine past, present, and future. Those who do not, those "who are so wrapped up in self that they . . . require the notion of another selfish life beyond the grave to keep up any interest in existence," must surely be denied consolation. They might not want to die with no hope of reward, but their vain hopes for a life beyond the grave only prove that their lives on earth have dwindled "into something too insignificant to be worth caring about."[51] Like the harsh necessities of endlessness and death in "the Kingdome of God by Nature" pictured by Hobbes, this stern teaching of the religion of humanity is an antidote to the multitudes' vainglory.

To be born in servitude to this religion and these stories is not to reject reason or philosophy but to incorporate them into a larger framework of authoritative ends. Very few men have the discipline and virtue sufficient to recognize necessity but still master it. Most men will glory in a belief in their natural liberty; but their actions will honor enslavement to self-interest and cultural mediocrity. Toleration holds out the possibility that the few can persuade the many that other ways of life are both possible and desirable. And, if the many can be convinced that present and future forms of ordinary happiness are the creations of extraordinary men risking their happiness and their lives, self-interest and perhaps even social science can be enlisted as allies.

Mill's history of ideas is his bow to the traditional gods of liberalism: some few men can dedicate their lives to selfless service, even without the hope of heavenly reward. Men of ideas whose selfless lives are spent touching eternity will welcome annihilation. Such men, having mentally acted beyond the happiness of mere sensation, have transcended the temptations of ordinary pains and pleasures: "[W]hen all [life's] pleasures, even those of benevolence, are familiar [and] . . . nothing untasted and unknown is left to stimulate curiosity and keep up the desire of prolonged existence," truly free men "would gladly lie down and take their eternal rest."[52] Mill's notion of what constitutes happiness for these men (these forerunners of future men) so transcends the happiness of ordinary pains and pleasures as to constitute either subversion or redemption at the very center of his liberal doctrine. Should we praise Mill's faith or damn his blasphemy? "They who have had their happiness can bear to part with existence, but it is hard to die without ever having lived."[53]

The joys of freedom which virtuous men experience and the passions by which they are driven have little to do with liberal laws and morality or with the moral philosophy which shaped them. Free men can bear to give up that kind of happiness because they have always been living partly in another world—that of ideas binding them to mankind's entire history and destiny. The image of happiness and politics and authority which Mill finally suggests, then, is not strictly that claimed by a religion of humanity which opens up an empty vista of individual annihilation and species endlessness. Rather, Mill seems finally to have left us where Hobbes and Locke did— with two worlds: one regulated by the logic of laws and morality; the other only promised by images and hopes that escape necessity. Politics mediates these worlds and citizenship consists of duties in both.

The realm of politics and the gods of liberalism once again meet, attended by risk, temptation, and freedom. Locke's picture of speculative religious faith as both powerless and all powerful symbolically represents the height of this most fortunate ambiguity—one which can always redeem the tradition of liberalism from the endlessness of laws and manners as well as from the slavelike necessities spoken in the language of mere truth. Mill's most utopian hopes for the power of ideas and his most trusting faith in the men who would dare to dream new ones binds him closely to Locke and, more tenuously perhaps, binds the tradition of liberalism to the possibility of political freedom.

Conclusion

Two centuries after Anthony Ascham, the Engagement pamphleteer, wrote of men born to two worlds, James Fitzjames Stephen, a utilitarian, defended a belief in the "end of the world" as a way of affirming human freedom. The conception of the end of the world is welcome, he said, because

> It is an opportunity for the spiritual nature of man to defy its material antagonist. It is an elevating thought that at some time . . . all that we see, and touch, and weigh, and measure, will cease to be, and that the spirits of men will be recognized, for good or for evil, as the real substances of which the heavens and the earth are accidents. Whether such an anticipation is true or false, it is at least splendid; and it gives the lie to much of that sham magnificence with which, in a scientific age, things intrinsically dead and soulless are invested by false associations.[1]

Liberalism from Hobbes through the utilitarians has often been held intrinsically dead and soulless. The certainties of its moral sciences are purchased, so the criticism goes, with a conception of man that denies his capacity for freedom and transcendence. In such accusations it is not recognized that criticisms of this type were made first and most vigorously by those within the tradition of liberalism itself. Stephen was a self-professed follower of Hobbes and a tenacious defender of Bentham's theory of law. He shared with Mill doubts about the sufficiency of Bentham's moral theory, calling for the explicit and political reintroduction of a belief in heaven and hell, a solution he thought superior to Mill's religion of humanity in preventing the dominance of "sham magnificence."

Whatever the merits of Stephen's criticisms of Mill's religion of humanity, it, too, is an attempt to uphold the "spiritual nature of man" and to make that affirmation the obligatory ground of liberalism. For better or worse,

216

this religion, expressed as a history of ideas, has become contemporary liberalism's sacred story in which all free men must place themselves, lest all men lapse into ways of life intrinsically dead and soulless. This study of the liberal tradition has been an attempt to recover neglected parts of that story and to show its importance to those who contributed its most important chapters. It remains now to draw some more speculative conclusions regarding its meaning for political life and freedom. These conclusions are necessarily tentative, but they nevertheless must be entertained if we are to judge the limits and possibilities of liberalism within the larger enterprise of political philosophy.

Freedom, Necessity, and Liberty

In liberal political philosophy, the assumption that man is born to liberty is always allied to a denial of free will. An empirically based psychology of desire and aversion or of pain-pleasure calculation must necessarily deny the efficacy of an autonomous "will" so that an empirically grounded legal and moral theory can be created. This same conclusion can be drawn simply by viewing the "state of nature" as a learning environment: material reality must dominate ideas, actions, and consciousness. It was not by chance that Locke, Hume, Bentham, and Mill shared Hobbes's position in denying free will. An affirmation of free will is found in these same writings, however, when the assumption is made that man is born in history and servitude. I have tried to show the nonparadoxical nature of this conclusion by examining the problem of capital punishment and death. A willingness to risk one's life and safety, whether as a soldier, citizen, or criminal, decisively refutes the arguments made against the possibility of free will: men in history are always portrayed as having this willingness while men in the state of nature and in natural history are not.

These two differing views of free will necessarily complicate the liberal notion of freedom. The denial of free will is the starting point for the construction and defense of "rule of law" and what is now termed "negative" liberty. This idea of freedom—most especially the right to create one's own obligations by voluntary private agreements—has nothing directly to do with political freedom and is as compatible with de facto theories of political obligation as it is with authoritarian regimes. In principle, objective standards exist for judging the extent of the legal freedom in any society and for measuring the individual and collective benefits which its exercise produces. Further, the maximum exercise of liberty of this kind is a precondition for proving the truth of the moral sciences constructed on a denial of free will: economics, jurisprudence, and psychology are both true and useful only under these conditions and therefore constitute a primary means of creating intellectual order and social discipline in a liberal theory of politics.

This latter feature—the ordering capabilities of systematic self-interest—is especially evident in nineteenth-century utilitarianism. Less evident is the way in which this idea of self-disciplining liberty is also a feature of seventeenth-century solutions to the politically destabilizing effects of free will in religious matters. The major weapon in Leviathan's arsenal for the defeat of religiously inspired pride is the guarantee of equal legal liberty. This weapon remains foremost, even in the more complacent mixed theories of government found in Locke, Hume, and Smith. No matter what the factual origins of political power, so long as it is primarily exercised to protect legal liberty most men will become immunized against appeals to exercise their political freedom against the standing government.

The assumption that man is born to servitude affirms free will and the exercise of political freedom—whether that freedom is exercised for good or for ill. This seeming paradox is less puzzling when we recall three specific expressions of it—religious, historical, and psychological. First, in seventeenth-century formulations, the struggles resulting in the acquisition or loss of political power are seen as part of sacred history presided over by God. Men's actions, in victory or in defeat, are portrayed as either acts of subservience to God's will or acts in vile subservience to a lust for godlike dominion. In both cases, however, the measure of the action can never be found in the morality of self-preservation and rational calculation, the grounds of legal and negative liberty. Indeed, the final measure of political action will only be evident at the end of the story; until then the exercise of political freedom is an act of prophetic faith. Is it any wonder that the "Kingdome of Darknesse" which Hobbes seeks to vanquish is a term taken from the most mystical and prophetic book of the New Testament?

A second expression of this paradoxical notion of political freedom is found in the historical explanations given for the rise of legal liberty. In contrast to state-of-nature and natural-history explanation, individual self-interest is not adduced as a direct motive for creating the political conditions supportive of legal liberty. All historical explanation pointing to changes in religious belief are the most obvious cases of this kind. Less obvious are the following: reliance on standing paternal-political power (Locke); discovery of the benefits of magistracy in wartime (Hume); the rise of sentiments of moral equality caused by widespread commerce and cooperative modes of production based on division of labor (Smith); and the creation of a culture of reform by disinterested intellectuals (J. S. Mill).

A third explanation of the paradox linking the assumption of servitude to political freedom is found in psychological theory. In all of the writings which address political freedom, the capacity for its responsible exercise is granted to very few men. In contrast, legal liberty is the preserve of the many because most men through all of history follow their self-interest within any social, economic, religious, and political context in which they happen to live. A liberal regime differs only marginally from others in that it encourages more rational and secular expressions of self-interest and in ways which achieve more predictable and economically productive forms of behavior. The epistemological starting point of the tabula rasa is the counterpart to men in the state of nature: neither assumes a capacity in men to think and act beyond the given context of pleasure and pain or, in Austin's phrase, the context of involuntary suffering. The creation and maintenance of contexts—political, moral, and legal—is the preserve of the few. Hobbes's sovereign by conquest; Locke's metaphoric captain and crew sailing the tumultuous sea of the many; Locke's and Hume's praise of minority religious dissenters; Mill's faith in the saving remnant of high-minded reformers: all point to some men freed from the prevailing force of material and moral coercion by their subservience to a consciously chosen set of ends requiring political action. All who act in this way acquire a consciousness of freedom as they acquire a mastery of their characters. All other men participate on this level of freedom only indirectly and through the efforts of others. Reason in most men is subservient to their ordinary passions, and therefore men do not comprehend the context within which their reason is exercised. Even Mill gauged the possibilities of reason in political choice to be extremely limited when he said that "most men . . . must in the last resort, fall back upon the authority of still more cultivated minds, as the ultimate sanction of the convictions of their reason itself."[2]

Equality, Democracy, and Liberty

The religious, historical, and psychological expressions of a paradox in liberal notions of freedom have a direct impact on the question of the relationship of liberalism to political democracy. Which assumption—man born to liberty or man born to servitude—best serves to connect liberalism to democracy? One need not search hard to find hostility to political democracy in all of the writings we have examined. It seems to me, however, that this hostility takes two very different forms. One form offers an egalitarian alternative and a barrier in principle to political democracy; the other provides a model of political action from which a justification for democratic participation in politics can be constructed. The egalitarian alternative begins with the notion that all men are equal because all men are born under the same set of natural necessities symbolized by the right of self-preservation. A regime of legal liberty not only preserves the dominance and prestige of this class of motives, it teaches that all who claim any resources on the basis of higher ones can be "exposed" as hiding base ones. When such claims are rejected, the moral equality of all is thereby assured. The political agency required to achieve this result may well be a single, impersonal Leviathan, but it could also be the constitutional mechanism sketched out in Hume's "Idea of a Perfect

Commonwealth" or the legislature in a political culture defined and dominated by shifting coalitions of economic interests.

The working ideal of this form of equality is shared privilege.[3] The moral equality of interests frees men to try to become better off than their fellows by acquiring more resources. If this process requires political action, the furthest moral reach of that action is to destroy politically protected bastions of high privilege in order to create many smaller bastions in their stead—which bastions are attacked in turn. Tocqueville's *Democracy in America* explores the dynamics of this model of equality. A satisfactory level of equality can never be achieved: small differences loom ever larger, but as privileges become increasingly widespread it is more difficult to mobilize majorities against them. More ominously, concerted political action of any kind becomes increasingly difficult if a society's central value is equality of self-interest. The reason "why revolutions will become more rare" and all political action increasingly difficult is that privatization (Tocqueville termed it "individualism") proceeds unchecked with the decline of great threats to moral equality. Men lose their capacity to heed political leaders, especially the ones who point to more subtle and dangerous forms of domination than those money can buy. Whether a single Leviathan or many legislators rule, the pleasures of this kind of equality "are every instant felt, and are within the reach of all; . . . in order to taste them nothing is required but to live."[4]

Tocqueville's analysis was not lost on Mill.[5] Mill's admitted hostility to democracy is addressed to this kind of egalitarianism. Even Hobbes and Locke, who first held out the promise of moral and legal equality, betrayed some contempt for those who took it unreservedly, for, in so doing, they committed themselves to a life bounded by natural depravity, a "desire for power after power" until death. This same promise also seems in principle to preclude political democracy. In Locke, the right of political participation must be restricted to those who in fact have enough property to constitute a link between a regime of legal-moral equality and the material benefits received from it. This link presumes a pervasive but mild corruption, in that political participation can be extended only as men can show their immunity both to higher and to lower motives. Despite some rather devastating doubts, Hume and Smith seemed to welcome political participation by a broadly defined middle class but only insofar as they trusted the socialization effects of commerce, industry, and luxury. The utilitarians wanted participation extended even further, but part of the cost was the suggestion that an entire class of the citizenry be placed in penitentiaries because it was deemed objectively incapable of obeying the law. More generally, all writings within this framework assume that popular political action is never to be undertaken with the end of governing, but only to limit and check standing governors. Here, too, is an inherent barrier to the idea of political democracy, for in any conflict between governing and participation, the latter must necessarily lose. So long as inequality is the end of individual liberty, political democracy will remain of secondary value.

The other form of hostility to political democracy is more ambivalent. It begins with men born to servitude and history but sees some forms of servitude as the basis for political freedom. Again, in Tocqueville's terms, the "exalted pleasures" of political liberty tend to be enjoyed by only a few because this liberty requires "sacrifices and great exertions."[6] Exercise of this liberty is often dangerous to the claim of a moral equality of interests because some men ask others to give them their trust and resources for a collective end. We should not disguise the fact that the literature of liberalism is full of warnings against most of these requests. Ascham warned the many against being herded out of their houses like horses to risk life and limb in the name of another's vanity; Hobbes thought most men were moderate and sensible unless seduced by the few who were obsessed by a love of power; Locke feared the "giddy multitudes" when inflamed by religious demagogues. Better that all men pursue proximate goals, chained to the necessities of their bodies, interests, and goods. But not always. Ascham, Hobbes, and Locke also spoke of the body of the truly faithful as a community of equals. The destruction of despotism and the institution of legal liberty require this community. This model of citizenship and equality has both millennialist (utopian) and charismatic features. Membership in a community of equals is independent of property, office, and status. Equality is an end to be achieved and not the starting line in a race for privilege; membership, not separation, is the greater goal.[7] The liberty celebrated is not the power to act on one's desires but a communal freedom to shape common ends of life.

The capacities for collective political action of this kind are multiplied in proportion to one's freedom from the ordinary passions and interests which animate civil society. This is seen most clearly in the millennialist and charismatic elements which accompany discussion of this model of action. Although Hobbes warned against designing men, especially under cover of religion, he also made his Leviathan Vicar of Christ and thus an earthly representation of the body of the faithful. Some from among Locke's giddy multitudes might become both sober and brave by emulating the practices of the dissenting sectarians. And surely John Stuart Mill, for all his praise of an educated elite, assumed that the bonds uniting the community of moral reformers were more egalitarian and liberating than shared credentials or class status. Not material interests and power, but opinions and ideas found in books and pamphlets, speeches and conversations, constitute the ligaments binding together this model of community. These words differ radically from the contractual word bonds sanctioned by the power of the sword and fear of death. Words denoting common ends are not the property or right of any individual but belong to each member only by virtue of his willingness to serve those ends. Mill most eloquently describes this kind of community as

> having its root no longer in the instinct of equals for self-protection, but in a cultivated sympathy between them . . . no one being now left out, but an equal measure being extended to all. . . . [T]he true virtue of human beings is fitness to live together as equals; claiming nothing for themselves but what they as freely concede to every one else; . . . preferring, whenever possible, the society of those with whom leading and following can be alternate and reciprocal.[8]

This model of community and political action is simultaneously democratic and aristocratic—democratic in its openness to all, aristocratic in that it requires the willingness to recognize some men as more faithful to the shared ends than others. Thus, the standard of citizenship includes judgments concerning a man's character as well as his actions and position. In both democratic and elitist guises, political life and action are independent of the distinctions created in civil society with its presumption of a moral equality of interests. Indeed, the very possibility of a community of equals presumes that interests must be ranked, that some pleasures *are* higher ones. Democratic politics is, then, a possibility only to the extent that a community of equals can be created and can include the vast majority of the citizenry.

History of Ideas, Social Science, and Analytic Philosophy

From time to time in this study, I have suggested that a history of ideas seems appropriate to men "born to servitude" while social science and analytic philosophy are appropriate to men "born to liberty." I have also suggested that liberal political thought, addressing men born to both worlds, utilized all three modes of understanding. Since I used Hobbes's *Leviathan* as the model for these distinctions, some more explicit conclusions should now be offered regarding these suggested relationships. At first glance, Hobbes seems uncompromisingly hostile to any notion of politics resting on a history of ideas. His "Kingdome of Darknesse" mocks the men and institutions claiming possession of historic wisdom, and he pits his own logic and science against the entire corpus of scholasticism. And if further proof were needed, Hobbes's aphorism at the conclusion of his masterpiece reads, "if it bee well considered, the praise of Ancient Authors, proceeds not from reverence of the Dead, but from the competition and mutual envy of the Living."[9] Hobbes neither praises ancient authors nor contends with others over the meanings of their texts. But he does place more than his own mind against them and the history of their ideas. He uses the biblical text and sees its history and prophecy encompassing his science and his politics, as well as their traditions and authorities. He contends mightily with others over the meaning of that text and its story, because he, like Locke, knows the political, moral, and intellectual consequences which ride on the outcome.

In their use of the Bible, both Hobbes and Locke incorporate a history of ideas in order to create and sustain a new system of ideas which purportedly rests on fact and logic. In this respect, their use of a history of ideas is the counterpart to their reliance on preexisting (historical) sources of political authority to sustain a new and ahistorical civil society. These preliberal ideas and the political authorities they legitimate serve another purpose as well: servitude to both can be a means of liberating the minds and bodies of men from despotic meanings of the texts and despotic rulers. Biblical history and prophecy can make the conclusions of unaided reason obligatory and liberal regimes a part of human and sacred history. This convergence of the conclusions of logic, science, and faith can become a political reality only if some men—including Hobbes and Locke—willingly subordinate their happiness and safety in order to tell others the meaning of this story.

The languages appropriate to men born free—social science and analytic philosophy—can never constitute a separate story. A liberal political philosophy entirely bounded by these two languages, like the first half of *Leviathan*, can never produce authoritative ends which constitute the story of human freedom. Only the assumption of a subservience to a more comprehensive tradition of ideas connects the enterprise of analytic philosophy and social science to political life and to political freedom. John Stuart Mill's critique of utilitarianism and the dissolving effects of analytic philosophy is a necessary prelude to his attempt to construct a logic of the moral sciences beginning with the capacity of man to create his own story and thus his own nature. In recounting the effects of exercising this capacity, merely empirical social and psychological truths are inadequate. Both history and human nature are created within the framework of speculative truths, that is, within the story of philosophy itself. For Mill, this story is both a history and a prophecy of freedom.

The creation of a moral, legal, and political theory based on the assumption that man is born to liberty is the most distinctive achievement of liberalism. Modern analytic philosophy and social science are part of this assumption and achievement. In contrast, both the tradition of political philosophy and the assumption that man is born to obligations are much older; they, too, are part of liberalism, but not its exclusive product or property. To the same degree, the idea of individual liberty grounded on the moral equality of interests is the hallmark of liberal thought, while ideas of political freedom and a community of equals are only incorporated into liberalism from other traditions.

Because of these differences, we today can tell different stories about liberalism, one bounded by its exclusive categories and the other including the more inclusive traditions of philosophy. In recovering the chapters which liberalism contributes to this latter story, I have also tried to show that the former one has major defects: alone it cannot tell us much about political freedom, whether experienced in our own consciousness or seen in the action and speech of others. Social science and analytic philosophy share these same defects.

An understanding of liberalism from the exclusive perspective of the former story has another grievous defect: it teaches that social science and analytic philosophy together now embrace all of the knowable subject matter of politics and represent the culmination of the tradition of systematic political thought. I have tried to show that an understanding of liberalism from the perspective of both stories demonstrates the vacuity of that teaching. Those who created the framework and much of the substance of social science and analytic philosophy knew the limited reach and the dependence of their creations upon other ideas and other traditions. This knowledge of limits was built into the dual structure of their writings and serves to remind us that freedom is not the exclusive property of either part. Mill feared utilitarian doctrines because the utilitarian story of freedom claimed to be the exclusive one, teaching us not to take seriously any other stories and thus the memory of philosophy itself. Mill's answer is my own: freedom must be located in a history of ideas which preserves the entire tradition of political philosophy—especially those parts of liberal political philosophy which incorporate and extend that tradition.

Notes

Introduction

1. Anthony Ascham, *What Is Particularly Lawful During Confusions and Revolutions of Government* (London, 1649), p. 161.

2. John Locke, *Two Tracts on Government* (Cambridge, 1967), ed. and with an Introduction by Philip Abrams, pp. 230–31.

3. John Stuart Mill, "The Utility of Religion" in M. Lerner, ed., *Essential Works of John Stuart Mill* (New York, 1961), p. 416.

4. Jean-Jacques Rousseau, *Emile*, trans. B. Foxley (New York, 1911), p. 252.

5. John Locke, *The Second Treatise of Government* (New York, 1952), no. 139.

6. Hannah Arendt, *The Life of the Mind*, vol. 1, *Thinking* (New York, 1978), p. 45.

Part One

1. Thomas Hobbes, *Leviathan, or the Matter, Forme and Power of a Commonwealth Ecclesiasticall and Civil* (New York and London, Everyman's Library, 1950), pt. II, chap. 31, pp. 318–19. Hereafter cited as *Leviathan*, part, chapter, and page. *English Works*, ed. Molesworth (London, 1841), vol. 5, p. 194. Hereafter cited as *E.W.*

2. D. P. Gauthier, *The Logic of Leviathan* (Oxford, 1969), p. 201, tells his readers that those who seek to understand "the positive structure and content of Hobbes' moral and political system may safely omit" his own five-page concluding discussion of the last half of *Leviathan* and presumably the text itself. For a bibliographic survey of this alternative, see Charles D. Tarlton, "The Creation and Maintenance of Government: A Neglected Dimension of Hobbes's Leviathan," *Political Studies* 26 (September 1978): 307, n.1.

3. Howard Warrender, *The Political Philosophy of Hobbes* (Oxford, 1957), chaps. 13–15, and M. M. Goldsmith, *Hobbes's Science of Politics* (New York, 1966), pp. 214–17.

4. Sheldon Wolin, *Politics and Vision* (Boston, 1960), pp. 273–74 and 335–37, and C. B. MacPherson, *The Political Theory of Possessive Individualism* (Oxford, 1962), pp. 224–29, stress the expediential use of supernatural religion in Hobbes and, later,

in Locke. F. C. Hood, *The Divine Politics of Thomas Hobbes* (Oxford, 1960), reverses the emphasis and maintains that Hobbes's entire theory of politics is structured and explained by Christian tradition, despite Hobbes's attacks on Catholicism, episcopacy, and Presbyterianism. Michael Oakeshott's Introduction to *Leviathan* (Oxford, 1960), p. xlvi, n., maintains that the last half of *Leviathan* renders irrelevant Hobbes's discussion of natural law in the early parts of the books. Oakeshott concludes, pp. xliv–xlv and lxii–lxiii, that Hobbes constructed a civil religion by transforming Christian belief into a civil theology. Leo Strauss, *The Political Philosophy of Hobbes* (Chicago, 1963), chap. 5, charts the relevance of Hobbes's writings on religion, but tends to see Puritanism as falling outside Judeo-Christian tradition.

5. For this meaning of religion as history, J. G. A. Pocock, "Time, History and Eschatology in the Thought of Thomas Hobbes," *Politics, Language and Time* (New York, 1973); on the specific role of millennial theology and radical politics in seventeenth-century England, J. G. A. Pocock, *The Machiavellian Moment* (Princeton, 1975), chaps. 1, 2, 11, 15; Christopher Hill, *The World Turned Upside Down, Radical Ideas During the English Revolution* (Harmondsworth, England, 1975), chaps. 6–19; in seventeenth- and eighteenth-century America, Alan Heimert, *Religion and the American Mind* (Cambridge, Mass., 1966); Sacvan Bercovitch, *The Puritan Origins of the American Self* (New Haven, 1975), and "The Typology of America's Mission," *American Quarterly* 30 (Summer, 1978): 135–55.

6. Many such criticisms of Hobbes's *Leviathan* are addressed only against the first half and for deficiencies which Hobbes clearly addresses in the second half although in the unfamiliar language and categories of supernatural religious belief. Hanna Pitkin, "Hobbes's Concept of Representation—I," *American Political Science Review* 58 (June 1964): 340, concludes that Hobbes's theory of representation suggests "a world of machines, whose behavior is programmed explicitly in advance. Such beings would have no need of concepts like motive and intention, trust and sympathy." Ellen Wood, *Mind and Politics, An Approach to the Meaning of Liberal and Socialist Individualism* (Berkeley, 1972), contrasts English and Continental theories of self as if the former perspectives were wholly confined within a logic of material interest. The capacity for social altruism and community loyalty was seen as lacking in the formulations of Hobbes when, in fact, he pointed precisely to these effects flowing from supernatural religious belief.

7. Irene Coltman, *Private Men and Public Causes* (London, 1962), esp. pp. 11–26 and pp. 197–239; A. Woolrych, "Oliver Cromwell and the Rule of the Saints," in R. H. Parry, ed., *The English Civil War and After, 1642–1658* (Berkeley, 1970); W. E. Prall, *The Agitation for Law Reform During the Puritan Revolution* (The Hague, 1966); George Mosse, "Thomas Hobbes: Jurisprudence at the Crossroads," *University of Toronto Quarterly* 15 (1945–46): 346–55; Quentin Skinner, "History and Ideology in the English Revolution," *Historical Journal* 8, no. 2 (1965): 151–78; "The Ideological Context of Hobbes' Political Thought," *Historical Journal* 9, no. 3 (1966): 286, and "Conquest and Consent: Thomas Hobbes and the Engagement Controversy," in G. E. Aylmer, ed., *The Interregnum: The Quest for Settlement, 1646–1660* (Hamden, Conn., 1972); J. A. W. Gunn, *Politics and the Public Interest in the Seventeenth Century* (London and Toronto, 1969), esp. pp. 55–108; Margaret A. Judson, *From Tradition to Political Reality: A Study of the Ideas Set Forth in Support of the Commonwealth Government in England, 1649–1653* (Hamden, Conn., 1980); John M. Wallace, *Destiny His Choice, The Loyalism of Andrew Marvell* (Chicago, 1968); and Perez Zagorin, *A History of Political Thought in the English Revolution* (London, 1954).

Chapter One

1. Thomas Hobbes, *The Elements of Law,* ed. F. Tönnies (London, 1889), was completed before 1640. Hereafter referred to as *Elements. De Cive,* or *The Citizen,* ed. S. Lamprecht (New York, 1949), was completed in 1642. *Leviathan* was written from 1649 to 1651 and published in 1651.

2. *Elements,* p. 2; *De Cive,* p. 21; Hobbes also does this in *Elements,* following essentially the same progression followed in *Leviathan.* Compare *Elements,* I, 2–9, to *Leviathan,* I, 1–7.

3. *Leviathan,* I, 1, p. 7; I, 2, pp. 10–11.

4. Ibid., I, 3, pp. 16 and 18. Conversely, Hobbes speaks here of thoughts without passion as wandering, "inconstant . . . impertinent one to another, as in a Dream."

5. Ibid., I, 3, p. 18.

6. Ibid., I, 3, pp. 19 and 20. Prudential knowledge has the same status as action.

7. Ibid., I, 6, pp. 40 and 39.

8. Ibid., I, 5, p. 36. See *Elements,* p. 26.

9. Ibid., I, 4, p. 23.

10. Ibid., I, 5, p. 37.

11. Ibid., I, 4, p. 27.

12. Ibid., I, 5, p. 36; I, 6, p. 49. Italics mine; I, 6, p. 42. See also ibid., I, 7, p. 51; I, 9, p. 67; and Goldsmith, *Hobbes's Science of Politics,* pp. 1–14. In the dedicatory epistle to Henry Lord Pierrepont of "Six Lessons to the Professor of Mathematics," Hobbes writes, "Of arts, some are demonstrable, others indemonstrable; and demonstrable are those the construction of the subject whereof is in the power of the artist himself, who . . . does no more but deduce the consequences of his own operation. Civil philosophy is demonstrable, because we make the commonwealth ourselves" (*E.W.,* 7:184).

13. *Leviathan,* I, 6, pp. 49 and 50.

14. Ibid., I, 5, p. 34. Both science and opinion take place among men. Hobbes speaks of inequalities from acquired wit both in terms of "talent" or virtue and power. The latter inequality I discuss in Chapter 2, below.

15. *Elements,* p. 26.

16. *Leviathan,* I, 5, pp. 33–34.

17. Ibid., I, 7, pp. 52–53.

18. *Elements,* p. 27, and *Leviathan,* I, 7, p. 52.

19. *Leviathan,* I, 7, pp. 53–54.

20. Ibid., I, 8, pp. 54–58, passim.

21. Ibid., I, 8, p. 58.

22. Ibid., I, 8, pp. 58–59.

23. Ibid., I, 8, p. 59.

24. Ibid., I, 8, pp. 60–61. And see *Elements,* p. 52, for another example of prophets.

25. *Leviathan,* I, 8, pp. 61–62 and 55. In Part IV, Hobbes's attack on the "kingdome of darknesse" is addressed to those who attempt to create philosophy from the Bible; they are like men who pretend to be prophets.

26. Ibid., I, 8, p. 57.

Chapter Two

1. *Leviathan*, I, 10, p. 69.
2. Ibid. MacPherson, *Possessive Individualism*, pp. 29–46, contains an extensive discussion of Chapter 10 of *Leviathan*, and shows its relationship to Hobbes's treatment of power in *Elements* and other writings.
3. *Leviathan*, I, 10, p. 70. Science is not an element of power. Because science "is of that nature, as none can understand it to be, but such as in a good measure have attayned it," science is "not eminent."
4. Ibid., I, 10, p. 75.
5. Ibid., I, 11, pp. 79–80. Italics mine. In *Elements*, pp. 47–48, Hobbes compares the search for felicity to a race which all men must run. Hobbes does not argue that all men seek to be foremost in the race for power, but that, in order to maintain one's relative position, power must be continuously sought.
6. *Leviathan*, I, 11, p. 83. See also, *A Dialogue Between a Philosopher and a Student of the Common Laws of England* (Chicago, 1971), ed. and with an Introduction by Joseph Cropsey, pp. 96–97 and 143. Hereafter cited as *Dialogue*.
7. *Leviathan*, I, 11, pp. 85–86, and I, 12, p. 87.
8. Ibid., I, 12, p. 87.
9. Ibid., I, 12, pp. 87–88.
10. Ibid., I, 12, p. 89.
11. Ibid., I, 12, pp. 90–91.
12. Ibid., I, 12, p. 91 and p. 96.
13. Ibid., I, 12, p. 97.
14. Ibid.
15. Ibid., I, 10, p. 70.
16. Ibid., I, 12, pp. 97–98.
17. Ibid.
18. Ibid., III, 32, p. 326. *Elements* does not contain an equivalent section devoted to the "seed of religion" and "Government of Religion." Immediately following a chapter on power and manners (9) and one on differences of wit among men and madness (10), *Elements* contains a long chapter on the status of men's knowledge of "things supernaturall." Hobbes states that all men can have "knowledge" of "the first power of all powers, and first causes of all causes." This knowledge, however, is without content and this god is "incomprehensible." Knowledge of a god who intervenes in the affairs of men and who has an effect on individual men is faith.
19. *Leviathan*, I, 11, p. 80.
20. Ibid., I, 12, p. 88. Italics mine.
21. Ibid., I, 10, p. 78.
22. MacPherson, *Possessive Individualism*, p. 40, refers to a "market in power" but does not recognize that this market is hopelessly distorted by religious belief and by the political relationships which flow from religious ties.
23. *Leviathan*, I, 4, p. 27.
24. Ibid., I, 12, p. 88.
25. Ibid., I, 12, p. 89.
26. See Goldsmith, *Hobbes's Science of Politics*, chaps. 1–3, on the god of nature, natural causal order, and human nature in Hobbes.

Chapter Three

1. *Leviathan*, I, 13, p. 101.
2. Ibid., I, 6, p. 48. By "voluntary" Hobbes means a process of deliberation (appetite and aversion) ending in the will—that is, doing or forebearing to do an action.
3. Wolin, *Politics and Vision*, pp. 248–72, contains an extensive discussion of the problem of names in Hobbes, and concludes that Hobbes's sovereign arbitrarily imposes names, ultimately by an act of power. I maintain in this chapter and the next that civil law in Hobbes's meaning was essentially without content, that it existed to enforce private agreements. Only with respect to doctrinal articles of faith and modes of worship (cf. above, chap. 5) does Hobbes's sovereign seem arbitrarily to name good and evil actions.
4. *Leviathan*, I, 8, p. 64. In the context quoted, Hobbes states that the biblical god left man in this position, because the Bible contains only prophecy for post-apostolic men, not law.
5. Ibid., I, 13, p. 103.
6. Ibid., I, 14, p. 117.
7. Ibid., I, 13, pp. 102–3. Compare with I, 11, pp. 79–80.
8. Ibid., I, 13, p. 105.
9. Ibid., I, 13, p. 104. Italics mine.
10. Ibid., I, 14, p. 109.
11. Ibid., I, 14, p. 107.
12. Ibid., I, 14, pp. 107–8.
13. Ibid., I, 14, pp. 110–14.
14. Ibid., I, 14, pp. 107–9.
15. Ibid., I, 14, p. 113.
16. Ibid., I, 15, pp. 124–25. Italics mine. "Justice of Actions," Hobbes states, "is by Writers divided into *Commutative*, and *Distributive:* and the former they say consisteth in proportion Arithmeticall; the later in proportion Geometricall. Commutative therefore, they place in the equality of value of the things contracted for; And Distributive, in the distribution of equall benefit, to men of equall merit. As if it were Injustice to sell dearer than we buy; or to give more to a man than he merits."
17. Ibid., I, 14, p. 117. A further possibility in this formulation is not simply to rely on fear but systematically to wage war on pride and glory. See Wolin, *Hobbes and the Epic Tradition of Political Theory*, William Andrews Clark Memorial Library (Los Angeles, 1970), pp. 23–50. The parallel of this enterprise and seventeenth-century Puritanism is apparent.
18. *Leviatian*, I, 14, p. 117.
19. Ibid., I, 14, p. 122. Italics mine.
20. Ibid., I, 14, p. 114.
21. Ibid., I, 15, pp. 118–19.
22. Ibid., I, 15, p. 119.
23. Ibid., I, 15, p. 123.
24. Ibid. Hobbes distinguishes between injustice of manners (the disposition to do injury) and injustice of actions. The latter presupposes a contract. Morality is invisible, so the only measurable standard of morality is legality, or some close analogue to legality. When an injury is committed, the actor's disposition is presumed to be clear.

25. Gratitude, the fourth law of nature mentioned in *Leviathan*, is portrayed as a type of quasi-contract: "For no man giveth, but with intention of Good to him-selfe." This law and the rest all share one of these two features: (a) the actions they urge are utterly incapable of measurement, even if they would be made into civil laws; (b) they merely indicate technical necessities in order for men to get close enough to create a government or to take care of dividing property which is not within the control of determinate men. As "moral virtues" in a civil state, they would, in fact, describe the informal habits of men related to each other largely by arm's-length agreements.

26. Ibid., I, 15, p. 132.

27. Ibid., I, 15, p. 133. When Hobbes examines the "kingdom" of a god known only by natural reason, he calls it "Metaphorical." Cf. ibid., II, 31, p. 307. On the relationships of this metaphorical kingdom to the real kingdom of God revealed in the Bible, see Chapter 5.

28. Ibid., II, 31, pp. 308–9.

29. Ibid., II, 31, p. 317.

30. Ibid., II, 31, p. 312.

Chapter Four

1. *Leviathan*, I, 31, p. 315.

2. *E.W.*, 5:194.

3. ". . . because neither mine nor the Bishop's reason is right reason fit to be a rule of our moral actions, we have therefore set up over ourselves a sovereign governor, and agreed that his laws shall be unto us, whatsoever they be, in the place of right reason, to dictate to us what is really good. In the same manner as men in playing turn up trump, and as in playing their game their morality consisteth in not renouncing, so in our civil conversation our morality is all contained in not dis-obeying of the laws" (ibid.). See also, *Dialogue*, p. 140.

4. *Leviathan*, I, 13, p. 113.

5. Ibid., I, 16, "Of Persons, Authors, and Things Personated." In "Hobbes's Concept of Representation," Professor Pitkin summarizes Hobbes's concept of au-thorization found in Chapter 16 of *Leviathan:* "Sometimes Hobbes speaks as if a man who has the right to do an action, commissions someone else to do it for him. At other times, Hobbes describes a man making himself owner of, making himself responsible for, what someone else is going to do. In both cases the rights and privileges accrue to the one who is authorized, the obligations and responsibilities to the one who authorizes." Wolin, *Politics and Vison*, pp. 275–81, also discusses representation in terms of "the naive assumption that, in a society of egotists, all that was needed to erase the conflict between public and private ends was the creation of a public, institutionalized ego."

6. *Leviathan*, II, 18, pp. 145–51. A specification of this "right" is the fourth right of sovereignty: "that whatsoever he doth, it can be no injury to any of his Subjects" (ibid., II, 18, p. 148).

7. Ibid., II, 26, p. 227.

8. This criticism takes the form of arguing that there is no necessary relationship between morality and legality in Hobbes's formulation because of the motives which led men into civil society and/or because of the powers which the sovereign was "granted." Both Warrender, *Political Philosophy of Hobbes*, pp. 330–37, and MacPherson, *Possessive Individualism*, pp. 9–18, summarize mainly British writings which argue lack of relationship. K. C. Brown, ed., *Hobbes Studies* (Oxford, 1965),

contains four articles defending and attacking Hobbes on this point. Hood, *Divine Politics*, offers a fascinating and complex argument attempting to show that morality and legality in Hobbes are only related because Hobbes rested his whole case on faith. Cf. especially Chapters 3, 12, and 18. See also, Oakeshott, Introduction, pp. xliv–xlv and pp. lxii–lxiv. My argument in Chapter 5, above, is indebted to Hood and Oakeshott, though my conclusions are quite different from theirs, stressing the relationship between supernatural religion and a theory of history in Hobbes.

9. *E.W.*, 5:194, and see *Dialogue*, p. 140.

10. *Leviathan*, II, 18, pp. 149–50. Italics mine.

11. Ibid., I, 15, p. 119 (italics mine), and see *Dialogue*, pp. 72–73 and p. 143.

12. *Leviathan*, II, 30, p. 289.

13. To teach true opinion requires the same strategies and instruments by which "so many Opinions, contrary to the Peace of Mankind, upon weak and false Principles, have nevertheless been so deeply rooted in [the people]" (ibid., II, 30, p. 295). And see ibid., II, 30, p. 291, and *Elements*, pp. 183–84.

14. *Leviathan*, II, 30, pp. 291–92.

15. Ibid., II, 30, p. 292. In a specifically biblical context, see ibid., III, 40, p. 413.

16. Ibid., II, 30, p. 291.

17. Ibid., II, 28, pp. 273–74.

18. Ibid., II, 28, p. 273.

19. *Dialogue*, p. 78.

20. Ibid., p. 76. And see *Leviathan*, II, 28, pp. 269–70, for the distinction between corporal and monetary punishment. Here Hobbes only says that harm "inflicted upon one that is a declared enemy, [falls] not under the name of punishment." Mario Cattaneo's "Hobbes' Theory of Punishment," in Brown, *Hobbes Studies*, p. 275–97, compares Hobbes with Bentham, Beccaria, and other liberals regarding "the principles of the certitude of the law, the basis of the right to punish and the question of torture" (p. 283). He concludes that Hobbes is decidedly liberal and anticipates Bentham and Beccaria. Joseph Cropsey's Introduction to *Dialogue*, especially pp. 30–48, stresses Hobbes's liberal perspective on courts, heresy, treasons, and punishment. These conclusions are all warranted so long as Hobbes is treating the sovereign as a pure artifice. The entire range of criminal law and bodily punishment is restricted by Hobbes, however, because it falls outside of any conceivable authorization by the subjects.

21. *Leviathan*, II, 27, p. 251.

22. Ibid., II, 27, p. 256.

23. Ibid., II, 27, p. 258. In discussing why fear causes private revenges and why some of these revenges are not crimes, Hobbes stresses that the fear must be "Bodily Fear." Thus, to revenge "words of disgrace, or some little injuries" for which no civil law provides, because of fear of falling into contempt, "is a Crime: For the hurt is not Corporeall, but Phantasticall." Hobbes stresses this distinction so that no man will seek revenge on the basis of "fear of spirits . . . of strange Dreams and Visions" (ibid., II, 27, pp. 256–57).

24. Ibid., II, 27, pp. 249–50, and ibid., I, 13, p. 104.

25. Ibid., II, 27, p. 260. Hobbes states earlier that "Of the Passions that most frequently are the causes of Crime, one, is Vain-glory, or a foolish over-rating of their own worth; as if the difference of worth, were an effect of their wit, or riches, or blood, or some other naturall quality, not depending on the Will of those that have the Sovereign Authority" (ibid., II, 27, p. 254).

26. Ibid., II, 27, pp. 249–50, and pp. 262–63. Hobbes lists three defects of reasoning in this context: "Presumption of false Principles," "false Teachers, that either mis-interpret the Law of Nature . . . or by teaching for Lawes, Doctrines of their own," and "Erroneous Inferences from True Principles." No man, Hobbes concludes, "that pretendeth to the administration of his private businesse" can be excused from a crime alleging the defects listed above (ibid., II, 27, pp. 253–54).

27. Ibid., II, 29, pp. 277–78.

28. Ibid., II, 29, pp. 278–79. Italics mine. The framework Hobbes establishes here is a thoroughly "Puritan" problem, while his answer is the only one a Puritan could give who seeks to contain the effects of "Christian liberty." The most dangerous doctrine of all is "that Sanctity and Natural Reason, cannot stand together."

29. The public rewards promised in historical politics were not equally distributed, nor, in Hobbes's sense, were they based on "merit." But power-seeking through the channels of political and religious institutions was motivated, according to Hobbes, because the actors (and those allied to them) felt divinely inspired or were part of institutions which claimed such inspiration.

30. According to Hobbes's chapter on manners, man in his search for felicity is not to enjoy objects of desire "once onely, and for one instant of time; but to assure for ever the way of his future desire" (ibid., I, 11, p. 79).

31. *Elements*, p. 147.

32. *Leviathan*, I, 11 and 12.

33. Ibid., II, 26–28.

34. Ibid., I, 13, and II, 27 and 29.

35. Ibid., II, 24 and 30.

36. Ibid., II, 29, p. 275, and II, 30, pp. 289–90.

37. Ibid., II, 30, p. 290.

38. Ibid., III, 38, p. 387. Italics mine.

39. Ibid.

40. Ibid., II, 31, p. 307.

41. Ibid., III, 35, p. 357.

42. Christopher Hill, *Puritanism and Revolution* (London, 1958), pp. 50–122, summarizes the revolutionaries' use of pre-Conquest rationale for legal and political change.

43. Prall, *Agitation*, pp. 10–11 and pp. 50–98; and Donald Veall, *The Popular Movement for Law Reform, 1640–1660* (Oxford, 1970), chaps. 5–11, for the specific legal changes urged and instituted before and after the regicide.

44. See above, Part I, n.8; and Ivan Roots, "Interest—Public, Private, and Communal," in Parry, *The English Civil War*. On the use of Hobbes by defenders of the Commonwealth, see below, nn. 47, 48.

45. Christopher Hill, *Antichrist in Seventeenth-Century England* (Oxford, 1971), chap. 3, esp. pp. 98–123; *God's Englishmen; Oliver Cromwell and the English Revolution* (New York, 1970), pp. 211–50; *Puritanism and Revolution*, chap. 4; *The World Turned Upside Down;* articles by C. V. Wedgwood and Austin Woolrych in Parry, *The English Civil War;* and Judson, *From Tradition to Political Reality*, chaps. 1, 2.

46. Ernest L. Tuveson, *Millennium and Utopia: A Study in the Background of the Idea of Progress* (Berkeley, 1949), remains the most complete analysis of the political images of millennial periods. Pocock, *Machiavellian Moment*, chap. 12 and *Politics, Language and Time*, pp. 148–201.

47. John Dury, *Considerations Concerning the Present Engagement* (London, 1650), p. 13. In this pamphlet, unlike in another of his, *Objections Against the*

Taking of the Engagement Answered (London, 1650), Dury utilizes legal arguments, many of which appear to be taken from Anthony Ascham, *What Is Particularly Lawful During Confusions and Revolutions of Government* (1649), first published in 1648 and revised the following year to include portions of Hobbes's *De Cive;* hereafter referred to as *Confusions and Revolutions*. For an extensive listing of the pamphlet literature, consult J. M. Wallace, "The Engagement Controversy," *Bulletin of the New York Public Library* 68 (1964): 391–92; on Hobbes and this literature, see Skinner, "Conquest and Consent."

48. Title of Chapter 2, Marchamont Nedham, *Case of the Commonwealth, Stated,* Folger Library (Charlottesville, Virginia, 1969), first published London, 1650. Marchamont Nedham's newspaper, *Mercurius Politicus,* printed sections of what came to be known as Hobbes's *Elements of Law* under Tönnies's editorship; Thomas White, a Catholic and personal friend of Hobbes, wrote *The Grounds of Obedience and Government* (London, 1655), urging engagement to the Commonwealth; Ascham, *Confusions and Revolutions*.

49. Francis Osborne, "Advice to a Son," from *Works* (London, 1701), p. 59. Osborne wrote *A Persuasive to a Mutual Compliance* (London, 1652) in support of the Engagement.

50. Dury, *Considerations*, p. 5.

51. Dury, *Objections*, Preface and p. 2.

52. Dury, *Considerations*, pp. 10–12.

53. Ibid., p. 5, and see p. 3, on protection from civil injuries, and p. 13, on the test of de facto power consisting of whether or not courts and a law-making power are in force, "to whom both he [the sovereign] and they are accountable." Dury's stress on his audience as private men referred both to the idea of privacy as "Christian conscience" and to nonofficials. See also Osborne, "Advice to a Son," pp. 61–62, for a discussion of the relationship of private men to public power in a way that leaves out all hint of Christian liberty: "All we owe to Governors, is Obedience, which depends wholly on Power, and therefore subject to follow the same fate and perish with it: For Friendship can be contracted between none that stand so far remote from the Line of Parity" (pp. 61–62). Wolin, *Politics and Vision*, pp. 272–85, discusses the inherent weakness of Hobbes's sovereign primarily in these terms.

54. Ascham, *Confusions and Revolutions*, pp. 142–43.

55. Ibid., p. 144. From this, Ascham argues that civil war is much worse than foreign war because private legal and moral relationships are also involved (p. 146).

56. Ibid., p. 133. In answer to the objection that obedience "even in Lawfull Things to unlawfull Governours, doth assert those Governours as lawful," Ascham answers: "If it be upon a plenary Possession, such an Obedience only asserts the Irresistibility of their Power. In this Argument [i.e., in Ascham's answer to the objection], there is no place for a distinction of a Government establisht with Long rooting, or without rooting: For if we sinne in doing Lawfull or unlawfull things under either, the Lapse of time . . . takes not away sinne either" (p. 137).

57. Ibid., p. 150 (Ascham's italics).

58. Ascham contends that there are three ways open to men to "evidence" or learn knowledge of religion and its relationship to justice: public authority, reason common to all men, and private revelation. In convincing others, public authority "(as Largest) prejudges from the other two, and the second from the last." This is the case because revelation "hath the greatest proofs for it selfe within but hath the least Evidence for it selfe without; and therefore cannot be offer'd either as the Sentance of a Judge, or as the Reason of a Doctour." Reason construed either logically as speech or

morally "as it relates to Prudentiall habits and Chiefly to the Virtue of Justice" must yield to authority (ibid., pp. 150–51).

59. Ibid., see pp. 152–53.

60. Ibid., p. 153.

61. Ibid., pp. 153–54.

62. Ibid., p. 157. Note his distinctive use of capitalization and plurals.

63. Wallace, "The Engagement Controversy," attributes *The Bounds and Bonds of Public Obedience* (London, 1649) to Ascham, even though it was generally attributed to Francis Rous. Whoever wrote it, the argument is considerably less systematic than in *Confusions and Revolutions.* The latter pamphlet's arguments were obviously utilized by Dury in *Considerations.* Wallace notes the wide influence of Ascham's *Confusions and Revolutions.*

64. The money argument was probably added to counter the demands of the most radical of the Puritan sects for an entirely new set of laws to be written. See Prall, *Agitation,* Chaps. 4 and 5, on Puritan lawyers' defense of the common law in the early 1650s.

65. Ascham, *Confusions and Revolutions,* p. 157.

Chapter Five

1. *Leviathan,* III, 32, p. 322. Warrender, arguing strictly from the motivational features in the state of nature, claims that even the god of nature is not strictly required to make Hobbes's theory of obligation logically coherent. Since one can choose to be an atheist, he argues from Hobbes, a fortiori one does not have to be a Christian. Warrender tends to discount Hobbes's discussion of will to obedience, which I have maintained places Hobbesian subjects outside of the motivational necessity implicit in the state of nature. Warrender transforms motivational necessity into prudence. See his *Political Philosophy of Hobbes,* pp. 299–329, for a summary of the argument. Hood, *Divine Politics of Hobbes,* pp. 57–126, contains an extensive discussion of obligation and its relationship to the "will to obedience," concluding that within the framework of Parts I and II of *Leviathan,* "Moral obligation is a mystery, of which Hobbes wrote . . . only in terms of theistic belief, or of philosophic fiction" (p. 126).

2. *Leviathan,* III, 36, p. 378–79.

3. Ibid., III, 42, p. 496. Italics mine. Contrast with the conditional language Hobbes uses when discussing the worship of a god known only by reason: "And that which is said in the Scripture, *It is better to obey God than men,* hath place in the kingdom of God by Pact, and not by Nature" (ibid., II, 31, p. 317; Hobbes's italics).

4. Cf. ibid., I, 16, pp. 134–37. Pitkin's analysis, "Hobbes's Concept of Representation," omits any discussion of representation found in Part III, *Leviathan.*

5. This argument is summarized in Chapter 33 of *Leviathan,* and is explicated in Chapters 35–37 and 40 of Part III. The status of this kingdom at various periods in Old Testament history is actually more complex than the summary given here. See Pocock, "Time, History and Eschatology," pp. 170–76; and Patricia Springborg, "Leviathan and the Problem of Ecclesiastical Authority," *Political Theory* 3 (August 1975): 294–97.

6. *Leviathan,* III, 41, pp. 425–28.

7. Ibid., III, 42, p. 433.

8. See ibid., III, 40, pp. 408–14.

9. Ibid., III, 40, p. 417.

10. Ibid., III, 41, p. 424.

11. Ibid., II, 31, p. 312.

12. Ibid., III, 42, p. 435, and see ibid., 40, p. 409: "As for the inward *thought* and *beleef* of men, which humane Governours can take no notice of . . . they are not voluntary, nor the effect of laws . . . and consequently fall not under obligation."

13. All quotations from Charles and Katherine George, *The Protestant Mind of The English Reformation, 1570–1640* (Princeton, 1961), pp. 237, 356, 367. See ibid., pp. 181–223 and 306–72, and Philip E. Hughes, *Theology of the English Reformers* (London, 1965), pp. 224–62, on the combination of radical theology and expediential and conservative institutionalism of the Anglican reformation. Hall (1574–1656) was bishop of Norwich; Whitgift (1530–1604) was archbishop of Canterbury; Sanderson (1587–1663) was bishop of Lincoln.

14. *Leviathan*, III, 43, p. 516.

15. Ibid., III, 38, p. 399.

16. Ibid., III, 38, p. 393.

17. Ibid., III, 36, pp. 378–79.

18. Ibid., III, 42, p. 457.

19. Ibid., III, 42, p. 448.

20. Chapter 42 of *Leviathan*, Part III, is more than one-tenth of the entire book. This should not be surprising, given the full title of *Leviathan*.

21. Ibid., III, 42, p. 450.

22. Ibid., III, 42, p. 456. The implication of Hobbes's view for religious freedom was not missed. In 1821, Bentham wrote "Summary View of a Work, Intituled Not Paul, But Jesus" (London, 1821). Francis Place claims to have put the book, *Not Paul, But Jesus* (London, 1823), together for Bentham under the pseudonym "Gamaliel Smith, esq." See Elie Halévy, *The Growth of Philosophic Radicalism* (Boston, 1955), p. 544.

23. *Leviathan*, III, 42, p. 498.

24. Ibid.

25. Ibid., III, 43, pp. 519 and 526.

26. Ibid., III, 43, pp. 517 and 519.

27. The phrase is from the Book of Revelation in the context of the "fifth monarchy" (16:10–11). On this central image in millennialist thought, see Tuveson, *Millennium and Utopia;* Woolrych article in Parry, *The English Civil War;* and Hill, *Antichrist in Seventeenth-Century England*, pp. 98–123.

28. *Leviathan*, IV, 47, p. 612.

29. Ibid.

30. Ibid., IV, 47, pp. 612–13.

31. Ibid., IV, 47, p. 613. Italics mine.

Chapter Six

1. *Leviathan*, I, 12, pp. 88–89.

2. Ibid., II, 30, p. 290.

3. Ibid.

4. See Wolin, *Hobbes and the Epic Tradition*, pp. 19–33 and pp. 41–50.

Part Two

1. For discussions of Lockean scholarship, consult John Dunn, *The Political Thought of John Locke* (Cambridge, 1969), pp. 5–10 and pp. 203–67; Hans Aarsleff, "Some Observations on Recent Locke Scholarship," in John Yolton, ed., *John Locke:*

Problems and Perspectives (Cambridge, 1969); Peter Laslett, Introduction, in John Locke, *Two Treatises of Government* (Cambridge, 1960).

2. Dunn, *Political Thought of Locke,* and Richard Ashcraft, "Faith and Knowledge in Locke's Philosophy," in Yolton, *John Locke,* both address the larger structure of Locke's thought. Professor Dunn's primary purpose is to locate the argument of the *Two Treatises* in the history of Locke's intellectual life. Professor Ashcraft's intention is to reestablish "the seventeenth-century context within which the *Essay Concerning Human Understanding* was written" (p. 94).

3. John Locke, *The Second Treatise of Government,* ed. and with an introduction by T. P. Peardon (New York, 1952), no. 11 and nos. 87–89, on punishing power, and nos. 134–58 on legislative power. Hereafter cited as *Second Treatise,* paragraph number. The difference between executive power and legislative will is most clearly expressed in conflicting interpretations of Locke. Compare, for example, Richard Cox, *Locke on War and Peace* (Oxford, 1960), and Willmoore Kendall, *John Locke and the Doctrine of Majority Rule* (University of Illinois, 1941).

4. Three features of the *Second Treatise* constitute the main ground of contrast: civil society independent of a political executive; an implied constitutional separation of powers; and a theory of resistance and revolution.

5. Ashcraft, "Faith and Knowledge"; Dunn, *Political Thought of Locke.*

Chapter Seven

1. Locke's major writings on the power of government over religious belief and church polity are: *Two Tracts on Government* (1660–62); *Essay on Toleration* (1667); *A Defense of Nonconformity* (1682); *A Letter Concerning Toleration* (1689) (in Latin, 1685); *A Second Letter* (1690); *A Third Letter* (1692); and, left unfinished at his death in 1704, *A Fourth Letter.* Locke's major writings on the relationship between Christian belief and political life are: *The Reasonableness of Christianity as delivered in the Scriptures* (1695); "A Vindication of the Reasonableness . . ." (1695); and "A Second Vindication of the Reasonableness . . ." (1697).

2. See Sterling Lamprecht, *The Moral and Political Philosophy of John Locke* (New York, 1962), pp. 152–53, on the background of the four letters on toleration; Mario Montuori, Introduction to *A Letter Concerning Toleration,* Latin and English Texts (The Hague, 1963), pp. xv–l, for an extensive discussion of the publishing history of the first letter; and J. W. Gough, *John Locke's Political Philosophy* (Oxford, 1973), chap. 8. A late-nineteenth-century essay on Locke's *Letters,* occasioned by a publication of Locke's *Works,* puts the position occupied by the "First Letter" this way: "[I]f an abstract of it were republished without saying where it came from—in some provincial newspaper, for instance—no one would think that it was anything else than a summary of what the editor himself, and all his predecessors for generations before him, had been continually saying on the same topic" (James Fitzjames Stephen, *Horae Sabbaticae,* reprint of articles contributed to the *Saturday Review,* vol. 2 [London, 1892], pp. 157–59).

3. Peter Laslett in the Introduction to the *Two Treatises,* pp. 92–105, thinks it inappropriate to view the *Second Treatise* as political philosophy at all. When reading Locke's *Essay Concerning Human Understanding,* we see Locke as an epistemologist doing philosophy; when reading the *Second Treatise,* we see Locke as a kind of "doctor" doing "empirical medicine" (pp. 98–99).

4. From title of preceding chapter (46), *Leviathan.*

5. *Leviathan,* "A Review and Conclusion," pp. 619–20.

6. "First Letter," *The Works of John Locke in Ten Volumes* (London, 1823 ed.), 6:23. Hereafter all references to the four "Letters on Toleration" will be cited "First (or "Second," etc.) Letter," *Works*, volume no.: page. Cf. also, ibid., pp. 5–6.

7. "Second Letter," *Works*, 6:64.

8. "First Letter," *Works*, 6:40; and see, "Second Letter," ibid., p. 62.

9. "First Letter," *Works*, 6:10. Locke realized, as did Hobbes, that churches and churchmen can induce obedience to moral rules on the basis of biblical faith if the church members stand in fear of divine punishment.

10. Ibid., pp. 9–10 and p. 13.

11. "Third Letter," *Works*, 6:144. Locke's "Fourth Letter" is devoted almost exclusively to a defense of this distinction, *Works*, 6:549–74. Hobbes discusses the distinction between knowledge and belief in relationship to Christian prophecy in these contexts: (a) when asking if we can distinguish a "true prophet" from a false one (*Leviathan*, III, 32); (b) when asking if we can know who has authority to translate written prophecy into law (III, 33); and (c) when asking if we can know what is required for salvation (III, 43). His conclusions in all three contexts are the same as Locke's: We can "know" natural law but we can only "believe" the Bible.

12. "First Letter," *Works*, 6:21.

13. Ibid., pp. 29–39.

14. Ibid., p. 41.

15. Ibid., pp. 29, 31, and 33. Hobbes also speaks of the intention of the worshipper as definitive in this regard, *Leviathan*, IV, 45, p. 570. Both Hobbes and Locke recognize the historical fact of diverse forms of outward worship and both hold that these forms rest on opinions and belief.

16. "First Letter," *Works*, 6:39–40. Italics mine. Compare *Leviathan*, II, 26, p. 245; III, 32, p. 322; III, 39, p. 409; and III, 42, p. 457.

17. "First Letter," *Works*, 6:40. Compare *Leviathan*, III, 42, p. 498, and III, 43, pp. 521–22, for a similar relationship.

18. "First Letter," *Works*, 6:41–42. Italics mine.

19. Ibid., p. 41.

20. Ibid., p. 45.

21. All quotations are from ibid., p. 42.

22. Ibid., p. 45. Hobbes's sovereign is charged with the negative task. Cf. *Leviathan*, II, 30, pp. 288–96.

23. "First Letter," *Works*, 6:45.

24. Ibid., p. 46. Italics mine.

25. Ibid.

26. Ibid., p. 47. In all the exceptions to the principle of toleration, Locke subjects the prophetic church to the standards of natural law and natural religion, thereby placing civil law as the final standard regarding beliefs which touch on political obligation.

27. Ibid., p. 13. This idea is more clearly expressed in Locke's theological writings. See, for example, his relative denigration of the Epistles and his stress on the Gospels in *On the Reasonableness of Christianity*, ed. and with an Introduction by George W. Ewing (Chicago, 1965), nos. 247–51. Hereafter cited as *Reasonableness*.

28. "First Letter," *Works*, 6:17.

29. Ibid., p. 48.

30. Ibid., p. 50. Italics mine.

31. In the Introduction to John Locke, *Two Tracts on Government* (Cambridge, 1967), pp. 30–81, Philip Abrams explores the more "Hobbesian" features of these early writings, especially those which concern sovereign control over external acts

and dress related to worship. Robert Kraynack, "John Locke: From Absolutism to Toleration," *American Political Science Review* 74 (March 1980): 66–68, maintains that Locke's early absolutism and later liberalism rest on the same principles.

32. "First Letter," *Works*, 6:51.

33. Compare ibid., pp. 51–54 and pp. 18, 21, 23, and 46. See discussion in Lamprecht, *Moral and Political Philosophy of Locke*, pp. 154–55.

34. John Dunn, *Political Thought of Locke*, pp. 79–83.

Chapter Eight

1. See above, chap. 7, n.1. Locke's theological writings also include three posthumously published works: *A Paraphrase and Notes on the Epistles of St. Paul . . . [and] An Essay for the Understanding of St. Paul's Epistles . . .* (1705–7); *A Discourse on Miracles* (1706); and *An Examination of Father Malebranche's Opinion of Seeing all Things in God* (1706).

2. On Locke's early concern with the relationship of morality and revealed religion, see S. von Leyden, Introduction, in John Locke, *Essays on the Law of Nature* (Oxford, 1954), pp. 60–82. On the controversy surrounding publication of the *Reasonableness*, see John Yolton, *John Locke and the Way of Ideas* (Oxford, 1956), pp. 62–64 and pp. 174–75, and George Ewing, Introduction, in John Locke, *Reasonableness*.

3. Locke suggests precisely this apologetic purpose in *Reasonableness* and the two "Vindications." See, for example, "Second Vindication," *Works*, 7:188–265. See John C. Biddle, "Locke on Reasonable Christianity," *Journal of the History of Ideas* 37 (July–September 1976): 411–22, on Locke's intentions. An indication of the different intellectual contexts Hobbes confronted can be seen in his stated purpose for Parts III and IV of *Leviathan*. Hobbes's effort appears to be directed more toward convincing Christians that the logic of natural law is not a threat to faith. Hobbes was thereby popularly thought an atheist while Locke was, if not welcomed by Anglican churchmen, at least supported by some of the more free-thinking ones.

4. *Reasonableness*, no. 241, pp. 170–71, and no. 243, p. 178.

5. Ibid., no. 241, p. 170.

6. Ibid., no. 242, p. 173.

7. Locke more rigorously locates the time when the Gospels end and the Epistles begin.

8. Locke promises a "demonstrable" science of morality to fulfill this duty, but fails to keep this promise. Dunn, *Political Thought of Locke*, pp. 203–67, discusses this issue in terms of a theory of morality and of political obligation. And see below, n. 20.

9. *Reasonableness*, no. 243, p. 176. Italics mine.

10. "Second Vindication," *Works*, 7:352. See also, ibid., p. 231. Hobbes makes the same argument in *Leviathan*, III, 43, pp. 518 and 521.

11. "Second Vindication," *Works*, 7:358.

12. Ibid., p. 382.

13. Ibid., p. 358. Hobbes repeatedly makes this argument, but only in reference to private men, not the sovereign. The principles of biblical interpretation in Locke's writings are identical with those of Hobbes. The Old Testament mixes universally valid law (natural law) with "peculiar" ceremonial and political law, therefore furnishing no certain guidance for salvation by works. The New Testament Epistles are addressed to particular problems of extant church organizations. Thus, only the

Gospels tell of the conversion of the gentiles in a context not obscure, particular, or open to the possibility of dominion-serving interpretation.

14. "Second Vindication," *Works*, 7:232–33. See *Leviathan*, III, 42, p. 498, and III, 43, p. 521.

15. "Second Vindication," *Works*, 7:229. See *Leviathan*, III, 43, pp. 515–16 and p. 528.

16. "First Letter," *Works*, 6:37. In this context, "legislator" means "sovereign," for the "executive" is simply enforcing God's commands.

17. Ibid., p. 38.

18. "Second Vindication," *Works*, 7:229.

19. In *Leviathan*, I, 12, pp. 97–100, Hobbes discusses Christian church history in exactly these terms when he explains the logic of the dissolution of moral and political orders.

20. *Reasonableness*, nos. 239–45, and John Locke, *An Essay Concerning Human Understanding*, 2 vols. (New York, 1961), bk. IV, chap. XVIII (hereafter cited as *Essay*, book, chapter, paragraph). See also, Ashcraft, "Faith and Knowledge," pp. 214–23.

21. *Reasonableness*, no. 241, p. 170.

22. See Wolin, *Politics and Vision*, pp. 314–31, on Locke's notion of pain avoidance and its use in subsequent liberal political theory.

23. *Essay*, bk. II, chap. XXI, no. 71. See also ibid., nos. 5 and 15. Lamprecht, *Moral and Political Philosophy of Locke*, pp. 89–94, remarks on the similarity between Hobbes and Locke on the question of willing and punishment, but argues that Locke was simply inconsistent in attempting to reconcile this part of his *Essay* and later writings on natural law, especially his own discussions of natural law in his *Second Treatise*.

24. *Essay*, bk. II, chap. XXI, no. 44.

25. Ibid., no. 31. See also, ibid., nos. 35, 36, and 37.

26. Ibid., no. 33.

27. Ibid., no. 19. Hobbes's position on the relationship between power and will is similar. See Part One, Chapter 1, above.

28. *Essay*, bk. II, chap. XXI, no. 18. Locke scholars always seek to resurrect elements of autonomous reason in Locke's politics, despite Locke's own denials in his epistemology. See Patrick Riley, "Locke on 'Voluntary Agreement' and Political Power," *Western Political Quarterly* 29 (March 1976):136–45.

29. *Essay*, bk. II, chap. XXI, no. 42.

30. Ibid., no. 43.

31. Ibid., chap. XXVIII, no. 5. Note that the lawmaker does provide for punishment but does not give rewards except by refraining from punishment. Compare with Hobbes's discussion in *Leviathan*, II, 28.

32. *Reasonableness*, no. 245, p. 185.

33. *Essay*, bk. IV, chap. XVIII.

34. Ibid., bk. II, chap. XXI, no. 45, and see no. 34.

35. Wolin, *Politics and Vision*, pp. 306–12; Richard Ashcraft, "Locke's State of Nature: Historical Fact or Moral Fiction?" *American Political Science Review* 62 (September 1968):898–915; Robert A. Goldwin, "John Locke," in Leo Strauss and Joseph Cropsey, eds., *History of Political Philosophy* (Chicago, 1963), pp. 242–52; Macpherson, *Possessive Individualism*, pp. 197–221 and pp. 238–47.

Chapter Nine

1. *Reasonableness,* no. 238, pp. 165–67.
2. See David Hume, *Dialogues Concerning Natural Religion,* ed. Nelson Pike (Indianapolis, 1970), pp. 114–15. Hume has Cleanthes state as a general principle what Locke held to be the proper role of Christian belief: "The proper office of religion is to regulate the hearts of men, harmonize their conduct, infuse the spirit of temperance, order and obedience. . . . When it distinguishes itself, and acts as a separate principle over men, it has departed from its proper sphere, and has become only a cover to faction and ambition."
3. *Essay,* bk. IV, chap. XIV, nos. 2 and 3, on the use of experience, sensory impression, and judgment "in the greatest part of our concernments, [where] He has afforded us only the twilight . . . of probability." And see Biddle, "Locke on Reasonable Christianity," p. 412 and p. 417; Ashcraft, "Faith and Knowledge," pp. 208–14.
4. See John Dunn, *Political Thought of Locke,* pp. 254–61, and Ashcraft, "Faith and Knowlege," pp. 214–23.
5. *Second Treatise,* no. 11. Locke makes the familiar distinction here between criminal and civil justice. In the former, the state (society in this case) has an overriding interest in punishment. In the latter, property or anything of value is in dispute between two private parties or a dispute has arisen involving the meaning of some contractual promise or negligence was charged with the intention of collecting damages.
6. Civil injury: e.g., a breach of contract, a dispute over ownership, or a tort. This distinction between crime and injury implies that the "public" is directly threatened only by the former.
7. *Second Treatise,* nos. 31–34, and see 36.
8. Ibid., no. 35.
9. Ibid., no. 37.
10. Ibid., no. 51.
11. Ibid., nos. 17 and 18.
12. Ibid., no. 37.
13. Ibid., nos. 36 and 40.
14. Ibid., no. 42.
15. Jean-Jacques Rousseau, "Discourse on the Origin and Foundation of Inequality Among Men," in *The First and Second Discourses,* ed. R. Masters (New York, 1964), p. 148.
16. *Second Treatise,* no. 41.
17. Rousseau, "Discourse on the Origin . . . of Inequality," p. 162.
18. *Second Treatise,* nos. 44 and 45.
19. Ibid., no. 50. In this sense, value (money) is an attribute of men outside of politics; punishment (penalties) is an attribute of government. See Locke's definition of political power, ibid., no. 3.
20. Ibid., no. 40.
21. Ibid., nos. 49, 50, and 51. Italics mine.
22. *Essay,* bk. II, chap. XXVIII, no. 6.
23. In concluding Chapter V, "Of Property," Locke flatly states that, at first, "there could . . . be no reason of quarreling about title . . . no temptation to labor for more than [a man] could make use of . . . nor for encroachment on the right of others" (*Second Treatise,* no. 51).

24. The argument is actually more complex than this. Theft would be a clear motivation for those who are without any property except their own labor. In the case of disputes about title and over contractual agreements exchanging property, the lack of settled civil law (as opposed to criminal law) and impartial judges could lead to situations where force would be used. Significantly, Locke rarely uses the threat of theft as a motive for men to create civil authority, even though the thief symbolizes for him punishment-use of state power. Rather, he speaks of men joining into separate political communities to "settle the property which labor and industry began" (*Second Treatise*, no. 45).

25. Ibid., no. 11.

26. Ibid., no. 16. In the case of theft, guilt and innocence are quite clear. In "civil cases," however, the situation would generally be cloudy in the state of nature. Lacking specific rules governing contractual interpretations, procedures for determining title to property, and even rules defining fault in cases of negligence, both parties to disputes can feel "wronged" without either of them challenging property and possession per se. Even in this case, however, he who first uses force is guilty. In this "civil law" context, then, the immediate possessor can be assumed to be in the right; physical control would determine ownership.

27. Ibid., no. 20.

28. Ibid., no. 22.

29. Ibid., nos. 134, 151, and 143, and see nos. 152 and 153.

30. Ibid., no. 152.

31. Locke uses the term "rebellion" to apply to those who use force against law (of nature); in that sense, governmental coercion against law puts the government in the position of rebellion. See ibid., no. 226.

32. Ibid., nos. 96 and 132. Italics mine.

33. Ibid., nos. 172 and 232. So clearly does Locke identify tyrannical government with theft that, in picturing the "civil law" functions of the state, he views bias on the part of government in deciding private disputes as, like theft, the utilization of force to take someone's property. "[T]hey who are in power, by the pretense they have to authority, and the temptation of force they have in their hands, and the flattery of those about them" are the ones most likely to constitute a general threat to property (ibid., no. 226). See also ibid., no. 180, on rights which flow from conquest and the way in which Locke seeks to preserve property; and ibid., no. 139, on the power of sergeants "with absoute power of life and death," who cannot "dispose of one farthing of [a] soldier's estate or seize one jot of his goods." Even if absolute monarchies establish and enforce just dealings between subject and subject (i.e., civil law), who "is to think that men are so foolish that they take care to avoid what mischiefs may be done them by polecats or foxes, but are content, nay, think it safety, to be devoured by lions." Men in this situation would lack protection "from harm or injury on that side where the strongest hand is to do it" (ibid., no. 93).

34. James Mill, *Essay on Government*, ed. and with an Introduction by Currin V. Shields (New York, 1955), pp. 67–75.

35. Thomas Macaulay's famous critique in the *Edinburgh Review* of 1829 was partially accepted by John Stuart Mill, who, however, had his own fundamental criticisms of it. See above, pp. 180–84.

36. Mill, *Essay on Government*, p. 49.

37. See Dunn, *Political Thought of Locke*, chaps. 10–13, and Abrams, Introduction to *Two Tracts*, pp. 30–83, on the political and intellectual context within which the *Two Tracts* was written.

38. *Two Tracts*, p. 124. The Latin *Tract* phrasing is slightly different.

39. Abrams, Introduction to *Two Tracts*, pp. 3–29 and pp. 84–111.
40. *Two Tracts*, p. 230. Italics mine.
41. Ibid., p. 231. Italics mine.
42. Ibid. Italics mine.
43. See n.33, above.
44. Confirmation of this view is provided in Richard Ashcraft, "Revolutionary Politics and Locke's *Two Treatises,*" *Political Theory* 8 (November 1980).

Chapter Ten

1. See Locke's explanations for the movement linking "two" states of nature (chap. 5 of the *Second Treatise*) and his discussion of naturally changing political forms in history (chaps. 6, 7, and 14). These chapters are stressed in Ashcraft, "Locke's State of Nature," pp. 908–914. Macpherson, *Possessive Individualism*, pp. 197–221, covers essentially the same ground, but with an emphasis on Locke's economic argument. Gordon Schochet, *Patriarchalism in Political Thought* (New York, 1975), chap. 13, discusses Locke's theory of changing paternal/political relationships and its importance to Locke's meaning of consent. Ronald Meek, *Social Science and the Ignoble Savage* (Cambridge, 1976), chaps. 1 and 2, discusses Locke's role in the development of a theory of history based on changing modes of subsistence.
2. *Second Treatise*, nos. 71 and 76. See also ibid., nos. 106 and 107.
3. Ibid., nos. 107 and 111. See also ibid., no. 108.
4. Ibid., nos. 76, 94, and 107. See also ibid., no. 61, and all of chap. 14 on prerogative; and Schochet, *Patriarchalism*, pp. 87–98.
5. *Second Treatise*, nos. 162, 107, and 111. Almost exactly stating what became Hume's central argument, Locke makes clear that the rise of arts (craftsmanship), not politics, was determinate in changing moral and legal relationships: "Government is everywhere antecedent to records, and letters seldom come in amongst a people till a long continuation of civil society has, by other more necessary arts, provided for their safety, ease, and plenty" (ibid., no. 101).
6. Ibid., no. 160; and ibid., no. 107, on the lack of oppression in early societies.
7. Ibid., no. 94. Italics mine.
8. Ibid., no. 174. In the *Essay*, the one example Locke uses to show that morality could be a demonstrable science is " 'where there is no property there is no injustice' . . . a proposition as certain as any demonstration in Euclid" (bk. IV, chap. III, no. 18). Hobbes makes the identical argument in *Leviathan*, I, 15, p. 119, but then argues that property depends on the prior construction of political power to enforce contractual agreements. And see *Reasonableness*, no. 252, and *Essay*, bk. IV, chap. XX, nos. 2–6.
9. *Second Treatise*, no. 101.
10. Ibid., no. 139.
11. Ibid., no. 11.
12. Rousseau, *Emile*, p. 252.
13. See Schochet, *Patriarchalism*, chaps. 12 and 13, contrasting Hobbes and Locke on the family and political authority.
14. Nonapocalyptic and nonrevolutionary forms of being "born in servitude" are equally supportive of this plane of action. Duties grounded in tradition, nationality, intellectual culture, or simply habit make legitimate non-self-interested actions in defense of a "way of life." Both Dunn, *Political Thought of Locke*, pp. 148–64, and

Schochet, *Patriarchalism*, chap. 13, point to the importance of Locke's more conservative social assumptions which embrace duties beyond interest and calculation.

15. *Reasonableness*, no. 243, p. 176. Italics mine. And see ibid., nos. 241 and 242.

Part Three

1. *Leviathan*, I, 13, p. 104.

2. Leslie Stephen, *History of English Thought in the Eighteenth Century* (New York, 1962), 1:28–49, 262–90, and 2:68–108; John Plamenatz, *The English Utilitarians* (Oxford, 1958), chaps. 1–3. Symbolic of the shift is the rejection of both a "state of nature" and a "social contract."

3. John Austin, *Lectures on Jurisprudence or the Philosophy of Positive Law*, 3d ed., rev. and ed. Robert Campbell (London, 1869), p. 468. Hereafter cited as *Jurisprudence*. This work, containing fifty-seven lectures, was compiled after Austin's death in 1861. The first six lectures were published during his lifetime in 1832 under the title *The Province of Jurisprudence Determined*. . . . This latter work was republished in 1954 (London), with an introduction by H. L. A. Hart, and contains a valuable bibliography of nineteenth- and twentieth-century comment on Austin's lectures, pp. xix–xxi.

4. Leslie Stephen, *The English Utilitarians* (London, 1900), 1:304.

5. John Stuart Mill, *On the Logic of the Moral Sciences*, ed. with an Introduction by Henry M. Magid (Indianapolis, 1965), p. 15.

6. *Leviathan*, II, 31, pp. 318–19.

Chapter Eleven

1. Adam Ferguson, *An Essay on the History of Civil Society*, 6th ed. (London, 1793), p. 204.

2. Adam Ferguson (1723–1816) was professor of pneumatics and moral philosophy at Edinburgh and an associate of David Hume, Adam Smith, Thomas Reid, Dugald Stewart, Francis Hutcheson, and other luminaries of the Scottish Enlightenment. See David Kettler, *The Social and Political Thought of Adam Ferguson* (Columbus, Ohio, 1965), chaps. 3, 5, and 7; Gladys Bryson, *Man and Society: the Scottish Inquiry of the Eighteenth Century* (Princeton, 1945), chaps. 2–6; Ronald Meek, *Social Science*, chap. 5; Duncan Forbes, *Hume's Philosophical Politics* (Cambridge, 1965), chaps. 2–5 of pt. 1, for discussion of Scottish political and moral philosophy of this period.

3. Quoted from W. L. Taylor, *Francis Hutcheson and David Hume as Predecessors of Adam Smith* (Durham, 1965), pp. 41–42. Smith's remarks are from his 1748 public lectures in Edinburgh. And see Meek, *Social Sciences*, pp. 107–30. In his *The Theory of Moral Sentiments*, in *Adam Smith's Moral and Political Philosophy*, ed. with an Introduction by Herbert W. Schneider (New York, 1948), pp. 246–47, Smith contrasts the man of "humanity and benevolence" with the "man of system." "The man whose public spirit is prompted altogether by humanity and benevolence will respect the established powers and privileges even of individuals, and still more those of the great orders and societies into which the state is divided. . . . The man of system, on the contrary, is apt to be very wise in his own conceit, and is often so enamoured with the supposed beauty of his own ideal plan of government that he cannot suffer the smallest deviation from any part of it." Hereafter cited as *Moral Sentiments*.

4. *Moral Sentiments*, p. 250.

5. Hume, *Dialogues*, pp. 114–15.

6. David Hume, *An Enquiry Concerning the Principles of Morals*, in *Essential Works of David Hume*, R. Cohen, ed. (New York, 1965), p. 190.

7. David Hume, *A Treatise of Human Nature*, in *Hume's Moral and Political Philosophy*, H. Aiken, ed. (New York, 1948), bk. III, pt. II, sec. 1, p. 55. Hereafter cited as *Treatise*.

8. Ibid., III, II, sec. 2, p. 55 and p. 64.

9. Ibid., III, II, sec. 2, p. 56. Hume does not stress this argument and evidences little concern with how men originally learned rudimentary forms of cooperation. Neither Hume nor his Scottish colleagues liked to dwell on the sexual aspect of marriage. They tended to reduce marriage to the more manageable category of "general benevolence." Thus, Hume in *An Enquiry Concerning the Principles of Morals*, p. 274, argues that "Love between the sexes begets a complacency and good-will very distinct from the gratification of appetite" and serves to show "general benevolence in human nature, where no real interest binds us to the object." Francis Hutcheson argued that sexual attraction leads to "an equal friendly society," "a state of friendship," "an amiable society" by marriage and offspring. From Bryson, *Man and Society*, p. 179.

10. *Treatise*, III, II, sec. 2, p. 58. And see Adam Smith, *Wealth of Nations* (New York, 1937), bk. 5, chap. 1, pp. 669–70.

11. *Treatise*, III, II, sec. 2, p. 62.

12. Ibid., III, II, sec. 4, p. 80.

13. Ibid., III, II, sec. 5, p. 86.

14. By viewing the earliest forms of property as resulting from the constant conjunction of person and object, Hume obviates the need to speak of labor, value, money, and the rise of inequality. Hume's formulation assumes scarcity, money, and inequality sufficient to compel the sale of labor.

15. *Treatise*, III, II, sec. 5, p. 87.

16. Ibid., III, II, sec. 5, pp. 86–87.

17. Ibid., III, II, sec. 6, p. 90.

18. Ibid., III, II, sec. 6, p. 93.

19. For Smith's discussion of the rise of justice, see Adam Smith, *Lectures on Justice, Police, Revenue and Arms*, in Schneider, *Adam Smith*, p. 477. Smith duplicates Hume's series; see ibid., pt. I, division III, nos. 1–5 and 9–10. Albert O. Hirschman, *The Passions and the Interests* (Princeton, 1977), pt. 2; and Meek, *Social Science*, chaps. 2 and 4, for a more general discussion of Scottish Enlightenment notions of the development of law.

20. Jeremy Bentham, *Theory of Legislation*, trans. from the French edition of Etienne Dumont by R. Hildreth, ed. and with an Introduction by C. K. Ogden (New York, 1931), pp. 94–95. The organization of the book is indicated in n. 65, below. There are two additional English editions of *Theory of Legislation*: Boston, 1840, trans. Hildreth, 2 vols., and Oxford, 1914, trans. C. M. Atkinson, 2 vols.

21. *Theory of Legislation*, p. 108. Bentham discusses this principle in terms of gambling, so that "a loss which diminishes a man's fortune by one fourth, will take away more happiness than he could gain by doubling his property." Like gambling, "the sum to be lost [by the old possessor] bearing a greater proportion to the reduced fortune than the same sum to the augmented fortune [of the new demandant], the diminution of happiness for the one will be greater than the augmentation of happiness for the other."

22. Bentham can calculate "happiness" because it has a strict money value—except when one has too little for subsistence. The problem is, even within this static

framework, "The excess in happiness of the richer will not be so great as the excess of his wealth" (*Theory of Legislation*, p. 103).

23. Ibid., p. 110. Italics mine.

24. Ibid., p. 111. "Nothing but law can encourage men to labors superfluous for the present, and which can be enjoyed only in the future. Economy has as many enemies as there are dissipators,—men who wish to enjoy without giving themselves the trouble of producing. Labor is too painful for idleness; it is too slow for impatience. Fraud and injustice secretly conspire to appropriate its fruits. Insolence and audacity think to ravish them by open force. Thus security is assailed on every side; ever threatened, never tranquil, it exists in the midst of alarm" (p. 110).

25. Ibid., p. 115.

26. Ibid., pp. 96–97. The chapter title is "Ends of Civil law." "Of these [four] objects of the law," Bentham states, "security is the only one which necessarily embraces the future. Subsistence, abundance, equality, may be considered in relation to a single moment of present time; but security implies a given extension of future time, in respect to all that good which it embraces. Security, then, is the preeminent object." For use of these concepts in his economic writings, consult George Stigler, *Essays in the History of Economics* (Chicago, 1965), pp. 70–74. An excellent analysis of Bentham's role as a political economist is found in W. Stark's *Jeremy Bentham's Economic Writings*, 3 vols. (London, 1952). Prefacing each of the three volumes is a summary of Bentham's theory of utility and money. Bentham's *The Philosophy of Economic Science* (vol. 1, pp. 79–120, in Stark's collection) repeats the discussion of "political good," in terms of subsistence, abundance, equality, and security, found in *Theory of Legislation*, but here solely in the context of economic theory.

27. *Theory of Legislation*, p. 116.

28. Austin, *Jurisprudence*, p. 468.

29. *Moral Sentiments*, p. 62.

30. *Jurisprudence*, p. 426. Italics mine. In the "Notes and Fragments" following this lecture Austin refers to Hobbes's *Leviathan*, ch. VI; Locke's discussion of "Power and Will" in his *Essay on Human Understanding;* and Bentham's discussions of "voluntarism" in *Principles of Morals and Legislation*. Supporting his argument that "dominion of the will [is] limited to bodily organs" and that, therefore, will is part of a cause-effect chain, he refers to James Mill's epistemology (*Jurisprudence*, p. 425 and pp. 429–30).

31. *Jurisprudence*, p. 474. Some italics omitted.

32. Ibid., p. 418. In discussing this distinction, Austin refers to Bentham's *Theory of Legislation*.

33. Jeremy Bentham, *The Limits of Jurisprudence, Defined*, ed. with an Introduction by Charles Warren Everett (New York, 1945). More recently published, with textual additions, as *Of Laws in General*, ed. and with an Introduction by H. L. A. Hart (London, 1970). Hereafter cited as *Limits*.

34. *Limits*, pp. 295–96.

35. Ibid., pp. 309–10.

36. Bentham says: "What I pay to the state, a creature of reason with which I have no quarrel, affects me only with that sort of chagrin I should feel if I dropped the same money into a well" (*Theory of Legislation*, p. 321).

37. *Ancient Law* was first published in 1861. The edition used here was published by J. M. Dent and Sons (London, 1954). A series of lectures delivered at Cambridge in 1887, *Lectures on the Early History of Institutions* (London, 1875), are an extension of some of the themes in *Ancient Law* and in *Village Communities East and West* (New York, 1886).

38. *Ancient Law*, p. 11 and p. 5. Note how similar this is to the congruence of "right and convenience" in Locke's "first" state of nature.

39. Ibid., pp. 8–10.

40. Ibid., p. 14–15.

41. Ibid., p. 46. Like equity in Rome, utilitarianism in England, Maine says, had its greatest effect on the courts, not on legislation. See generally pp. 43–66 and *Lectures on the Early History of Institutions*, pp. 342–400, for an extensive analysis of state of nature and consent theory in Hobbes, Bentham, and Austin.

42. *Ancient Law*, p. 25. See ibid., pp. 40–41, where Maine discusses the "primary phenomenon" of moral progress as the "real" cause of legal change. This phenomenon is wholly economic.

43. Ibid., p. 89. Maine's use of *patria potestas* as the "germ" out of which the modern "law of persons" developed is also an argument for the divorce of "politics" from "law," for early *potestas* was both political authority and the unit of private legal action. See also *Early History of Institutions*, p. 379, where Maine, referring to *Ancient Law*, argues that "the authority of the Patriarch or Paterfamilias over his family is . . . the element or germ out of which all permanent power of man over man has been gradually developed." Progress in civil law is completed when every legal actor is a bundle of rights and duties respecting things of value; thus the phrase "from status to contract."

44. *Ancient Law*, pp. 79–80. In *Village Communities*, p. 332, Maine states: "It is not because our own jurisprudence and that of Rome were *once* alike that they ought to be studied together—it is because they *will be* alike" (Maine's italics).

45. *Ancient Law*, p. 232.

46. Ibid., p. 229.

47. *Jurisprudence*, p. 417, makes this same point.

48. *Early History of Institutions*, pp. 392–93.

49. *Treatise*, III, II, sec. 7, p. 100, and sec. 8, p. 107.

50. For a more systematic discussion of the relationship between criminal law and political loyalty, see E. Eisenach, "Crime, Death and Loyalty in English Liberalism," *Political Theory* 6 (May 1978): 213–32.

51. *Treatise*, III, II, pp. 102–3, and see D. Forbes, *Hume's Philosophical Politics*, pp. 74–77.

52. David Hume, "Of the Original Contract," *Essays: Moral, Political, and Literary* (Oxford, 1963), p. 468. Hereafter referred to as *Essays*.

53. Ibid., p. 468: "The necessities of human society, neither in private nor public, will allow of such an accurate inquiry; and there is no virtue or moral duty but what may, with facility, be refined away, if we indulge a false philosophy in sifting and scrutinizing it, by every captious rule of logic, in every light or position in which it may be placed." And see, *Enquiry Concerning . . . Morals*, sec. III, pp. 189–206, and App. III, pp. 278–84.

54. *Treatise*, III, II, sec. 10, p. 114.

55. Ibid., III, II, sec. 9, p. 111. Restated as the title of an Engagement pamphlet, *Plenary Possession Makes Lawful Power*.

56. Treatise, III, II, secs. 7–10; *Enquiry Concerning . . . Morals*, sec. IV.

57. "Of Refinement in the Arts," *Essays*, p. 278.

58. Ibid., p. 284. "Of Commerce" discusses the role of luxury in lightening civic burdens (*Essays*, pp. 261–62).

59. For a more complete discussion of the relationship of Bentham's legal theory and natural history, see E. Eisenach, "The Dimension of History in Bentham's Jurisprudence," *The Bentham Newsletter* 4 (Spring 1980).

60. *Moral Sentiments,* p. 250.
61. *Theory of Legislation,* p. 48.
62. Ibid., p. 49.
63. Ibid., p. 52. Although the converse is also true, "the seed of good [industry] is not so productive in hopes as the seed of evil is fruitful in alarms" (p. 53).
64. Ibid., p. 55.
65. "Principles of the Penal Code" is the title of the third and last section of *Theory of Legislation.* Other than preliminary classifications and subdivisions (chaps. 1–3), the entire definition of "offences" is in terms of alarm (chaps. 4–14). Bentham's *Theory of Legislation* is divided into three sections: "Principles of Legislation," "Principles of the Civil Code," and "Principles of the Penal Code." The first nine chapters of "Principles of Legislation" follow the exact order of the first chapters of "Principles of the Civil Code." The two following chapters are concerned with "an analysis of political good and evil" and "reasons for erecting certain acts into offences." The second section, "Principles of the Civil Code," consists of three parts. The first concerns the relationship between economy, industry, property, and alarm. The other two parts are concerned with titles to property, wills, and private relationships (family, master-servant) and do not concern us. "Principles of the Penal Code," is subdivided into four parts. The first, "Of Offences," is nothing but a discussion of alarm and the specific circumstances which increase or decrease alarm. The second, "Political Remedies Against the Evil of Offences," is an attempt to show how alarm can be decreased by devices which significantly diminish the primary or "first order evils." The third, "Of Punishments," is a discussion dealing with offenses which do create alarm. The fourth, "Indirect Means of Preventing Offences," is self-explanatory.
66. *Limits,* p. 297.
67. Ibid., pp. 309–10, and see pp. 295–97 on circumstances where this is the case.
68. *Theory of Legislation,* p. 310. Bentham uses the example of a guardian who embezzles from a ward. Other than for restitution and costs, the guardian should not be punished because his act is an offense "which none but such as are responsible can commit. Where compensation is certain punishment is needless" (*Limits,* pp. 296–97). Needless to add, embezzlement creates no general alarm.
69. Title of chap. 3, "Principles of Legislation," *Theory of Legislation,* p. 6.
70. Ibid., p. 470.
71. *Limits,* p. 290.
72. Ibid., pp. 307 and 310.
73. *Theory of Legislation,* pp. 322–57.
74. Ibid., p. 385.
75. Ibid., pp. 373–93, passim. And see Letwin, *Pursuit of Certainty,* pp. 173–75, for a more complete summary of Bentham's crime-prevention remedies based on systems of detection and information.
76. *Theory of Legislation,* p. 400.
77. Mill's article originally appeared in a supplement to the sixth edition of the *Encyclopaedia Britannica* (1818) and was reprinted in the seventh edition, from which the quotation is taken. Hereafter cited as "Prisons."
78. "Prisons," pp. 575–76.
79. Ibid., pp. 576–77.
80. Ibid., pp. 577–78.
81. Ibid., p. 578. Gertrude Himmelfarb's essay "The Haunted House of Jeremy Bentham," in her *Victorian Minds* (New York, 1968) is a study of the Panopticon plans of Bentham spanning a period of twenty years followed by an additional twenty

years in which "he grieves over its defeat." James Mill praises Bentham's prison and prison reform plans so fully that he concluded little remained but to "travel in his steps." See *Victorian Minds*, pp. 79–80, on how closely Mill followed Bentham's plans.

82. "Prisons," p. 581.

83. *Jurisprudence*, p. 469, and see pp. 467–72, comparing prisons, political sanctions, and scientific proof.

84. Ibid., p. 471 and pp. 416–17 and pp. 517–24.

85. Ibid., p. 871.

86. Ibid., p. 774.

87. Ibid., p. 776.

88. Ibid., pp. 771–72.

89. Ibid., p. 771.

90. Ibid., p. 519. See pp. 281–87 on Austin's general distinction between free and despotic government. He concludes, p. 289, that no government has any "legal rights against its own subjects."

91. See above, n.20, for translations and n.65 for an outline of its structure.

92. *Autobiography*, in *John Stuart Mill, A Selection of His Works*, ed. John Robson (New York, 1966), p. 256.

Chapter Twelve

1. John Stuart Mill, *Utilitarianism*, in *John Stuart Mill, A Selection of His Works*, pp. 187–88.

2. David Hume, *The Natural History of Religion*, ed. H. E. Root (London, 1956), p. 21. Hereafter cited as *Natural History*.

3. *Natural History*, p. 28.

4. Ibid., p. 38. "Could men anatomize nature," Hume continues, "they would find, that these causes are nothing but the particular fabric and structure of the minute parts of their own bodies and of external objects; and that, by a regular and constant machinery, all the events are produced, about which they are so much concerned. But this philosophy exceeds the comprehension of the ignorant multitudes" (p. 29). Compare to Hobbes, *Leviathan*, I, 11, p. 86: "And they that make little, or no enquiry into the naturall causes of things, yet from the feare that proceeds from the ignorance it selfe, of what it is that hath the power to do them much good or harm, are enclined to suppose, and feign unto themselves, severall kinds of Powers Invisible; and to stand in awe of their own imaginations."

5. *Natural History*, p. 43, and see pp. 25–26 and pp. 48–54.

6. Ibid., pp. 47–48.

7. Ibid., p. 67.

8. Ibid., pp. 71–72.

9. In *Dialogues*, Hume pits man's capacity for "art and contrivance" against his capacity for justice and morality, arguing that "the moral qualities of men are more defective in their kind than his natural abilities" (p. 113). To trust morality (and, therefore, law) to the more certain faculties of contrivance is the conclusion of the skeptical Philo (pp. 115–16). And see *Enquiry Concerning . . . Human Understanding*, secs. V, X, and XI.

10. *Dialogues*, pp. 114–15.

11. "Superstition and Enthusiasm," *Essays*, pp. 78–79.

12. Adam Smith, *Wealth of Nations*, bk. 5, chap. 1, pp. 740–66 on other proposals such as low pay for clergy, scientific education for the professions, and frequent and

gay "public diversions" to counteract "that melancholy and gloomy humour which is almost always the nurse of popular superstition and enthusiasm" (p. 748). See Joseph Cropsey, *Polity and Economy: An Interpretation of the Principles of Adam Smith* (The Hague, 1957), pp. 79–87, on Smith's proposals regarding religion. Jeremy Bentham, *Church of Englandism and Its Catechism Examined* (London, 1818), pp. 297–98, was quite outspoken on the utility of sects: "Schism, it has been observed already, is conducive to truth in doctrine: it is no less so to goodness in [church] discipline. By the very nature of the case, a sort of auction is established. The article put up and bid for is public favour. The bidders are the several sects; led—such of them as have leaders—by their respective chosen instructors. The auction is a perpetual one: the biddings are in good behaviour . . . and which, if it be not in every point that which is most conducive to general happiness, differs not from it very widely, and, under the protection of freedom will approach nearer and nearer to the mark continually, in proportion to the degree of freedom which has place. So many of these competitors, so many mutual *spies*—so many eventual *informers*—against that sect, in the conduct of which, if any such there be, mischief in any shape is to be found. *Spies*—informers—by these names are designated so many sorts of agents, to the function of which, necessary as they are in every government, the experience had of the ill use, which, in proportion as the government has been ill-constructed, has been made of them, has been given an ill name: but, in the case here in question, there is no ill but in the name."

13. David Hume, *Enquiry Concerning . . . Human Understanding*, p. 78.

14. *Natural History*, pp. 21 and 31. See also, *Treatise*, III, II, sec. 2; *Enquiry Concerning . . . Human Understanding*, sec. XI.

15. See Forbes, *Hume's Philosophic Politics*, pp. 64–65, on Hume's assumptions about the declining power of religious belief in contemporary England.

16. The decline of religious belief is also accompanied by a weakening of institutional barriers among classes of people; economic prosperity and leisure place a premium on literacy and encourage sociability and thus the sharing and diffusion of opinion.

17. *Moral Sentiments*, pp. 114–15.

18. Ibid., p. 117.

19. Ibid., pp. 120 and 125.

20. Ibid., pp. 122–23.

21. Ibid., p. 124, and David Hume, *Enquiry Concerning . . . Morals*, p. 279.

22. *Moral Sentiments*, p. 146, and see pp. 122–23.

23. Hume, *Enquiry Concerning . . . Morals*, p. 279.

24. *Moral Sentiments*, p. 116. And see Hume, *Enquiry Concerning . . . Morals*, pp. 185–89.

25. *Moral Sentiments*, pp. 73–75 and pp. 248–50. Hume stresses in his essays "Of Commerce" and "Of Refinement of the Arts," *Essays*, that without commerce and the talents to which commerce gives rise, the positive virtues of generosity would not be possible. He stresses, furthermore, that generosity was to be proportional to "rank," or economic means, as a way to contain it. Smith tends to expand on the notion of benevolence in order to merge benevolence with religion, or "universal benevolence." And see Bentham, *Theory of Legislation*, pt. 4, chap. 16.

26. Hume, *Treatise*, II, I, sec. 11, pp. 40–47. Hume's discussions of sympathy and sentiment are within the context of differential rank and wealth; and see Smith, *Moral Sentiments*, pp. 91–107, pp. 116–20, and pp. 209–18, on rank, place, wealth, and sympathy.

27. "Of Refinement in the Arts," *Essays*, p. 286.

28. *Moral Sentiments*, p. 116. Forbes, *Hume's Philosophical Politics*, pp. 176–79, explores the various meanings of "middling rank" as used in Hume's writings; Donald Winch, *Adam Smith's Politics* (Cambridge, 1978), pp. 70–102, summarizes Smith's theory of rank, commerce, and political capacity and compares it to the theories of Hume, Ferguson, and other contemporaries.

29. Quoted from Hirschman, *Passions and Interests*, p. 90.

30. *Moral Sentiments*, p. 104.

31. Ibid., p. 127, and see also, p. 117 for Smith's discussion of the inner conflict between the demands of justice and the feelings of benevolence.

32. Ibid., p. 93. And see *Enquiry Concerning . . . Morals*, p. 238, n.4.

33. *Moral Sentiments*, pp. 212–14; *Treatise*, II, II, sec. 5. Smith, in *Lectures on Justice, Police, Revenue, and Arms* in Schneider, *Adam Smith*, p. 287, begins his discussion of public law by referring to his earlier discussion of wealth in *Moral Sentiments*. Hume covers this fully in *Treatise*, II, I, secs. 7–12.

34. *Moral Sentiments*, pp. 93–94. That Smith thought these sentiments illusory, see pp. 211–12 on the costs of starting poor and attempting to become very rich; and Hirschman, *Passions and Interests*, pp. 100–102.

35. Hume, "Of Refinement in the Arts," *Essays*, p. 286; and see his "Of the Middle Station of Life," ibid., pp. 579–84; Smith, *Moral Sentiments*, pp. 223–24.

36. A summary and complex resolution of this discussion is in Forbes, *Hume's Philosophical Politics*, chaps. 3–6. And see Sheldon Wolin, "Hume and Conservatism," *American Political Science Review* 48 (December 1954): 999–1016.

Chapter Thirteen

1. *Moral Sentiments*, p. 141. And see pp. 73–90 for Smith's discussion of internalizing others' feelings through sympathy. Hume's discussion of sympathy is in *Treatise*, III, III, sec. 1, "Of the Origin of Natural Virtues and Vices"; II, II, "Of Love and Hatred"; and *Enquiry Concerning . . . Morals*, secs. VII and VIII. Networks of sympathetic bonds define and sustain personality. Hume's discussion of "personal identity" in *Treatise*, I, IV, sec. 6, and Appendix, goes further to maintain that self-consciousness includes the feelings and mental states of others. Smith's reformulation of the golden rule is "to love ourselves only as we love our neighbor or, what comes to the same thing, as our neighbor is capable of loving us" (*Moral Sentiments*, p. 88).

2. Austin, *Jurisprudence*, p. 162. "Strictly speaking . . . [general] utility is not the measure to which our conduct should conform, nor is utility the test by which our conduct should be tried. It is not in itself the source or spring of our highest or paramount obligations, but it guides us to the source whence these obligations flow. It is merely the *index* to the measure, the *index* to the test" (ibid., p. 160). Utilitarian reformers were so confident of the capacity to reduce the need for passion and physical punishment to support political life that even the utility of natural religion as a system of moral duties was called into question. John Stuart Mill, *Autobiography*, sec. II, discusses his early Benthamite views; and see his essays "Nature" and "Utility of Religion" in *Essential Works of John Stuart Mill*. Jeremy Bentham and George Grote (Philip Beauchamp) wrote an attack on natural religion called *An Analysis of the Influence of Natural Religion on the Temporal Happiness of Mankind* (London, 1822). Stephen, *The English Utilitarians*, 2:338–61, discusses this and related Benthamite writings. See also Halévy, *Philosophic Radicalism*, pp. 291–95.

3. Hume, *Enquiry Concerning . . . Human Understanding*, sec. IV, lays the foundation for this division. Forbes, *Hume's Philosophical Politics*, pp. 91–102, and pp. 193–230, stresses Hume's philosophical reliance on political authority and institutions, not rational standards of law and economic life.

4. *Theory of Legislation*, p. 428. Bentham adds that "the sentiment of benevolence is liable to deviate from the principle of general utility. It cannot be set right except by instruction. Command and force do not avail" (p. 431).

5. Shirley Letwin, "Utilitarianism: A System of Political Tolerance," *Cambridge Journal* 6 (March 1953): 327–29, discusses Bentham's attack on benevolence as a cloak for intolerance and despotism.

6. Bentham, *Rationale of Reward* (London, 1825), p. 93.

7. *Theory of Legislation*, p. 321.

8. *Jurisprudence*, p. 305.

9. Ibid., n. "u," pp. 288–89, and p. 298.

10. Sir Henry Maine, "Sovereignty and Empire," in *Early History of Institutions*, pp. 396–97.

11. John Austin, "A Plea for the Constitution," *Fraser's Magazine* (April 1859); Sir Henry Maine, *Popular Government*, 2d ed. (London, 1886). And see J. S. Mill's review of Austin in *Dissertations and Discussions*, 4 vols. (Boston, 1868), 4:51–69.

12. Jeremy Bentham, *Book of Fallacies*, Bowring ii, p. 401.

13. John Stuart Mill, "Bentham," *Dissertations and Discussions*, 1:412.

14. Ibid., p. 402. Italics mine.

15. Mill, *Logic of the Moral Sciences*, pp. 117–18.

Part Four

1. "Coleridge," *Dissertations and Discussions*, 2:70.

2. The essay by John Rees, "The Thesis of the Two Mills," *Political Studies* 25 (September 1977): 369–82, is a discussion of the ways in which this duality has been perceived in recent studies.

3. On method, Alan Ryan, *John Stuart Mill* (New York, 1970), chap. 13; on interpretation of the utility principle, Samuel Gorovitz, ed., *Mill: Utilitarianism, Text and Critical Essays* (Indianapolis, 1971); on democracy, compare Joseph Hamburger, *Intellectuals in Politics: John Stuart Mill and the Philosophic Radicals* (New Haven, 1965), Dennis Thompson, *John Stuart Mill and Representative Government* (Princeton, 1976); Graeme Duncan, *Marx and Mill* (Cambridge, 1973); and Maurice Cowling, *Mill and Liberalism* (Cambridge, 1963); on economics and social class, see the discussion in Duncan, *Marx and Mill*, pp. 209–37; on differing conceptions of liberty, Isaiah Berlin, *Four Essays on Liberty* (Oxford, 1969), pp. 118–72.

4. R. P. Anschutz, *The Philosophy of J. S. Mill* (Oxford, 1953), p. 5.

5. Robert Denoon Cumming, *Human Nature and History: A Study of the Development of Liberal Political Thought*, 2 vols. (Chicago, 1969), esp. 1:21–83 and 2:320–449.

6. *Utilitarianism*, in *John Stuart Mill, A Selection of His Works*, p. 187.

7. *Autobiography*, in *John Stuart Mill, a Selection of His Works*, pp. 280–82.

8. *Utilitarianism*, p. 187.

9. *Autobiography*, p. 283.

10. *Utilitarianism*, p. 188.

11. *Autobiography*, p. 270.

12. "The Spirit of the Age," in *Essays on Politics and Culture*, ed. Gertrude Himmelfarb (New York, 1962), p. 9 and p. 25.

Chapter Fourteen

1. *Logic of the Moral Sciences,* p. 117; and John Stuart Mill, *Auguste Comte and Positivism* (Ann Arbor, 1961), p. 102.

2. *Auguste Comte,* p. 101.

3. *Logic of the Moral Sciences,* pp. 117–18.

4. See Appendixes A and B of *Logic of the Moral Sciences,* pp. 151–56, for the changes and deletions.

5. Evidence of Mill's reliance on Hume's *Natural History of Religion* is most evident in his essay "Utility of Religion," in *Essential Works of John Stuart Mill,* pp. 418–20.

6. *Auguste Comte,* pp. 111–13; and see "Spirit of the Age," p. 45.

7. "Utility of Religion," p. 406.

8. Ibid., pp. 408–9. Italics mine.

9. Ibid., pp. 410–11.

10. *Leviathan,* I, 12, p. 97.

11. "Utility of Religion," p. 416. Italics mine.

12. Ibid., pp. 417 and 421.

13. "A Few Observations on the French Revolution," *Dissertations and Discussions,* 1:82–83.

14. "Spirit of the Age," p. 45.

15. James Fitzjames Stephen, *Liberty, Equality, Fraternity,* ed. and with an Introduction by R. J. White (Cambridge, 1967), p. 133.

16. Bentham, *Natural Religion,* pp. viii, and 121–39, passim.

17. "Utility of Religion," p. 402, p. 404, and p. 417. Like Locke, Mill speaks of "the small limits of man's certain knowledge," and our experience as "a small island in the midst of a boundless sea" (p. 420).

18. Ibid., p. 405. And see *On Liberty* in *John Stuart Mill, A Selection of His Works,* pp. 66–67. Mill here is one short step away from Cleanthes's judgment in Hume's *Dialogues,* p. 16. Cleanthes's judgment of Locke was wrong.

19. "Utility of Religion," p. 425.

20. R. J. White, Introduction to *Liberty, Equality, Fraternity,* pp. 1–18, and Noel Annan, *Leslie Stephen, His Thought and Character in Relation to His Time* (Cambridge, Mass., 1952), chap. 7.

21. *Liberty, Equality, Fraternity,* p. 119. Locke's theory of toleration is discussed in *Horae Sabbaticae,* 2:157–73.

22. "Bentham," in *Essays on Politics and Culture,* p. 88. This discussion of Hume was dropped when republished in vol. 1 of *Dissertations and Discussions.*

23. "Professor Sedgwick's Discourse," in *Dissertations and Discussions,* 1:97–98. Italics mine.

24. "Reorganization of the Reform Party," in *Essays on Politics and Culture,* p. 324.

25. Ibid., pp. 308–18, for the incredible ambivalence toward working-class suffrage in 1838; for the enthusiasm with which he greeted the Hare system of weighted voting in 1859, see "Recent Writers on Reform," in *Dissertations and Discussions,* 4:80–100; and for his own proposals for plural voting, see "Thoughts on Parliamentary Reform," in ibid., 4:5–50. All three of these writings indicate an attempt to escape the political logic of ordinary utilitarian interest doctrine. Thompson, *Mill and Representative Government,* pp. 99–112, summarizes Mill's position on plural voting and the Hare system. Duncan, *Marx and Mill,* pp. 217–37, contains an excellent discussion of Mill's cultural and elitist perspectives. For a counterset of

perspectives on Mill in this regard, see Hamburger, *Intellectuals in Politics*, pp. 234–72.

26. "On the Probable Futurity of the Labouring Classes," in *Principles of Political Economy*, 2 vols. (New York, 1900), 2:265–75.

27. *Principles of Political Economy*, p. 271. And see *On Liberty*, p. 85. "The honor and glory of the average man is that he is capable of following the initiative . . . of a highly gifted and instructed One or Few. . . ."

28. *On Liberty*, p. 44.

29. "Coleridge," in *Dissertations and Discussions*, 2:70–72 and 76.

Chapter Fifteen

1. See *Autobiography*, chap. 2, and *Utility of Religion;* and see R. J. White, "John Stuart Mill," *The Cambridge Journal* 5 (November 1951): 93–94.

2. "Nature," in *Essential Works*, p. 381.

3. Ibid., p. 380. In case his readers might miss his point, Mill adds: "In sober truth, nearly all the things which men are hanged or imprisoned for doing to one another are nature's everyday performances."

4. Ibid., pp. 395 and 379.

5. "Austin on Jurisprudence," *Dissertations and Discussions*, 4:236 and 234.

6. *Autobiography*, pp. 256–57.

7. "Austin on Jurisprudence," *Dissertations and Discussions*, 4:278.

8. *Utilitarianism*, pp. 213–14.

9. Ibid., p. 216. "The feelings concerned are so powerful . . . that *ought* and *should* grow into *must*, and recognized indispensability becomes a moral necessity, analogous to physical" (p. 216). Italics in original.

10. Ibid., p. 216.

11. See *Logic of the Moral Sciences*, p. 31, n.3, for the importance Mill gives to this discussion of sentiments of justice for a future science of society.

12. *Utilitarianism*, pp. 213–14.

13. "The Spirit of the Age," pp. 40–50; "Civilization," *Dissertations and Discussions*, 1:186–231, on the causes of this condition.

14. *Auguste Comte*, pp. 84–85.

15. *Logic of the Moral Sciences*, p. 17.

16. *Autobiography*, p. 305.

17. Jeremy Bentham, *Theory of Legislation*, p. 110.

18. *Utilitarianism*, p. 187.

19. J. F. Stephen, "The End of the World," *Essays by a Barrister*, p. 5.

20. *Utilitarianism*, p. 198.

21. "The Limitations of Morality," *Essays by a Barrister*, p. 112–13. And see "Hume's Essays," *Horae Sabbaticae*, 2:382–85.

22. *On Liberty*, p. 78.

23. "Utility of Religion," p. 416.

24. Quentin Skinner, "Some Problems in the Analysis of Political Thought and Action," *Political Theory* 2 (August 1974): 294–95.

25. Locke, *Reasonableness*, no. 241, p. 171, and no. 236, p. 164. In *On Liberty*, p. 46, Mill speaks of the energies of the intellectual ferment in the recent past as "well nigh spent" requiring a "fresh start" through the reassertion of "our mental freedom."

26. "The Spirit of the Age," p. 19; and see Appendix, *Dissertations and Discussions*, 1:418–25; and *Logic of the Moral Sciences*, pp. 130–31.

27. Austin, *Jurisprudence*, discusses ideas of will by referring to Hobbes's *Leviathan*, Locke's *Essay*, and Bentham's *Principles of Morals and Legislation*. Both James and John Stuart Mill wrote extended commentaries on others as a vehicle for their formal philosophical writings. Leslie Stephen, *English Thought in the Eighteenth Century*, is the first formal "history of ideas" in England; he later wrote *Hobbes*, English Men of Letters series (London, 1929), and *The English Utilitarians*, the last of whose three volumes is on John Stuart Mill. James Fitzjames Stephen, Leslie Stephen's brother, wrote a long series of articles and reviews on, among others, Locke, Hobbes, Berkeley, Bentham, Austin, and Maine. These articles are all reprinted in *Horae Sabbaticae*, and *Essays by a Barrister*. To complete the circle, James Fitzjames Stephen then wrote *Liberty, Equality, Fraternity*, a critique of *On Liberty*. On the Stephen brothers, see Annan, *Leslie Stephen*. On John Stuart Mill, see Cumming, *Human Nature and History*, 2:320–58, for a discussion of the importance of "light from other minds" in Mill's conception of political ideas.

28. *Reasonableness*, no. 243, p. 180.

29. *Leviathan*, III, 33, p. 327. Hobbes's italics.

Chapter Sixteen

1. *Autobiography*, p. 303.

2. "Coleridge," *Dissertations and Discussions*, 2:51. Mill is quoting Coleridge.

3. Mill is certainly aware that an institutional conservatism can accompany the preservation of high intellectual culture and that institutions can in turn be centers of opposition to reform. Mill's stress on ideas rather than institutions and his insistence on the broad diffusion of ideas counters this logic of institutional interests. In this way, the bonds which really connect men in the future will be invisible and thus independent of all institutions with their attendant interests and privileges.

4. *Logic of the Moral Sciences*, p. 103. And see ibid., pp. 51, 81, and 118.

5. Ibid., p. 102. *On Liberty*, p. 15, speaks of "utility in the largest sense, grounded on the permanent interests of man as a progressive being."

6. *Reasonableness*, no. 245, p. 185.

7. Locke, "First Letter," *Works*, 6:9–10.

8. *Auguste Comte*, p. 86. And see, *Logic of the Moral Sciences*, pp. 37, 51, 81, and 103.

9. *Logic of the Moral Sciences*, pp. 22–23.

10. *Utilitarianism*, p. 227.

11. Ibid., p. 170. *On Liberty*, chap. 3, is almost entirely devoted to a comparison of past, present, and future regarding the declining need for religion and physical coercion.

12. "Utility of Religion," p. 416.

13. Mill, *Principles of Political Economy*, 2:261–65.

14. John Stuart Mill, *Representative Government* (Chicago, 1962), chaps. 1–4, and see Cumming, *Human Nature and History*, 1:36–60.

15. *Representative Government*, pp. 44–45.

16. *On Liberty*, p. 85.

17. *Utilitarianism*, pp. 190 and 199.

18. *Logic of the Moral Sciences*, chaps. 5 and 9–13. Cumming, *Human Nature and History*, 1: chap. 3, and 2: pt. 4 gives the fullest explication of Mill's perspectives on the limits of the social sciences, experience, and experiment. Professor Cumming uses the term "history" to refer to the scientific and empirical grounding in English liberalism and "human nature" to refer to a "reflexive" tradition. Douglas G. Long,

Bentham on Liberty (Toronto, 1977), chap. 13, discusses the utilitarian ideal of a social science.

19. *Utilitarianism,* pp. 188 and 194.
20. Ibid., pp. 171 and 195.
21. *On Liberty,* chap. 4, discusses the limits of law on actions and the reach of coercive opinions on ideas and actions and introduces "experiments in living." In *Logic of the Moral Sciences,* chaps. 10 and 12, Mill speaks of speculative ideas having no relationship to interests, desires, and aversions and of an "art of life" independent of empirical and abstract or "geometrical" methods of science.
22. *Logic of the Moral Sciences,* p. 51, and see ibid., p. 47.
23. Ibid., pp. 144–45. And see Ryan, *John Stuart Mill,* chap. 13, on the role of aesthetics; Cowling, *Mill and Liberalism,* pp. 106–21, on values in Mill's conception of social science; and, Cumming, *Human Nature and History,* 2:380–88 and pp. 399–408, on the relationship between Mill's *Autobiography* and his discussion of poetry, art, and internal culture.
24. *On Liberty,* p. 100. Italics mine. Pains of this sort, continues Mill, are, "as it were, the spontaneous consequences of the faults themselves," and are not to be thought of as punishments by others (p. 99). Austin, *Jurisprudence,* p. 211, excludes the "law of opinion" from the category of law simply because the authors of the punishments "have no formed intention of inflicting evil or pain upon those who may break or transgress it."
25. "Utility of Religion," p. 424.
26. Ibid.
27. Ibid., p. 423; and see *Logic of the Moral Sciences,* pp. 146–48.
28. *Reasonableness,* no. 238, pp. 165–66.
29. Ibid., no. 241, p. 170.
30. John Stuart Mill, *The Subjection of Women* (London, 1906), pp. 71–72.
31. *Utilitarianism,* p. 182.
32. *Logic of the Moral Sciences,* chap. 8. See Cumming, *Human Nature and History,* 2:280–94, on the meaning of Mill's rejection of an abstract political and moral philosophy.
33. *On Liberty,* p. 53.
34. *Logic of the Moral Sciences,* app. A, pp. 152–53.
35. *On Liberty,* p. 85.
36. Ibid.; and see "The Spirit of the Age," *Essays on Politics and Culture,* pp. 11–20.
37. Quoted from Cowling, *Mill and Liberalism,* p. 65. And see *Logic of the Moral Sciences,* chap. 5 on ethology, and chap. 9 on political ethology; and Cumming, *Human Nature and History,* 1:60–62.
38. Letwin, *Pursuit of Certainty,* pp. 1–10, draws these conclusions in tracing the influence of Hume and Bentham through John Stuart Mill to Beatrice Webb. And see Noel Annan, "John Stuart Mill," in J. B. Schneewind, *Mill: A Collection of Critical Essays* (Notre Dame, 1969), pp. 41–45, on Mill's spirit living on in Fabianism.
39. *Logic of the Moral Sciences,* pp. 9–11, and app. C, p. 157. And see "Theism," *Essays on Politics and Culture,* pp. 461–78, for Mill's critique of Protestantism in its later liberal forms. As Mill concludes in this ostensibly most sympathetic treatment of traditional religion: "The notion of a providential government by an omnipotent Being for the good of his creatures must be entirely dismissed." Only the few, through "the cultivation of severe reason," can participate "in the imagination" in being a

helpmate to a less than omnipotent Being without a perversion of their judgment (pp. 479 and 481). And see "Utility of Religion," pp. 428–29.

40. See chap. 15, n.27, above. And see Cumming, *Human Nature and History,* 2:320–28, on the relationship between history of ideas, Mill's mental history, and Mill as representing modern liberalism. Professor Cumming, ibid., 2:359–88, leaves out of consideration the role of religion and religious ideas in Mill's mental history and in the structure of Mill's humanism.

41. Hume, *Natural History,* p. 75.

42. "Coleridge," *Dissertations and Discussions,* 2:18–25 and 45–49. Ryan, *John Stuart Mill,* pp. 105–24 and 234–55; and Cumming, *Human Nature and History,* 2:296–307, stress the new location which Mill gives to politics by his stress on internal culture.

43. *On Liberty,* p. 45.

44. Ibid., p. 54.

45. Ibid., p. 46.

46. "Utility of Religion," p. 427. In the companion essay, "Nature," Mill asks, "Is there any moral enormity which might not be justified by imitation of such a Deity?" (ibid., p. 426). Mill here repeats Hume's argument in *Natural History,* pp. 70–73.

47. Stephen, *Liberty, Equality, Fraternity,* pp. 241–42, rejects such a religion on precisely those grounds, calling it "a huge Social Science Association embracing in itself all the Exeter Halls that ever were born or thought of." Such a religion "is not fitted to take command of the human faculties, to give them their direction, and to assign to one faculty a rank in comparison with others which but for such interference it would not have." He attributed to Mill's religion of humanity these weaknesses but did not have access to "Utility of Religion," published posthumously in 1874. For Stephen's other writings on the weaknesses of a nonsupernatural religion and the importance of heaven and hell to the success of Utilitarian political, moral, and legal theories, see *Essays By a Barrister,* pp. 120–40, and *Fortnightly Review* 18 (1872): 644.

48. Hume, *Natural History,* p. 53. John Austin expressed a similar vexation: "In case the good of those persons considered singly or individually were sacrificed to the good of those persons considered collectively or as a whole, the general good would be destroyed by the sacrifice. . . . When it is stated strictly and nakedly, this truth is so plain and palpable that the statement is almost laughable. But experience sufficiently evinces, that plain and palpable truths are prone to slip from the memory: that the neglect of plain and palpable truths is the source of most of the errors with which the world is infested" (*Jurisprudence,* p. 161).

49. *Logic of the Moral Sciences,* pp. 136–37, and see p. 118, n.11.

50. John Stuart Mill, *An Examination of Sir William Hamilton's Philosophy* (London, 1865), p. 213. James Fitzjames Stephen refers to this discussion on personal identity by Mill, concluding that Mill was avoiding "with needless caution, the inferences which his language suggests, namely an implicit belief in a future state or a final time, a past, present, future state all in one—a state which . . . transcends time and change" (*Liberty, Equality, Fraternity,* p. 246).

51. "Utility of Religion," p. 429.

52. Ibid., pp. 429–30. At the start of *Logic of the Moral Sciences,* Mill states that men do have the power "to conquer . . . character" and thus to shape our future. He calls this moral freedom and concludes that "none but a person of confirmed virtue is completely free" (p. 15).

53. "Utility of Religion," p. 429. The appropriate hell for these depraved men, says Mill, would be the necessity to live forever, endlessly acting out desire after desire after desire. And see his justification of capital punishment, *Hansard's Parliamentary Debates*, 3d ser. (1868), pp. 1947–55; and discussion by L. W. Sumner, "Mill and the Death Penalty," *The Mill Newsletter* 11 (1976): 2–7.

Conclusion

1. Stephen, *Essays by a Barrister*, pp. 137–38. And see chap. 16, n.50, above.
2. "The Spirit of the Age," p. 19.
3. I owe this formulation to Wilson C. McWilliams, "On Equality as the Moral Foundation for Community," in Robert H. Horwitz, ed., *The Moral Foundations of the American Republic* (Charlottesville, Va., 1977), pp. 183–92 and 198–203.
4. Alexis de Tocqueville, *Democracy in America* (New York, 1961), 2:116.
5. See Mill's review of *Democracy in America*, vol. 2, prefacing the Schocken edition (New York, 1961), especially pp. xxxi–xli.
6. Tocqueville, *Democracy in America*, 2:116.
7. See McWilliams, "On Equality," pp. 183–98. For a more general discussion of the relationship between coercion and freedom, see Benjamin R. Barber, "Forced to be Free: An Illiberal Defense of Liberty," in *Superman and Common Men* (New York, 1971).
8. Mill, *The Subjection of Women*, pp. 71–72.
9. *Leviathan*, IV, "A Review and Conclusion," p. 629.

Index